An Act of Genocide

An Act of Genocide

Colonialism and the Sterilization of Aboriginal Women

Karen Stote

Fernwood Publishing • Halifax & Winnipeg

Editing: Penelope Jackson
Cover design: John van der Woude
Printed and bound in Canada

Published by Fernwood Publishing
32 Oceanvista Lane, Black Point, Nova Scotia, B0J 1B0
and 748 Broadway Avenue, Winnipeg, Manitoba, R3G 0X3
www.fernwoodpublishing.ca

Fernwood Publishing Company Limited gratefully acknowledges the financial support
of the Government of Canada through the Canada Book Fund and the Canada Council
for the Arts, the Nova Scotia Department of Communities, Culture and Heritage,
the Manitoba Department of Culture, Heritage and Tourism under the
Manitoba Publishers Marketing Assistance Program and the Province of Manitoba,
through the Book Publishing Tax Credit, for our publishing program.

 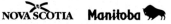

Library and Archives Canada Cataloguing in Publication

Stote, Karen, 1980-, author
An act of genocide : colonialism and the sterilization of Aboriginal
women / Karen Stote.

Issued in print and electronic formats.
ISBN 978-1-55266-732-3 (pbk.).--ISBN 978-1-55266-754-5 (epub)

1. Native women--Health and hygiene--Canada. 2. Native women--
Canada--Social conditions. 3. Sterilization (Birth control)--Law and
legislation--Canada. 4. Sterilization (Birth control)--Government
policy--Canada. I. Title.

HQ767.7.S76 2015   363.9'70971   C2015-900658-9
                        C2015-900659-7

Contents

If you have come to help me,
you are wasting your time.
But if you have come because your liberation
is bound up with mine, then let us work together.

Aboriginal Activists Group, Queensland, 1970s

Acknowledgement

Researching and writing this work has been much more than an academic exercise and as with all works, it did not get written in isolation. It was inspired, shaped and fueled by countless people with whom I have been fortunate enough to engage, either face to face or through correspondence, books and documentaries. It is meant as a statement of solidarity with those who have consistently resisted an unjust system which treats all of us poorly and continues to deny Indigenous peoples the right to exist on their own terms — it is offered in the belief that a better world is possible. This manuscript began as a doctoral dissertation and was made possible through much support and encouragement. To the Department of Native Studies at St. Thomas University and all those I met during my time there, thank you for stimulating many of the ideas found in this work, for providing an environment where real learning could take place and for employing me in times when I needed a job! To my supervisory committee, Andrea Bear Nicholas, Linda Eyre and Linda Kealey, for helping me through the longest part of this journey each in your own way, and to David Bedford, Nicole O'Byrne and Pamela Palmater for your constructive criticisms and encouraging comments as this work took its final shape as a PhD thesis. Thank you to Ward Churchill and Mary Eberts whose comments on sections of this work did much to strengthen some of the arguments made within. The Social Sciences and Humanities Research Council of Canada provided financial assistance without which much of this work would have been difficult to complete. A big thank you is due to Fernwood Publishing for supporting this work and bringing it forward in its current form. Finally, to my family, my friends and my partner: thank you for loving me, supporting me and always reminding me of the beauty and hopefulness of life.

Preface

Since I began this project, people have often asked about this research and once filled in they tend to respond in one of two ways. Some react with a sense of disbelief that they have been kept in the dark about this piece of Canadian history, and this is most often followed up with a statement referring to the fact that this must be something that happened long ago. Many Canadians carry a mistaken assumption that crimes and abuses against impoverished, marginalized and Aboriginal women are a thing of the past and that perhaps things are not perfect, but overall people are making out okay today. On the other end of the spectrum, some respond with various comments relating to the fact that although not ideal, something needs to be done about people having children they cannot afford. A practicing physician with whom I spoke retorted that today, those who should be reproducing are now seeking sterilization of their own volition while others are allowed to have as many children as they please. Someone else equated childbirth by poor women with the failure of pet owners to sterilize their animals as a step towards preventing overpopulation. In between those who think crimes committed by the state do not happen today and those who would promote the coercive use of the state apparatus for racist and/or economic ends are those who categorize this work as Aboriginal history. To all of this I would like to respond by clarifying what this work sets out to do and where it is coming from.

It is important to point out that although some of those coercively sterilized were Aboriginal, others, too, were also victimized by this practice. By focusing on Indigenous women, I do not mean to disregard this fact. I also do not purport to speak on behalf of Aboriginal peoples. I hope this work is useful to and serves as a statement of solidarity with Indigenous peoples here, but I believe it is left to those victimized by Canadian policies and practices to speak for themselves about their experiences and what these have meant for them, in their lives and as peoples. I have tried to provide a bigger picture which will, hopefully, help to inform these experiences and help us all understand many of the forces that influence how and why injustices like this happen. My main argument is that the consistent undermining of Aboriginal women and their reproductive lives through policies and practices like coercive sterilization has been part of a longstanding attack against Indigenous ways of life in an effort to reduce those to whom the federal government has obligations, and in order to gain access to lands and resources. Coercive sterilization should not be viewed in isolation from the larger context in which it has taken place, just as other policies such as residential schools cannot be separated from the larger purposes they have served, or their effects which continue to be felt

1

today. As Patricia Monture has written, the impact of these policies is greater than the sum of their individual wrongs and the harms extend to all Aboriginal peoples as individuals and communities. Even though the experiences of those impacted by Indian policy in Canada differ greatly, the ties between these originate in a system based on the expropriation of Indigenous lands and resources, and mediated by a government that has had the elimination of the "Indian problem" as a central goal since its very inception.

This work consists of a historical recount of Canadian bureaucrats, policy makers and so called humanitarians proposing, enacting and implementing policies and practices that have sought to open up access to or legitimate ownership over Indigenous lands and resources. It consists of a history of Canadian state, medical and philanthropic organizations subjecting Aboriginal peoples to practices and policies they, by and large, did not ask for or need, and for which they have yet to be compensated. In this sense, the history dealt with here is very much a Canadian history. Indigenous peoples have absolutely resisted, adapted and survived in the face of policies and practices such as those discussed, and they will most likely continue to do so into the future. By speaking of the victimization of Aboriginal women by Canadian laws and practices, I do not mean to deny this fact. Yet, this active and ongoing resistance is not the subject of this work. Through research and scholarship which highlights some of the injustices faced by Aboriginal peoples, I seek to call Canadians to task. In our ignorance and complacency many of us do not even recognize the harm that is being carried out in our names, let alone who its victims are or that those resisting desire something different than what we have to offer.

As Canadians, we must remember that if anyone does not belong, it is us. Aboriginal peoples existed in all their complexity, all their diversity and all their beauty and shortcomings before we came to these lands. Whatever reasons we give for our historical and present occupation of Indigenous territories, or our past and present treatment of the original inhabitants, we need to understand what brought us here and what has motivated our actions. These reasons are rooted in a capitalist system that, by its very nature, consistently seeks to maximize profits for the few through the exploitation of the earth and most often at the peril of its peoples. For many, the move to this side of the ocean was not necessarily by choice. State and private interests were also busy expropriating the lands and resources of Europe and in many respects they employed policies and practices similar in form to those wielded on Aboriginal peoples to do so. A primary motivation for the mass transference of people from one continent to another in the nineteenth and early twentieth centuries was indeed to relieve the state from the responsibility of dealing with the aftermath of these practices on the peoples of Europe. Some individuals and families came unwillingly, and countless others were enticed with the promise of a better life. Once here, settlers were given the opportunity to work as servants to a state which had so recently dispossessed them, and to aid in the continued creation of wealth by dispossessing the original inhabitants of these lands we call Canada. We are the ones who sought out Aboriginal peoples because they had and continue to have something that we want. It is Canadians who have not upheld our obligations through treaties or otherwise, and who are ultimately responsible for the policies, practices and horrendous abuses experienced by Aboriginal peoples. The fact that our existence has come to depend on what is not ours does not negate this fact. And, though it is left to Aboriginal peoples to reconstitute their institutions, ways and communities, it is also up to Canadians to hold our government to account for the dishonest, unsustainable and genocidal policies and practices it has imposed on Aboriginal peoples for far too long. Before Aboriginal peoples can reconstitute their lives in sustainable, meaningful and sovereign ways, these destructive policies and practices need to stop.

I have come to question the reliability of elected officials to accomplish this task. After spending countless hours sifting through government documents reporting the actions and words of bureaucrats, lawyers and members of parliament, I could not help but be struck by the tendency for rhetoric, ignorance and sometimes outright racism on the part of many of those who make decisions on our behalf. My already skeptical view of the political process in Canada has been eroded further. If the general population knew what was being said and done in their name, I can only hope they would be outraged. In concert with many others who have made this call previously, Canadians need to take up our responsibilities and become engaged in decision making about our lives by losing our ignorance. If more of us were willing to hold our government to account for its dealings with Indigenous peoples then perhaps we could all benefit from living in a more humane world. I have also come to question the role of academics in effecting change. My hope is that more academics will stand up to this challenge. In such a privileged position, we must remember that the ability to sit and write about reality is at the expense of those who must struggle every day just to continue to live it. We must be more forceful, more critical and more urgent in the tasks we undertake. We must seek to link struggles. We have more in common than many of us would like to think.

Before beginning, I also want to make a few final comments on my style and approach in writing this work. There are indeed many nuances in the provision of health services to Aboriginal peoples across Canada and this responsibility has been complicated by federal, provincial and territorial agreements. Matters are further convoluted by the fact that many Indigenous peoples have been denied federally provided services after moving off reserves for extended periods of time, or after marrying someone other than another Indian as defined under the Indian Act. This reality has made it difficult to find the exact location of many of the files relating to the sterilization of Aboriginal women in Canada. It has also led to disagreement among scholars on whether any generalizations can be made when speaking of Aboriginal health policies historically because services were not provided in an identical way across the country. Despite these difficulties, I argue that the larger context in which health policy was imposed was consistently one of colonialism and assimilation. I acknowledge that many nuances exist, but I believe that it is possible to speak of services provided to Aboriginal peoples without getting bogged down in bureaucratic wrangling and I have taken this approach in this work.

To ensure this work is both accessible and of practical use to the broadest possible audience, I have actively resisted the use of highly theoretical conversations abstracted from the world in which we live. I hope the reader finds that this enhances rather than detracts from the overall integrity of this work. I also do not purport a neutral objectivity when speaking of the consequences of policies and practices for peoples. We cannot be neutral on a moving train, as Howard Zinn aptly pointed out. There is a reality at hand and there are forces at work that have very real consequences for people. I want to call attention to this reality with hopes of effecting its transformation and creating a different vision of the future in which some no longer benefit at the expense of others. The analysis found in the forthcoming pages has been shaped greatly by the works of scholars and activists who have joined research and praxis in a way that seeks to address injustice and as such, as much as it seeks to inform, it is also politically motivated.

Finally, I have been taught that all terms referring to the Indigenous peoples of these lands are problematic. The terms Aboriginal, Indian and First Nations have colonial or bureaucratic origins and have been imposed in one way or another. They also homogenize the diverse original inhabitants. I acknowledge this and realize that none of these terms reflect the diversity of Indigenous nations. However, I use these terms because these are the ones that appear in the documents reviewed and they continue to represent who Indigenous peoples are to the Canadian government. I also use geographical terms, like "Canada," realizing this also does not acknowledge that the lands which make up this country are in fact the traditional territories of many different Indigenous peoples. I am confident that, in spite of this, the reader will be able to tell this work stands against the paternalistic and colonial practices that have for so long denied Indigenous peoples their identities and ways of life.

Introduction

Aboriginal peoples have been strategically and systematically targeted for assimilation into Canadian society. The control of women's reproductive capacities by the Canadian state has been central to this end. The imposition of Western medical practices on Aboriginal women since the founding of Canada, though often carried out under the pretense of a humanitarian concern by the federal government, has also allowed the state to maintain its colonial grip on and undermine the health and integrity of Aboriginal peoples. The coercive sterilization of Aboriginal women, rationalized as a means of protecting society and women from the burdens that additional births might bring, is an example of such an imposition. The details of how this practice was carried out and its implications have yet to be acknowledged in the historical record. Notions of race have also long permeated dealings with Aboriginal peoples in Canada. Eugenic ideology served as a convenient rationalization for the dire circumstances created by colonization and was instrumental in determining how to intervene in the lives of Aboriginal peoples. The disproportionate incidence of ill health and poverty in Indigenous communities became indicative of a lower racial evolution and a certain hereditary taint among them. Interventions were often guided by the view that the less evolved were a threat to society and this justified drastic intrusions in their lives. Primary measures advocated in the spirit of negative eugenics including marriage regulation, segregation and sterilization were all imposed on Aboriginal peoples at one point or another, and they all affected Aboriginal women in specific ways.

In Canada, the practice of coercive sterilization was carried out in several provinces but only two, Alberta and British Columbia, enacted formal legislation. From 1928 to 1973, at least three thousand people were sterilized in these two provinces under the direction of a provincially mandated Eugenics Board. In the province of Alberta, Aboriginal peoples were those to whom legislation was most applied as compared to their numerical significance in the general population. Despite this, no scholarship has yet referred specifically to or conducted in-depth study of this practice as it was imposed on Aboriginal peoples. This is a critical weakness, particularly if the claim of the Canadian government is to address the historical wrongs committed against Indigenous peoples. Therefore, a consideration of how, why and to what extent this practice was imposed on Aboriginal women is worthwhile. At the same time, this coercive sterilization needs to be considered within the broader context of colonialism, the oppression of women and the denial of Indigenous sovereignty.

In contrast to the lack of attention paid to the sterilization of Aboriginal women in Canada, in the United States, the sterilization of Native American women became public knowledge in the 1970s when, through the efforts of women and reproductive rights organizations, instances of abuse were brought to light. So many instances, in fact, that Dr. Constance Uri, a Native American physician involved in these investigations, publicly accused the government of genocidal intentions (Carpio 2004). Subsequently, the United States Government Accounting Office conducted an inquiry into sterilization practices of the Indian Health Service, the federal department responsible for the provision of health services to Native Americans. Even though the investigation encompassed only a limited number of Indian health regions, it confirmed that between 1973 and 1976, four out of twelve Indian Health Service regions sterilized a total of 3406 American Indian women without their informed consent (Torpy 2000). Despite its limited scope, this type of inquiry into the sterilization of Aboriginal women would shed much needed light on the practice as it transpired in a Canadian context.

Since that time, Native women have been considered a unique class of victims among the larger population facing sterilization because of the historical relationship between Indigenous communities and the federal government (Lawrence 2000; Smith 2005a). Due to an enforced dependence on services provided by the state, through the Bureau of Indian Affairs and Indian Health Services, sterilization rates experienced by Native American women have been directly related to funding priorities and a general lack of concern for the welfare of Indian communities (Lawrence 2000). A similar enforced dependence exists in Canada, yet an analysis of the factors motivating decision making on the part of the Department of Indian Affairs or the Department of National Health and Welfare has yet to be undertaken with respect to issues affecting the reproductive lives of Aboriginal women. Sterilization is also linked to other policies affecting Indigenous women and their children like adoption and foster care, which have seriously jeopardized the future of Native American communities as sovereign nations (Torpy 2000). These represent important connections that are only beginning to be made in Canada, where Aboriginal communities have also been subject to similar policies, whether through residential schools and the Sixties Scoop, or the more recent high rates of Aboriginal children being placed in state care as child and welfare services proliferate in Aboriginal communities (Blackstock et al. 2004; Chrisjohn and Young 2006; Cull 2006). Indeed, the struggle for reproductive rights for Native American women has always been one of not only being able to have children but also being able to keep them in their custody (Silliman et al. 2004). This point could be made when speaking of the experiences of Aboriginal women in Canada as well (Blaney 1995).

It is now clear that the federal agency responsible for the health of Native Americans abused its power to administer policy upon Indian women and used sterilization as a population control measure in the face of the high birth rate of Indian children and the perceived inability of Indian women to use other forms

of birth control (Smith 2002: 135–36). Despite court rulings mandating sterilization be based on informed consent, physicians often performed the procedure
for economic and social reasons, and women were sometimes coerced into the
procedure or not told at all (Lawrence 2000; Carpio 2004). A similar history is
beginning to emerge in a Canadian context and this work will show that historical
examples like those listed above happened here, too. The sterilization of Indigenous
women in the United States has been linked to a continued history of colonialism
and the quest to acquire Indian lands and resources. Considered part of the long
term strategy to remove Indigenous peoples from their homelands and limit the
number of those able to claim title and land rights, sterilization and the resulting
loss of children has endangered the sovereignty of Indian Nations while reducing
federal obligations (Ralstin-Lewis 2005; Silliman et al. 2004). Even though the
history of colonialism and enacted federal policies differs in a Canadian context,
these underlying goals of land dispossession and reducing federal obligations have
similarly motivated policies and practices toward Aboriginal peoples.

Due to the paucity of literature dealing with these issues as they relate to
Aboriginal women in Canada, this work seeks to begin that discussion. More
specifically, it seeks answers to the following questions: (a) What were the ideological, social, political and economic circumstances motivating the sterilization
of Aboriginal women? (b) When, where and to what extent has this practice taken
place? (c) What are the implications of this practice for Aboriginal peoples? To
these ends, I analyze Canadian policy toward Aboriginal peoples historically, and
link sterilization to other explicit government interventions in the areas of Indian
and public health. How have these worked in concert to maintain and perpetuate
an agenda set forth by the Canadian government? How and why have Aboriginal
women been targeted as reproducers of life? Throughout, I highlight the extent to
which scientific racism has served as ideological justification for the implementation of these policies and demonstrate the political and economic interests served.

Without getting bogged down in theoretical discussions, it is worth briefly
mentioning the historical materialist approach that has influenced the questions I
have asked and the conclusions to which I have come. As a central premise informing this discussion, I assume that policy is fundamentally shaped by and arises to
meet the needs of the mode of production. The practice of coercive sterilization
is also influenced by this context, and trying to understand why sterilization was
implemented in the first place is the starting point here. I show that the answer
to this question lay not within the practice itself but within the broader context
in which it arose. To put it differently, I begin from the premise that the mode of
production of Canadian society has been shaped by and depends on a history of
colonialism and the control of Indigenous lands and resources by the Canadian
state. I then show how the sterilization of Aboriginal women has arisen out of and
maintained these relations.

The capitalist and patriarchal productive relations that underlay Canadian society have also been made possible through the subordination and exploitation of women from colonizing countries and those in their asserted colonies (Mies 1986: 38). As producers and reproducers of life, women are impacted by the mode of production in ways that are specific to them, and their reproduction is viewed and treated differently based on the larger needs of the political and economic system (Gimenez 2005; Rousseau 2006). I consider the control of Indigenous reproduction within the historical context of colonialism, in the name of capitalist development, and within the context of the exploitation of women. While the productive and reproductive potential of some women was needed to settle and populate the newly founded nation, Aboriginal women, in their ability to reproduce future generations of Indigenous peoples, represented and continue to represent an impediment to the colonial project. This helps us better understand why at the same time as some women were encouraged to reproduce, Aboriginal women were subject to coercive policies in an effort to curb their reproduction — but both of these realities arose out of and helped ensure the functioning of the political economy. Coercive sterilization serves a different purpose and has different implications when applied to Aboriginal women because Aboriginal peoples live under colonial and assimilative conditions (Smith 2005a: 79–108).

This work links sterilization practices to government policy and other interventions in the lives of Aboriginal peoples under the veil of public health, and grounds these within the context of colonialism and the control of land and resources. I begin with a brief overview of the eugenics movement and the pseudoscientific ideology that legitimated sterilization as a viable public health intervention. I highlight the ideological climate of Canadian society toward Aboriginal peoples and the reasons why scientific racism represented a preferred ideological explanation for social phenomena in Indigenous communities. Why was exerting control over women's reproduction important to creating a eugenic vision of society and how, by adopting eugenic ideology, did some women compromise their own struggles and help support the sterilization of Aboriginal women? In order to understand the specific context out of which the sterilization of Aboriginal women arose, I then examine the history of Indian policy in Canada. Beginning with the year of Confederation of 1867, I conduct a historical review of the relationship between Canada and Aboriginal peoples, and the impact of policy on Aboriginal women. Central to the discussion is understanding the political and economic factors that led Indigenous ways of life to be undermined. How did the direct connection of Aboriginal women to the land, and their ability to produce future generations of Aboriginal peoples, lead them to be targeted in specific ways? This larger historical and material context allows us to understand coercive sterilization as one policy among many imposed in an effort to separate Aboriginal peoples from their lands, and to reduce the number of those to whom the federal government has obligations.

Following this, and covering roughly the time period during which formal sterilization legislation was in effect, from 1928 to 1973, I examine the extent to which the practice of coercive sterilization was applied to Aboriginal women in legislated and non-legislated form. Piecing together this history involves surveying proffered reasons for why Aboriginal women were targeted for sterilization and how this was justified. It also involves discussing other reproductive policies and practices that were imposed on Aboriginal women, including the promotion of birth control and the provision of abusive abortion services. Although evidence dealing with the sterilization of Aboriginal women has only just begun to be unearthed, I show that the context in which these took place was indeed coercive, and that even one having been allowed to happen represents an attack against Indigenous peoples.

I then discuss some of the factors leading to the repeal of sterilization legislation in Alberta and British Columbia. I examine the avenues of redress made available to sterilization victims in seeking compensation. Have reparations through the courts proven just? I show that rather than undertake open and honest efforts to make things right, both federal and provincial governments have sought to limit and/or deny responsibility for actions carried out on wards under their charge. By doing so, the state has constrained our knowledge of these crimes and shaped the parameters of how the sterilization of Aboriginal women is understood, as an individual crime committed by individual wrongdoers with no systemic nature or group implications.

The imposition of measures to prevent births within a group constitutes an enumerated act of genocide under international law, yet the sterilization of Aboriginal women is not generally considered within this context. I consider the extent to which this term is applicable to understanding the treatment of Aboriginal peoples by the Canadian state. The role of Canadian officials in defining and implementing this concept under international and domestic law is highlighted in order to demonstrate how our understanding of what constitutes genocide, and the avenues of redress available for crimes committed as a result of Indian policy in Canada, have been limited as a result. Even though genocide is not likely to arise in Canadian courts this does not negate the fact that when it is understood within its broader historical and material context, it is a proper descriptor of the treatment of Aboriginal women and their peoples. The larger question that remains, then, is what changes are needed in order to fully address the injustices of the past against Aboriginal peoples, and how are we to understand those injustices which continue to be perpetrated in the present? I conclude with some final remarks to this effect by referring to the voices of Indigenous peoples who have been consistently vocalizing to us the fundamental shift needed in order to fully respect Indigenous sovereignty and self-determination.

1. Eugenics, Feminism and the Woman Question

Eugenics as a scientific method of improving the "race" has served as one particular ideological justification for exerting control over the fertility of women. Under eugenic theory, women, as bearers of the next generation, were seen as responsible for "reproducing the race" both in a biological sense and in their role as reformers and child raisers. Eugenicists sought to actively encourage the reproduction of some women while at the same time seeking to ensure their cooperation in efforts to curb the reproduction of others through their support for measures like marriage regulation, institutionalization and sterilization. Many eugenicists were prepared to support certain rights for some women to the extent that these would help buttress the political and economic enterprise of nation building based on an inherently racist notion of who belonged. Alternatively, some feminists adopted eugenic ideology to strengthen their arguments for social reform, and in an effort to gain an increased role in public life by having their maternal role valued. A "eugenic feminism" was developed by these women who were involved in shaping North America in the late nineteenth and early twentieth centuries (Ziegler 2008). By making use of evolutionary theory to argue against their inferiority to men, these women were able to ensure a place in society for others like them by legitimating their roles as "mothers of the race" (Valverde 1992).

The reproductive potential of women is essential to the continuance of every way of life. Under the capitalist patriarchal mode of production, the reproductive capacities of women have been subverted, exploited and controlled in particular and specific ways to ensure its proper functioning (Federici 2004). It is this context which led to the relegation of women from colonizing countries to the private sphere, out of which the struggle for increased rights in the late nineteenth and early twentieth centuries arose. That which is commonly referred to as "first wave" feminism consisted of a wide range of women from a variety of political persuasions and with different political agendas. However, it was most often those who were Anglo-Saxon and middle or upper class and were prepared to employ dominant racist ideologies, and who generally did not question the system but sought to reform it from within, whose arguments were given prominence. In the absence of a fundamental critique of the historical and material relations that first led to their oppression as women, and through their uneasy alliance with eugenics, these women acquired a moral authority to impose relations of oppression on others, while achieving certain rights within existing structures and institutions.

Although the goals of eugenics and this feminism diverged, on a fundamental level they worked to support each other within the context of colonialism and capitalist expansion. In this sense, eugenic feminism functioned similarly to eugenics proper by obfuscating and perpetuating exploitative relations while benefiting private interests.

The Birth of an Idea

Though by no means unique to this time period, racist ideology has played a central part in explaining away the effects of capitalist expansion in newly formed and increasingly urbanized cities, first in Europe, then in North America during the late nineteenth and early twentieth centuries (Carew 1988a; Chase 1977; Pagden 1998; Rodney 1973; Sanders 1978). The basic purpose of a racist ideology is to deny the humanity of those who are being oppressed, to blame individuals for their miserable conditions and to divert attention away from those who are doing the oppressing. In the case of the burgeoning industrial capitalist state, the poor living conditions of the masses needed to be explained as due to individual failures. Eugenic ideology served this purpose. Granted, eugenics "meant different things to different people in different settings" (Dowbiggin 1997: 238). However, as an ideology, it has consistently allowed the destitute conditions of the poor to be explained, not as the result of an unequal distribution of wealth inherent to the political and economic system, but as due to innate characteristics inherent to the impoverished masses. Neither were the dire circumstances of Aboriginal peoples created by policies of land dispossession and cultural repression on the part of a colonial government, but rather they resulted from the inability or unwillingness of "primitive groups" to rise to a higher level of civilization. Consequently, and as is the case with any useful racist ideology, eugenics allowed business to continue for those benefiting from the exploitation of the lands, resources and labours of others.

In 1883, Francis Galton coined the word "eugenics" (Black 2003; Haller 1963; Kevles 1985). Implied in this term was the notion that society consisted of people(s) evolved to greater or lesser degrees in their biological, physical and moral capacities. Galton viewed those traits he saw as most common among the middle and upper classes, such as intelligence, good physical health and a high income, as indicative of a higher evolutionary development, and believed these could be inherited from one generation to the next. Alternatively, he argued that poverty and the many social vices which he considered manifestations of inherent traits in the lower classes could also be passed on from parent to child. Hence, the only way to exterminate these undesirable qualities was to eliminate the potential of people who manifested these traits to reproduce. With the help of Karl Pearson, a psychometrician and his protégé, Galton proceeded to rank people through the use of statistical methods and proposed to actively intervene in the reproduction of human beings by encouraging the selective breeding of the "fit" and by promoting state interventions, through the use of agencies of social control, to limit the reproduction of those deemed "unfit," whether this unfitness was mental, moral or physical (Black 2003: 18; Kevles 1985: 20–40). Encapsulated in this racist ideology were notions put forth by many of his predecessors who shared a concern that some should not reproduce.

In the late eighteenth century, Thomas Malthus wrote on the state of society at the height of the industrial revolution in England (Malthus 1878). In the face of exponential growth due to technological advances and the rise of industry came a drastic restructuring of daily life for working people. Having recently been subjected to land enclosures and Poor Laws, many of the newly dispossessed migrated to cities to find work for a wage. Life in urban centres was unsanitary and rife with poverty, malnutrition, overcrowding and unsafe working conditions (Chase 1977: 2–175; Perelman 2000). Malthus acknowledged the resulting high mortality rates of the working class, but was against state interventions to improve living conditions. He viewed these as the necessary stimulus to industry because they forced people to work for wages. From his perspective, any attempt to address these problems was immoral and against the laws of nature, and as such, he was against sanitary reform, increased medical care, higher wages or artificial means of controlling births. Poverty, disease and famine were nature's way of keeping the population in check since the poor had a much higher birth rate than the world could support (Chase 1977: 68–84).

Charles Darwin was a cousin of Galton and an avid reader of Malthus. He referred to his own theory of evolution as the ideas of Malthus "applied with manifold force to the animal and vegetable kingdoms" (Darwin 2001: 63). Darwin's theory was based on the idea that the variety of living organisms in existence resulted from the interaction of three principles: first, that all organisms reproduced; second, that each organism differed slightly from any other; and third, that all organisms competed for survival. He believed those organisms that were best able to adapt to or change in new situations would gradually outbreed those less well adapted, and this process, what he called "natural selection," could also bring about new species (Degler 1991: 6). Although he initially spoke only of the biological evolution of animal and plant life, his writings set the stage for racist conclusions to be drawn with respect to humans (Degler 1991: 8–14). This is most especially the case with his later work, *The Descent of Man*, in which he applied evolutionary theory to human societies. Here, Darwin spoke of human societies as consisting of different levels of civilization, with "savages" from the "lower races" as intermediates between animals and civilized people. The groups making up the different levels of civilization formed part of the same species, but those at the top were from European cultures. Any contact between groups stemming from colonial encounters would increase the evolution of the species as a whole despite the negative consequences this might present for some (Darwin 1871). Commenting on the impact of European colonialism for Indigenous peoples in the Americas he wrote, "wherever the European has trod, death seems to pursue the Aboriginal ... The varieties of man seem to act on each other; in the same way as different species of animals, the stronger always extirpating the weaker" (Nicholas 1989: footnote 30).

Herbert Spencer built on Darwin's ideas and applied evolutionary theory to social phenomena in what is now referred to as social Darwinism.[1] Spencer argued that social phenomena like discrepancies in wealth and their consequent outcomes like poverty, starvation and disease were also the result of competition between naturally occurring groups, and the middle and upper classes, with their higher intelligence and better health, were simply further along on the evolutionary path than their lower class counterparts (Chase 1977: 105–07). As such, Spencer was against any attempts to provide aid to the poor, arguing this would result in "unquestionable injury" for society because it would "put a stop to that natural process of elimination by which society continually purifies itself" (Degler 1991: 11). The "survival of the fittest" no longer referred to the biological evolution of a species, but to that of mental and social characteristics within the species as well. This social Darwinism became the preferred ideology of political economists who sought to justify systemic inequalities and to maintain the status quo. It also served to rationalize the rightness of the "civilizing mission" being carried out in European colonial possessions. Since Indigenous societies were at the lower end on the evolutionary path, contact with European life through colonization would either aid in their progression or lead to their natural demise (Chase 1977: 105–07).

A central difference between the ideas of Malthus or Spencer and those held by eugenicists like Galton was in what should be done about the increasing competition between social groups. Rather than let the struggle unfold naturally, eugenicists sought to actively intervene in reproduction in order to speed up this evolutionary process (Black 2003). Following the rediscovery of Gregor Mendel's work on the genetic transmission of dominant and recessive traits in peas, what Galton referred to as a "stirp" or germ plasm as the site of heredity in humans was replaced with the notion that parents could transmit social traits to their offspring through their genes.[2] Eugenicists now had the scientific propaganda necessary to sway public opinion to support measures aimed at reducing the reproductive capacities of those considered inferior (Wahlsten 1997).

These ideas were invigorated and brought to formal fruition in the United States through the work of individuals like Charles Davenport, a former professor of zoology before being appointed director of the Eugenics Records Office in 1910, who employed Mendelian principles to find ways to produce "superior humans" (Black 2003: 87–124). Through private funding from the Rockefeller and Carnegie Foundations, Davenport undertook research on the inheritance of mental deficiency, insanity, criminality and many physical conditions such as epilepsy, deaf mutism and eye defects (Black 2003: 87–124). Shortly thereafter, at the First International Eugenics Congress in 1912, a framework was laid out on how to practically apply eugenic principles to the breeding of social classes. Primary methods proposed at this Congress, and by the eugenics movement in years to come, were to encourage the reproduction of the fit and to enact restrictive marriage laws, implement eugenic public education campaigns and segregate and/or sexually sterilize the unfit. To some eugenicists, these would prove to be the most efficient methods of dealing with crime, poverty, sexual promiscuity and laziness caused by mental deficiency, all traits said to be rampant among the lower classes (Black 2003: 70–73). In the spirit of Malthus, Spencer and Galton, these phenomena were not considered symptoms of the political and economic conditions of the time, but rather the result of the inherent genetic inferiority of those most negatively affected by the rise of industrial capitalism. Presenting these assumptions as scientific truths enabled the eugenics movement to lobby for legislation aimed at inhibiting the ability of some to reproduce (Black 2003: 387). However, unemployment, poverty and many of the other social traits focused on by eugenicists cannot simply be reduced to natural laws. Such phenomena reveal fundamental flaws in capitalist society and adopting eugenic measures was motivated by political and economic interests (Perelman 1985; Marx 1990; Engels 1884). In practice, these measures helped justify doing nothing or very little to improve the lot of the greatest number of people while keeping the exploitative relations of production intact. Looking back on this history, Allan Chase writes:

> Few societal actions demonstrate the direct influence of Galton's brand of scientific racism on twentieth century governments more tragically than do the seven decades of forced sterilization of men, women and children for the crime of being poor in America ... [by] prompt[ing] state and national governments to make sterilization their weapon of choice against what the scientific racists called "the menace of racial pollution." (Chase 1977: 15)

Racism begins with the need of one people to exploit another and the development of an ideology to justify this exploitation (Carew 1988a: 16). Eugenics and its inherent racism was an ideology that obscured the material reasons for social inequalities and allowed those who advocated its proposed interventions to benefit from the disparities created by and required for the advancement of capitalism.

Eugenics in Canada
The late nineteenth and early twentieth centuries in Canada were characterized by a rise in population through large waves of immigration, increased urbanization and industry as well as the expansion of settlement into western parts of Canada (Lux 2001; McLaren 1990; Walker 2008; Palmer 1992). These conditions gave rise to the common problems experienced by other industrializing capitalist societies and they were sometimes met with similar ideological explanations and attempts to intervene. The improvement of public health through an understanding of heredity was the chief cause which served to rally supporters to eugenic interventions

like sterilization (McLaren 1990: 28). Concerns surrounding issues of crime and immorality, high infant mortality rates, venereal disease and prostitution, and the mental deficiency that was said to accompany these, could more easily be dealt with if they were explained as the result of the inherent defectiveness of certain people or groups. Eugenicists in Canada tended to target the "feebleminded," a catch-all phrase referring to those otherwise considered mentally deficient and who were found living among the masses, or those at a higher level of functioning who, once sterilized, could be more easily released from institutional care (McLaren 1990: 91, 93–96). William Hutton, former director of the Eugenics Society of Canada, wrote of the feebleminded:

> They are the people with mental capacities and abilities of children. In the cities they tend to drift towards the slums. Indeed, the slums are largely the product of the segregating of the subnormals ... for their benefit as well as for our own, we should control their reproduction. (Hutton, in McLaren 1990: 115)

There was a clear class bias to eugenic notions in Canada, and there were racial and gender biases as well. Although feeblemindedness could be found among those of British descent, most often this condition presented itself in the large waves of non-British immigrants in the early twentieth century (McLaren 1990: 46–67; Valverde 1991: 104–14). Feebleminded women in particular were considered primarily responsible for social problems through their apparent lack of concern for sexual and social norms, and their role in reproducing the next generation of feebleminded children (Grekul 2008: 247–66; McLaren 1990: 94). Aboriginal women were also a concern because they did not readily adopt expected social norms, and because their supposed sexual immorality represented a threat to the social order, especially when these sexual relations involved men from the settler population (Valverde 1991: 86, 116). Inhibiting the reproduction of the feebleminded through sterilization would prevent the social problems associated with this group from multiplying (McLaren 1990: 93–94).

Sterilization as a eugenic intervention represented a means of addressing public health problems in a way that was both individualizing and obfuscating of any potential systemic or structural causes. It also served private interests. Many directly benefited from their support for eugenic explanations of social problems. Historian of medicine Ian Dowbiggin has documented how professional interests drew many psychiatrists to eugenic explanations rather than any particular racial prejudice on their part, and how the profession was able to legitimize itself and expand as a result of its support for eugenics (Dowbiggin 1997). As more people turned to the psychiatric profession for the treatment of mental illness, as it was broadly defined, the number of violent or chronically ill patients who could not easily be discharged from institutions rose; the state, responsible for funding these institutions, was increasingly holding medical superintendents accountable for costs; and the newly emerging neurological profession claimed the institutionaliza-tion of mental patients was often unnecessary and sometimes positively injurious. As such, espousing eugenics alleviated blame for the inability of the psychiatric profession to "cure" the "mentally defective" in public hospitals, and this allowed it to become part of the public health movement outside the asylum through its promotion of preventative measures like sterilization (Dowbiggin 1997: 9–11). The psychological profession also carved a niche for itself by promoting intelligence tests as the primary means of identifying the feebleminded, and the role these professions played in implementing university curricula that promoted eugenics as science provided a veneer of legitimacy to calls for sterilization (MacLennan 1987; Normandin 1998).

Central in this role was C.K. Clarke, a major proponent of eugenic measures and founding member of the Canadian National Committee on Mental Hygiene (CNCMH), an organization that did much to rally government officials, academ-ics and reformers to the role psychiatry could play in addressing social problems (McLaren 1990: 109–13). The CNCMH rebuked simple institutionalization as a means of dealing with crime, prostitution, illegitimacy and venereal disease caused by mental deficiency. In lieu, the CNCMH argued for more effective and less expen-sive interventions aimed at prevention. While speaking of venereal disease in 1917, a year prior to the formation of the CNCMH, Clarke argued that feeblemindedness was rampant among female prostitutes. He accorded them primary responsibility for its spread, and because these women were unable to understand their respon-sibilities to the race, they should be identified through the use of mental tests and rendered harmless through sterilization (McLaren 1990: 73).

Social workers also supported arguments for sterilization. Historian Angus McLaren (1990: 49–50, 163) speculates that by attributing social problems to hereditary taint, social workers were able to rationalize their own limited successes in rehabilitating the poor while it enhanced their professional standing. However, the main supporters of eugenics in Canada were doctors, and some of its most vocal, women (McLaren 1990: 30–45, 128–44). Helen MacMurchy, the recently honoured advocate of public health reform in Canada from the early twentieth cen-tury, was an outspoken proponent of sterilization and a leading figure in securing a position for the medical profession in the formation of social policy and provision of services (Ottawa Citizen, October 5, 2012). MacMurchy argued that the high maternal and infant mortality rates experienced by poor women were indicative of the inefficiency, lack of energy, less than average intelligence and lack of ability to see the importance of detail that was inherent in this group (MacMurchy 1912: 61; McLaren 1990: 31). Her solution was to forcibly control their reproduction through sterilization, and until this was done, good citizens would continue to pay through their taxes for the lawlessness, dependency, ill health and incapacity of the subnormal. To this list of notable female doctors, we could add Madge Thurlow Macklin, who was active in the eugenics movement and argued that conditions ranging from cancer, to tuberculosis and idiocy were inherited. She also made explicit calls for the sterilization of the feebleminded (McLaren 1990: 128–44). Or Dr. Margaret Patterson, regarded as an expert on prostitution and vice, who was also involved in social purity work and called for the compulsory sterilization of those convicted of sexual offences (Valverde 1991: 48–49). McLaren provides two reasons for the involvement of doctors in the eugenic crusade. If conditions were caused by biology or heredity, rather than social, environmental or economic factors, this would strengthen the position of the medical profession as only they would be in a position to judge the proper direction of public health policy. Further, just as scientific methods were being applied in industry, it was hoped these principles would also be useful in other areas. Doctors managed to sway government and public health officials to turn to the medical sciences for efficient methods of social management and in doing so, made themselves the authority on all things related to health (McLaren 1990: 28–30).

It is important to note that the type of crude, biologically deterministic and individualistic explanation for the manifestation of social problems like that advanced through eugenics has existed in a constant tension with other explanations that stress the role of a healthy environment in ensuring a healthy population. Implicit in Galton's work was a rejection of Lamarkian theory, or the belief that human characteristics could be acquired after birth and subsequently passed on to following generations, and which considered education and the provision of a certain level of social services as useful interventions in public life (Gould 2002; Schwartz Cowan 1977; McLaren 1990: 14–18). Sometimes prominent figures advocated for both types of interventions. For instance, Clarence Hincks, also a member of the CNCMH and an ardent supporter of sterilization for those he described as "physically attractive moron girls," stated:

> I find myself favoring sterilization, not on eugenical grounds alone, but on euthenical ones as well. I have been struck by the fact that feebleminded mothers are notoriously incapable of bringing up their children, and I am convinced that they should not be given a chance to thwart healthy child development. Sterilization would prevent them from having the responsibility of child care. (Hincks in McConnachie 1987: 226, 246)

Advocates of eugenic measures sometimes acknowledged the effect that "euthenics" or environmental influences could have on individuals, and good parenting, nutritious food and the proper training of children were also important in preventing feeblemindedness (McLaren 1990: 92–98; Valverde 1991: 15–21). Yet, as McLaren writes, "It is important not to exaggerate the gap that separated the eugenicists and environmentalists. Although their methods differed, their goals of efficient social management were similar" (McLaren 1990: 112). Even as eugenic thinking fell into disrepute following the Second World War and was replaced with a more welfare-minded idea of social intervention, this did not put an end to eugenic speculation or biologically deterministic measures. Eugenic arguments for the sterilization of the most marginalized continued to hold water with some, and the practice continued at least into the 1970s (McLaren 1990: 156–64).

Ultimately, eugenic approaches to social and public health problems were supported because they were cost effective to society. As was stated by Frank Hodgins, Commissioner of the *Report on the Care and Control of the Feebleminded in Ontario*, solutions were to be considered with "due regard being had to the expenses involved in any such proposals ... and to the best way of securing economy therein" (Hodgins 1919: 3). Or again, as promoted by the Eugenics Society of Canada, "the sterilization of the unfit requires immediate attention as this problem directly increases taxation" (McConnachie 1987: 230). This cost effectiveness went beyond the fact that sterilization could potentially alleviate the financial burden caused by institutionalizing large numbers of people (McLaren 1990: 93). The idea that social problems could be addressed in this way served to blame the most vulnerable segments of the population for what were, in effect, systemic problems directly related to how wealth is produced and distributed in a capitalist system, and to the social relations that arise between groups as a result. Instead of viewing these historical and material conditions as setting the stage for social problems, eugenic approaches enabled the state to provide the appearance of addressing public health issues while these exploitative relations continued unabated. This type of position also fostered the racist and divisive notions held by middle class social reformers that considered the poor as the cause of all social misery. Professionals directly benefiting from the implementation of eugenic measures took it upon themselves to construct social problems in such a way as to obfuscate the material reasons for the impoverished circumstances of people, to blame victims for these circumstances and to propose solutions that were beneficial to themselves and their profession. McLaren states:

> This fear of the feebleminded was based on the assumption made by a large number of turn of the century commentators that mental deficiency was a cause of a host of social ills. For the middle class, of course, it was a comforting notion to think that poverty and criminality were best attributed to individual weakness rather than structural flaws of the economy. This explains why so many otherwise intelligent humanitarians supported the labelling, segregation, and ultimately sterilization of those designated subnormal. (McLaren 1990: 37)

Sterilization was a cheap and simple solution (McConnachie 1987: 233).

Eugenics and the Woman Question

Eugenic ideology worked to obfuscate the historical and material relations that gave rise to many of the social problems of Canadian society in the late nineteenth and early twentieth centuries by locating the causes of poverty, crime and illness within individuals. The adoption of proposed interventions like sterilization served as a cost-effective public health solution allowing systemic explanations to be avoided, private interests to benefit and exploitative relations to continue. In their efforts, eugenicists also encouraged the reproduction of the "fit," namely women of Anglo-Saxon, middle and upper class origins. Fearing a decrease in the birth rate due to their increased access to education, the pursuance of work outside the home and rising infant mortality rates, eugenicists sought to bring these women "back home" by enticing them to become crusaders to the eugenic cause.

For eugenicists, women were important to national progress (Burdett 1998: 45–59). As child bearers, they held the ability to produce future progeny and were viewed as either helping or hindering the forward march of civilization (Valverde 1992: 4). At the same time, involving some women in eugenic work, and granting credence to some of their arguments for reform, provided the appearance of a concern for the plight of women. Karl Pearson stated in reference to the question of whether suffrage should be granted to women:

> We have to first settle what is the physical capacity of woman, what would be the effect of her emancipation on her function of race-reproduction, before we can talk about her "rights," which are, after all, only a vague description of what may be the fittest position for her, the sphere of her maximum usefulness in the developed society of the future. (Pearson 1888: 371)

Pearson saw the role of women primarily as one of reproduction and any rights accorded should be tailored to that role exclusively (Rensing 2006: 38). More than this, the "civilizing" work done by some women was needed to aid in forming the nation and colonizing other peoples. Caleb Saleeby, an ardent eugenicist and obstetrical doctor in the early twentieth century Britain, commented on how to effectively establish nationhood in western Canada, "before nations can be founded the cooperation of women is indispensable" (Saleeby in Henderson 2003: 171–73). In another instance, he expressed fear that the diminishing birth rate was happening at a juncture when "the Peace Treaty adds another million square miles or so to our vast Empire, already famishing for men" (Saleeby in Devereux 2005: 23). He denounced "aberrant women," or those who refused both motherhood and the profession of "foster-motherhood" in favour of other employment. Only women who were willing to undertake their proper role as "mothers of the race" should be granted rights and privileges. On whether to grant the vote Saleeby stated:

> I believe in the vote because I believe it will be eugenic, will reform

> conditions of marriage and divorce in the eugenic sense, and will serve the cause of what I have elsewhere called "preventative eugenics," which strives to protect healthy stocks from "racial poisons." (Saleeby in Devereux 2005: 35)

In another instance, Havelock Ellis, the well-known writer on sexuality, was more explicit when he said:

> The breeding of men lies largely in the hands of women. That is why the question of Eugenics is to a great extent one with the woman question. The realization of Eugenics in our social life can only be attained with the realization of the woman movement in its latest and completest [sic] phase as an enlightened culture of motherhood. (Ellis 1914: 46)

In this sense, eugenics became the answer to the "woman question." Women in nineteenth century Western European societies were subordinated, and experienced an inequality that was said to originate at the point when private property and the monogamous family appeared and mother right ended (Engels 1976: 191–344; Bebel 1971; Kealey 1984). They had suffered a history of mistreatment and oppression as patriarchy was imposed, and later, with the rise of primitive accumulation and the removal of peasants from the land in Europe, a most notable and brutal instance of this being the witch hunts (Federici 2004; Mies 1986). These historical and material relations shaped the context of the struggle being waged by women at this time, and questions of what their proper place should be and what rights should be accorded to them, both in Europe and its newly formed colonies, were central. Eugenicists were prepared to go along with the fight for the "Woman's Cause" to the extent that this would aid the imperial project (Devereux 2005: 30–44).

This merging of eugenics with the woman question allowed for the development of a program of "scientific sex reform," or the reconstruction of the role of some women in society by granting them certain rights and influences (Dodd 1991: 203–30). These women were viewed, and many began to view themselves, as "scientific experts" and "mothers of the race" (Valverde 1991: 59–60; Valverde 1992: 3–26). The influence of eugenics on feminism shaped the struggle being waged in the late nineteenth and early twentieth century and provided material incentives for some to turn against others and reproduce the existing relations of colonialism and capitalist patriarchal oppression. American historian Linda Gordon (2002: 83) notes that every eugenic argument was in the long run more effective in the hands of antifeminists than feminists, and that its influence on feminist arguments reinforced the status quo rather than drastically altered society. The same can be said about the adoption of eugenic arguments by the feminist movement in a Canadian context. The rights argued for and granted to some women at this time did not fundamentally threaten the existing order of society, nor were they ever meant for all women. They were reserved for those who willingly accepted dominant versions of femininity and did not question the historical and material relations of production.

Eugenic Feminism: Maternal Feminists, Suffragettes and "Other" Women

Some elements of the feminist movement in Canada took an interest in eugenics, embraced its theory and saw in its rhetoric the possibility to advance their efforts to gain increased recognition in the political sphere, to legitimate the reform work they were carrying out and to provide an authority and respectability to the work conducted by women in the home. Historian Diane Paul states, "the history of eugenics has been presented so often as though it were simply the extension of nineteenth century social Darwinism ... that we have nearly lost sight of the fact that important segments of the Left (as well as the women's movement, which deserves to be treated as a separate category) were also once enthusiastic about the potential uses of eugenics" (Paul 1998: 596). The influence of eugenics can be seen in the arguments made by many feminists, suffragists and reformers in Canada in the late nineteenth and early twentieth centuries.

Feminists often challenged the sexist elements of evolutionary theory, or the idea that women did not contribute to natural selection, that they were passive participants in the perpetuation of the race and that their faculties were characteristic of the lower races, and hence, of a lower level of civilization (Valverde 1992: Newman 1999). In contrast to traditional theories of inferiority based on religious explanations, and which viewed women as a servant to men as ordained by God, evolutionary theory held the possibility of making women central actors in the advancement of civilization, as the creators of life.[3] Yet feminists often failed to question the underlying racism of this ideology and worked to reinforce racist notions by adopting them for their own purposes (Bacchi 1983; Fiamengo 2006; Gibbons 2014; Kealey 1979). They also did not necessarily question the underlying organization of the capitalist mode of production which had caused them to be devalued, exploited and excluded from public life. What resulted were demands by some that they be allowed a place within the existing structures of society, and a role in perpetuating racist and exploitative relations on others.

Two opposing models of woman emerged in Canada and the United States in the early twentieth century. American historian Wendy Kline (2002: 29) refers to the "mother of the race" as a socially responsible, moral and civilized woman who would shape the future of the race through child raising and civilizing others. Alternatively, the "moron girl" was an immoral and uncivilized girl, and a biological threat to the health and advancement of the race. Efforts by many maternal feminists to protect their homes and families through preventative programs aimed at ensuring healthier children were often coupled with fears that their children would come into contact with those deemed unfit, and some actively supported protective measures aimed at limiting the propagation of the unfit in hopes that this would also limit contact between their children and these "abnormals" (McLaren 1990: 94). A profoundly racist form of feminism arose that excluded certain women from the specifically Anglo-Saxon work of building the nation (Valverde 1992: 8). Many celebrated feminists in Canada toed this line and through their support of eugenics, helped maintain exploitative relations while gaining privileges for women of their own backgrounds.

Emily Murphy was a key figure in the struggle for suffrage and one of the "Famous Five" who succeeded in gaining the status of personhood for some women under the *British North America Act*.[4] However, at the same time, as she argued for increased rights for some, she lobbied for increased state intervention to curtail the liberties of others. Murphy was a key stimulator of public support for the sexual sterilization acts in both Alberta and British Columbia (McLaren 1990: 94). In her role as the first female Magistrate Court Judge, Murphy is said to have dispensed a "moral justice" and her Women's Court has been referred to as a "clearinghouse for the unfit" because she often argued that the women passing before her should be sterilized rather than incarcerated for their crimes (Henderson 2003: 159–208). Murphy viewed sterilization as a useful means of protecting women and children from sexual attack, of ending the crippling expense of incarceration, and of promoting the mental and physical betterment of the race (McLaren 1986: 140). In another instance, in response to criticism that sterilization might impinge on the private liberty of individuals, Murphy argued this concern must take a back seat to the larger social good (Sanders 1945: 186–89).

It is hard to conclude that the gains argued for and eventually achieved by Murphy and her fellow feminists were ever meant to apply to all women. When considering the state of Aboriginal peoples in Canada, Murphy wrote:

> One hardly knows whether to take the Indian as a problem, a nuisance, or a possibility ... Regarding his [sic] future we may give ourselves little uneasiness. This question is solving itself. A few years hence there will be no Indians. They will exist for posterity only in waxwork figures and in a few scant pages of history. (Kulba 2004: 121)

The idea that Aboriginal peoples were a "vanishing race" was held by many involved in nation-building and it was meant literally in that Indians were dying from disease and starvation, but also figuratively as some believed assimilation would bring about the end of the "Indian problem" in Canada (Kelm 2005). Scholar Cecily Devereux (2005: 121–23) highlights that Indians were considered the least desirable non-British group by eugenicists like James Shaver Woodsworth, who was heavily involved in missionary work in the West, and who believed the presence of Aboriginal peoples should be erased from the landscape. In *Strangers Within Our Gates*, Woodworth, who went on as the first leader of the Cooperative Commonwealth Federation (later to become the New Democratic Party) wrote of Aboriginal peoples in 1909, "there are still 10, 202 Indians in our Dominion, as grossly pagan as were their ancestors, or still more wretched, half civilized, only to be debauched" (Woodsworth 1909: 160). He continued:

> it is our duty to set him on his feet, and sever forever the ties that bind him either to his tribe or the Government. Both Church and State should have, as a final goal, the destruction and end of treaty and reservation life. (Woodsworth 1909: 159–60)

This "end" would be achieved by raising Aboriginal peoples to a higher level of civilization through their adoption of Christian habits and beliefs.

Feminist Nellie McClung spent many years writing pamphlets for the Methodist and the United Church Mission Services with which Woodsworth was involved. She pointed out years after his writings above that Indians had not yet disappeared through missionary activity, and reissued a call on behalf of the All People's Mission in Winnipeg and the Methodist Woman's Missionary Society asking people to "keep up the good work" of empire (Devereux 2005: 120–23). Her feminism was indeed racially motivated as it supported imperialist expansion. Providing some women the vote, McClung argued, would allow "the female conquering of racial poisons that threaten to pollute the empire's last best West" (Devereux 2005, 86). The threats she spoke of included tuberculosis, alcohol use and the sexual immorality of some women. Through her involvement with the Woman's Christian Temperance Union (WCTU) and the establishment of home missions, McClung sought to "conquer these poisons" by training "uncivilized" women, including immigrant, impoverished and Aboriginal mothers, in the arts of "mothercraft," or in how to breast and bottle feed, and in what constitutes good domestic hygiene and proper food preparation (Valverde 1992). In spite of her belief that assimilation represented a potential cure for "Indianness," in other cases, McClung saw the need for more direct eugenic interventions and she actively promoted sexual sterilization. In *The Stream that Runs Fast*, McClung wrote of her involvement in arranging a meeting between a doctor and the parents of an eighteen-year-old girl said to have behavioural and educational difficulties in order for her to have a sterilization operation. After seeing the girl a year later, then happy and neatly dressed, McClung said this was the result of the sterilization procedure (McLung 1945: 177–80; McLaren 1990: 100).

More generally, the social purity and moral reform movements in Canada, in their efforts to rescue "fallen women," employed this rhetoric in their activism (Valverde 1991: 58–67). As a result, they were able to legitimate their reform work aimed at regulating women and family life, and to provide a new and scientific importance to the work conducted by women in the home. Organizations like the WCTU, the Salvation Army and the National Council of Women all advanced arguments steeped in evolutionary theory, and all gave prominence to scientific experts in spite of the heavy religious influence on these groups. These organizations

had a significant impact on immigration policies and practices, and helped create a
climate in which some were considered undesirable, namely impoverished, "undo-
mesticated" and Aboriginal women (Valverde 1991: 32). Neither was the racism of
these organizations simply an external factor contaminating their feminism. It was
integral to their feminism, a feminism that held the reproduction and nurturing,
not of all human beings, but of the white Anglo Saxon Protestant "race" as corner-
stones (Valverde 1992). The social purity movement blamed women who failed
to adopt socially defined middle class values and roles for the deterioration of the
race, and in its efforts it made patriotic virtue of women's asexuality (Bacchi 1978:
460). Prostitutes, "loose women" and the feebleminded bore primary responsibility
for the breakdown of the family and the spread of public health concerns (Adams
1994). Promiscuity, venereal disease and pregnancy were often pathologized,
and women and girls were presumed to be suffering "individual, psychological or
psychiatric maladjustment" if they engaged in premarital sex, had more than one
sexual partner or gave birth to illegitimate children (Sangster 2002: 33; Sangster
2000: 11). Through the work of these reformers, and later through the influence
of the medical, psychological and social work professions, a juvenile and criminal
justice system was created with very clear gender, class and racial biases, and it was
assumed those at the bottom of the social ladder were more promiscuous (Sangster
2000: 7–8; Sangster 2001: 89).

Even when larger political and economic relations were acknowledged as responsible for the relegation of women to the private sphere, emphasis sometimes
quickly turned eugenic. This is seen in the case of the United Farm Women of
Alberta (UFWA) and their efforts to improve the lives of rural women and children.
Scholar Alexis Soltice argues the life of a typical farm wife in rural Alberta in the
early twentieth century could be reduced to one word: labour. She states, "Women's
sphere was defined long ago, not by women, but by men" and argues that women
were essentially the tools and chattel of men, performing what she refers to as the
"never ending tasks" of fieldwork and the household chores of cooking, cleaning
and laundry (Soltice 1996: 75). Or, as Nellie McClung pointed out, women, as
the "servants of men," often did the work of two people, receiving little in return
(Soltice 1996: 64). Soltice quotes Irene Parlby, President of the UFWA and member
of the Famous Five, who acknowledged the exploitation and economic dependency
of these women:

> Because the work of the married woman, in caring for her household, was
> supposed to be a labour of love, and of no economic value ... women
> were at first content to sell their work at far below its real value, and thus
> depress the wage scale for all workers. (Soltice 1996: 68)

However, as early as 1916, Parlby is again quoted, this time in her attempt to redefine
the role played by women as being crucial to public life:

> Until women — all women — are raised to a much higher standard and educated to realize that in their hands lies the remedy for all these evils, not by getting of the votes, and the passing of laws, but by searching with their own hearts, and thoughts, and lives — by their prayers, and resolutions, and ideals to bring forth only that which is good, by refusing to give themselves to men of low and ignoble lives. Only so shall the highest in the race be achieved, and sin and disease over! (Soltice 1996: 85)

At their most basic level women were defined by their ability to reproduce, both by eugenic ideology and by some feminists. As a solution to the subordination of women in this role, some feminists, through the use of the very ideologies employed to oppress them, turned this oppression into a maternal duty with very real racist implications.

Through an alliance of feminism and eugenics, racism and sexism also merge. German historian Gisela Bock (1983: 416) argues that racism and sexism concern all women, the "inferior" and "superior." She explains:

> Sexism, which imposed economic dependency upon superior women, could be used, and was used, to implement racism by excluding many women from the relative benefits granted to 'desirable' mothers and children and forcing them to accept the lowest paid jobs in the labour market hierarchy in order to survive. (Bock 1983: 416)

Eugenics and the support of some feminists for this ideology allowed for the establishment of specific roles for "superior" men and women, and reinforced different roles and labours for "superior" and "inferior" women in ways that perpetuated relations of exploitation. Both eugenics and the gains sought by feminists who advocated this ideology were based on the control of female reproduction; reproduction for the future of the race for some and the denial of the ability to reproduce for others. Eugenic feminism argued for "freedom" only for those who demonstrated the "fitness" to use this "freedom" appropriately, that is, within the confines of the existing relations of production (Franks 2005: 15). These insights can be applied to the Canadian context as well. The eugenic feminism advocated by reformers like McClung, Murphy or Parlby did not become the dominant discourse on the rights of women in the early twentieth century because it held the possibility for emancipation from relations of oppression and economic dependency. This feminism was given prominence because it reinforced these very relations. It met the requirements of the mode of production by further assimilating women into socially desired roles, and by providing a space for some to perpetuate oppressive relations on others.

Gains achieved from within the capitalist patriarchal system always have implications for all of those involved. Feminist Maria Mies writes, "the law of this 'progress' is always a contradictory and not an evolutionary one: progress for some means retrogression for the other side; 'evolution' for some means 'devolution for others;' humanization for some means 'de-humanization for others'" (Mies 1986: 76). Those gains achieved by feminists in the late nineteenth and early twentieth centuries in Canada, as they were partial and specific to Anglo-Saxon, middle and upper class women, were granted because they were more cost effective than doing what was required to acknowledge and address the reasons why women lacked control over their lives, fertility and subsistence in the first place (Franks 2005: 15–17). Sociologist Martha Gimenez expands:

> Feminist struggles for women's rights, though important for the attainment of substantial improvements in the opportunities and quality of life of many individual women, do not and cannot substantially alter the status of all women. Women's success in their struggle for economic, political, and civil rights does not alter the material conditions that created the problems that motivated those struggles ... political emancipation and the attainment of political and civil rights are inherently limited achievements because, though the state may abolish distinctions that act as barriers to full participation by all citizens, it does not abolish the social relations that are the basis for those distinctions and are presupposed by the very existence of the state. (Gimenez 2005: 28)

The very existence of the capitalist patriarchal state presupposes social relations that deny women (and men too) the ability to exist and provide for their own subsistence in the ways they so choose. It is these relations which gave rise to the economic dependency and exploitation experienced by women in the early twentieth century. For Aboriginal women (and men too), the existence of the Canadian state in its current form presupposes relations of colonialism and assimilation. These relations also make it so the control of Indigenous women's reproduction by the state has different manifestations and unique implications.

As the next chapter illustrates, there are connections between the material relations of colonialism and resource accumulation, the ideology of Aboriginal women as "unfit mothers," and state interventions in their lives and those of their children. Scholar Dean Neu highlights that land provides the basis of reproduction for both settlers and Indigenous peoples. Thus, the struggle over land is also a struggle over the rights and bases of reproduction for settlers and Indigenous peoples alike (Neu 2000: 275). The depiction of Aboriginal women as "inferior" or "unfit" becomes one means of securing land ownership, of further assimilating Aboriginal peoples into Canadian society and of denying their ability to reproduce (Cull 2006). If one considers these broader connections, the sterilization of Aboriginal women becomes simply one aspect of an historical assault directly related to other policies like residential schooling, the displacement of Aboriginal children from their families and the dismantling of traditional male–female social roles in Aboriginal societies.

Though not solely to blame, the mainstream feminist movement of the late nineteenth and early twentieth century played a role in allowing the relations of capitalism to continue, and in the process, it created a space for itself as a colonial agent by reinforcing sexist and racist notions of womanhood. By consequence, some participated in the colonization of Aboriginal peoples and their lands in ways that also made the sterilization of Aboriginal women more likely to occur. To more deeply understand many of the other reasons why sterilization came to represent a viable intervention in the lives of Aboriginal women we turn to a history of Indian policy in Canada. Considering the specific ways Indigenous women have been targeted for assimilation as well as the political and economic interests served will also allow us to better understand the unique implications of coercive sterilization for them and their peoples.

Notes

1. Despite the common misapplication of "the survival of the fittest" to Darwin, it was Herbert Spencer who coined the phrase. Social Darwinism is a term that has been most commonly employed by critics of this view, rather than the theorists themselves.
2. Mendel was an Austrian Monk who, while studying at the University of Vienna, experimented with the breeding of peas of different colours and shapes. He discovered that certain traits could be inherited from one generation to the next even when their presence was not apparent. Although Mendel was speaking of physical traits and not social characteristics, for eugenicists these were one and the same.
3. The biblical story of Genesis held that the first woman was created out of Adam's rib, as his servant.
4. Referred to as the "Famous Five," Emily Murphy, Nellie McClung, Irene Parlby, Louise McKinney and Henrietta Muir Edwards demanded that the Supreme Court of Canada answer on whether women were included as "persons" under Section 24 of the *British North America Act* of 1867. On 24 April 1928, the Supreme Court declared women were not persons. This decision was subsequently overturned by the British Judicial Committee of the Privy Council. Not all women were persons, however. Aboriginal peoples — both men and women — were not considered persons under Canadian law until 1951.

2. Indian Policy
and Aboriginal Women

Prior to European contact, Aboriginal women enjoyed a status drastically different from that held by women in Western European societies of the same time period. Although both Aboriginal women and men played a vital economic role in their communities, their tasks were complementary to each other. Women were responsible for meeting many of the needs of their communities, and even though there was a division of labour, this did not imply inferiority. Rather, men and women enjoyed the right of access to food, tools and other means of survival by their simple fact of existence (Anderson 1988; Buffalohead 1983; Klein 1983). Aboriginal women were also central decision makers in matters affecting social life and they enjoyed greater freedom in their sexual life than did European women (Carter 1997; Klein 1983). In Indigenous societies, land and many of the decisions regarding resource distribution were often under the control of women. In Iroquoian and Algonquin societies, for example, social organizations were largely matrifocal, matrilineal and matrilocal (Jamieson 1989: 113; Mann 2000: 117, 241). While bilateral kinship was respected, descent was often traced through the female line, husbands would often take up life in their wife's community and there was an immediate connection between Aboriginal women and the land because both had the ability to give life. This connection had a material basis arising from the fact that Aboriginal women often provided the subsistence base for their societies and were responsible for reproducing future generations, both biologically and socially.

Indigenous women were most often responsible for and had authority over harvesting life supporting products from the land. For example, women often cultivated rice, dried wild plant foods and roasted, transformed and distributed game, waterfowl and fish (Buffalohead 1983). Laura Peers has documented the trend in Western literature of minimizing the contributions of Aboriginal women to their societies (Peers 1996). Aboriginal subsistence is frequently said to be based primarily on hunting practices, with gathering done by women as only supplemental and incidental to the diet, thereby relegating Aboriginal women's work to the private sphere. However, Indigenous societies have traditionally had much more flexible subsistence bases provided by women, with large game added when it was available. And women were often central to decision making in these matters (Peers 1996: 39–50, 49). In Cree, Ojibway and other Algonquin societies, for example, women controlled the products of their labour, and had a high degree of control over the products of men's labour too, as they were often responsible for processing and distributing meats and other foods and resources (Bourgeault 1983; Etienne and Leacock 1980; Stevenson 1999).

Although Indigenous societies were diverse in their organizations, and the division of labour varied from one to another, evidence indicates that women were highly regarded in general. Despite this, European colonists, fur traders and missionaries tended to focus on the roles of men while diminishing the pivotal roles played by women. Aboriginal women were often perceived as drudges, serving only as slaves to men (Biard 1612; Bear Nicholas 1994; Denys 1908). Yet, as Anthropologist Eleanor Leacock states in reference to Montagnais society, "women retained control over the products of their labour. These were not alienated, and women's production of clothing, shelter … gave them concomitant practical power and influence, despite formal statements of male dominance that might be elicited by outsiders" (Etienne and Leacock 1980: 30). It is precisely because Aboriginal women were not divorced from the land or the products of their labour — in fact they had a direct and immediate connection to these, and enjoyed a freedom and ability to determine their own lives in a manner that was incongruent with what was to be imposed — that colonial policies targeted them in specific ways.

Through colonization there arose a clash of fundamentally opposed modes of production — those of Aboriginal societies and that of Western capitalism (Marx 1990: 931–40). Indigenous forms of life existed in fundamental opposition to the relations required for colonization, or the imposition of Western capitalism. Aboriginal societies were diverse, but they were not capitalist. The autonomy of men and women and the relations between them have often been referred to as egalitarian, and these relations are said to deteriorate only under specific conditions (Anderson 1988; Etienne and Leacock 1980). Within this context, colonists proceeded to distort and undermine the roles of Aboriginal women. If they had no connection to their means of subsistence and were oppressed by Aboriginal men, then the colonial relations that were being imposed could more easily be justified as acts of goodwill, or simply another variation of what was already in existence. This would also open up Aboriginal lands for exploitation.

For colonization to be successful, both Aboriginal women and men would need to be reduced to a marginal class within the capitalist mode of production. One way by which this is done is through assimilation. Assimilation allows for the termination of the legal line of descendants able to claim rights to the land and resources on which Canada depends for its existence. Hugh Shewell (2004: 29–32) tells us that "civilizing" Aboriginal peoples with the aim of making them into menial wage labourers and gaining access to lands and resources was one way of answering the "Indian Question." Assimilation has as its logical consequence that it also becomes increasingly difficult for Aboriginal peoples to practice their own ways. Therefore, assimilation is a twofold process involving the imposition of a particular way of life at the expense and with the destruction of the former. Another manner by which assimilation is carried out is by stripping Aboriginal women of the ability to control their reproduction and denying them the opportunity to raise their children in ways that are in keeping with their ways of life. Colonial policy has attacked the ability of Aboriginal women to reproduce, and short of eliminating this ability altogether, has sought to curb it, or confine it within socially accepted forms conducive to capitalist relations. In this respect, the relations imposed, though perhaps different in form, are very similar in content to those imposed on European women. Just as European women have been subverted from controlling their ability to exist autonomously through their separation from their means of subsistence, their relegation to the private sphere and by having their labour deemed non-productive, so too have their reproductive abilities been appropriated for capital, used to produce a working class of labour (Mies 1986: 74–111). For Aboriginal women, assimilation serves first and foremost to separate Aboriginal peoples from their lands and resources so that these can be incorporated and exploited under the mode of production being imposed. This was the underlying purpose of colonial policy and this continues to represent the goal of Indian policy in Canada. How this has been done since Confederation will be of interest here.

Historical Context and the Indian Act

As Canada became an independent nation-state, it inherited from the British Crown legal obligations toward Indigenous peoples. By the simple fact that Aboriginal peoples were here before the arrival of Europeans, they possess inherent collective rights to self-determination and to the lands and resources necessary to practice their ways of life.[1] As early as 1763, the Royal Proclamation explicitly acknowledged that Aboriginal peoples held title to the lands of North America and it established that this title could only be transferred to the Crown through treaty or direct negotiation with Indigenous peoples, with the promise that, in all cases, the Crown would provide security and protection to Aboriginal peoples.[2] The government of Canada acquired these responsibilities through section 91 (24) of the *Constitution Act*, 1867.[3] Further, the first treaties entered into with Great Britain, and later with the Canadian state, also established obligations on the part of the Crown and confirmed the status of Aboriginal peoples as sovereign nations on whose lands and resources Canada depends for its existence.[4] Since its formation, however, Canada has attempted to limit or eschew its obligations as they were and continue to be seen as too costly, as impeding assimilation and as standing in the way of capitalist expansion and resource development. Within this context, the Indian Act of 1876 was established, a piece of legislation that has had a devastating impact in all aspects of Indigenous lives. The imposition of this legislation has undermined central aspects of Aboriginal forms of life, has divorced Native peoples from their lands and has worked in concert with other colonial policies to further the assimilation of Aboriginal peoples by replacing existing relations with those more conducive to a capitalist mode of production. And, because capitalist relations are inherently patriarchal, part of the assimilative agenda has been to target Aboriginal women in specific ways.

The stated purpose of Indian policy was laid out early on, prior to the formation of Canada. A 1834 report commissioned by the British House of Commons to investigate expenditures in the colonies of the Crown stated that the Indian Department, established to distribute annual payments to Indians for their military alliance, was to be greatly reduced if not entirely abolished (Neu and Therrien 2003: 55). Scholars Dean Neu and Richard Therrien point out that the recommendations proposed in the final version of this report aimed to address various concerns of government. The military support provided by Indians was less needed by this time, yet their lands continued to be desired for settlement and resource expropriation. The Indian Department was also becoming financially burdensome. The report:

> addressed the[se] competing dilemmas of government. The specific costs associated with the Indian department would be reduced over time and, if the solutions were successful, Indigenous peoples would both be contained and civilized. Furthermore, over the long term, this strategy of containment would make it easier for colonial officials to buy and resell the land previously occupied by Indigenous peoples, since this land was no longer central to their subsistence. (Neu and Therrien 2003: 61)

Containment or assimilation of Indigenous peoples were the only viable policy options since the close watch of humanitarians and missionaries had effectively ruled out extermination and slavery (Neu and Therrien 2003: 61). With these aims in mind, responsibility for Indian Affairs was transferred to the Province of Canada in 1860, and then to the newly formed Canadian state, during which time it set out to assimilate Aboriginal peoples. In the words of Herman Merivale, permanent under secretary of the British Colonial Office, the goal was to obtain Indigenous consent to the usurpations made upon them, bit by bit (Neu and Therrien 2003: 65). The Indian Act served this purpose.

The Indian Act of 1876 consolidated all previous legislation relating to Aboriginal peoples while providing the government of Canada more authority over their lives in order to carry out the goals of "containment, civilization and assimilation."[5] This Act and its subsequent amendments criminalized many aspects of Aboriginal ways of life, undermined Indigenous political, economic and social institutions and imposed Canadian ones. This can be seen in the outlawing of traditional forms of government based on consensus and the imposition of band councils; the exclusion, until 1951, of women's participation in elections or public meetings; or through the criminalization of the Potlatch, a central means of forging alliances with other nations.[6] The Indian Act also included a formal definition of what constituted an Indian, and this definition was designed to limit the number of those to whom the federal government had obligations. A statement made by an unnamed official to the Joint Committee on Indian Affairs during its 1946–48 parliamentary hearings on the Indian Act makes plain the purpose of defining Indians under the Act. This official wrote:

> By the alteration of the definition of Indian by the Statute of 1876 the Dominion very substantially reduced the number of people for whose welfare it was responsible and by that action passed the responsibility on to the provinces for thousands of people, who, but for that statute of 1876, would have been federal responsibility for all time. (Canada 1996: 280; Palmater 2011a: 46)

Through this Act, Aboriginal rights to lands and resources as the original inhabitants of this land were replaced with "Indian rights," or rights to such things as annuity or treaty payments, or access to reserve lands based on a colonial government's limiting definition of who was considered an Indian. From the outset, the definition of an Indian was race-based and targeted Aboriginal women in specific ways.

Historian Sarah Carter states that legislation embodied within the Indian Act left women who were defined as Indian with fewer fundamental rights than any other women or men in Canada (Carter 1996; Jamieson 1978). This is evident in the very definition of an Indian under the Act as "any Indian man and his wife."[7] This definition was central in undermining property relations in Aboriginal societies, relations which were directly tied to the female line, by transferring this property to Indian men. For example, under Indian Act legislation, upon marriage a woman was reassigned to the band of her husband and only men could own property. Consequently, an Aboriginal woman who married someone other than another Indian man, and any of her children, ceased to be an Indian in the eyes of the Canadian government, ceased to have rights to land and became unable to transfer this connection to future generations.

If a child was born out of wedlock, the implications were sometimes different. Although Indian Act legislation has been amended several times, and this has changed who could or could not be considered an Indian in the eyes of the federal government, prior to a 1985 amendment, state-imposed criteria for band membership affected children differently (Fiske 1995: 6). Children born out of wedlock became members of their mother's band if no objections were raised. However, male children born out of wedlock to non-Indian women and Indian men were registered with the father's band; and sometimes female children were denied registration (Green 1985). Kathleen Jamieson writes that the imposition of European values of:

> private rights in land inherited through the male were an indispensable component of this system, which had as its corollary control and repression of the sexuality of the female ... The threat that women's autonomy posed to this system resulted in the development of a body of common law emphasizing the importance of legitimacy and the legal ownership by

a husband of a wife's generative capacity. The wife was in common law the property of her husband. Work (labour for pay) and the accumulation of goods were seen as an end in themselves ... The Indian married woman was thus seen as an appendage to her husband whether he was Indian or white. (Jamieson 1978: 13)

This legislation had the effect of separating Aboriginal women from the land by imposing patrilineality and instilling notions of female subordination. It also ensured the assimilation of Native peoples, if they were to survive at all, into the rising Canadian capitalist system by imposing notions of private property held only by men, whether Indian men, white men, or the Canadian state.

Many have written of the inherent sexism of the Indian Act and of Bill C-31 of 1985, which repealed the above mentioned clause (Joseph 1991; Lawrence 2003; Turpel 1993). Its repeal, however, does not automatically mean the reinstatement of previously excluded women. The onus remains on Aboriginal women to reapply for status, and the federal government has assigned band councils the task of deciding whether applicants should be reinstated as band members and share in treaty benefits or reserve lands. This has left many bands in a conflicting position. The reacceptance of individuals further taxes resources that are often inadequate to provide an acceptable standard of living to community members. Band councils are forced to choose whether to accept newly reinstated individuals without being provided the necessary resources for this to take place. As scholar Menno Boldt states, this government action was more self-serving than progressive as it has left band councils to "take the heat" for accepting or denying reserve residence to Indian women and their children (Boldt 1993: 207–16). Reinstatement of status by the federal government and reacceptance as a band member, then, is not always certain, and it leaves unaddressed the larger question of whether arguing for equal treatment under an Act specifically designed to destroy Aboriginal ways of life is the most effective way to address sexism and racism toward Aboriginal women (Turpel 1993). The Indian Act effectively made Aboriginal women the property of men and its specific focus on women has allowed government to reduce the numbers of those considered Indian by denying status to future generations of children (Palmater 2011a). This has allowed Canada to terminate a legal line of Aboriginal descendants and establish property rights to territory and resources without physically killing Aboriginal peoples (Chrisjohn et al. 2002).

Policies embodied in the Indian Act, which were fluid and altered as required to meet political and economic needs, served to destroy Indigenous forms of life and to reduce the numbers of those considered Aboriginal in the eyes of the federal government. Under the guise of education, residential schools were also geared toward this end (Bear Nicholas 2001; Chrisjohn and Young 2006; Milloy 1999). Residential and industrial schools were established in the 1840s in Upper Canada and were extended to the West in 1880, where they expanded rapidly in conjunction with settlement patterns. For over one hundred years, Canada forcefully removed Aboriginal children from their communities and sent them to these church-run institutions. These schools were never intended to educate, but to separate Aboriginal children from their way of life and to indoctrinate them in European ways. These also aimed to Christianize Aboriginal children, to inculcate within them clear roles for men and women within a nuclear family and to instruct them to become a subservient class of workers within the Canadian political economy (Canada 1996). In 1883, while discussing the education scheme being laid out for Aboriginal peoples, Member of Parliament Edward Blake highlighted the importance of targeting Indian girls. His statement also illustrates that racist ideology played a role in justifying Indian policy:

> If [we] leave the young Indian girl who is to mature into a squaw to have the uncivilized habits of the tribe, the Indian, when he married such a squaw, will likely be pulled into Indian savagery by her. If this scheme is going to succeed at all, you will ... have to civilize the intended wives ... I have known ... how difficult it is to eradicate that hereditary taint. (Canada 1883: 1377)

Leacock has also shown in her writing on the Naskapi Montagnais and the Jesuit program of colonization that the introduction of a European family structure, with male authority, female fidelity and the elimination of the right to divorce, was essential to civilizing and assimilating Indigenous peoples (Etienne and Leacock 1980: 24–42). Missionaries, who were instrumental in the policy of residential schools, also played a primary role in the imposition of Christian marriage on the adult population. Marriage was seen as a means of ensuring the assimilation of both Aboriginal women and their children into Canadian society. Scholar Karen Anderson states that Christian marriage and the transformation of women and men's means of interrelating was considered central to control of the entire society. As long as parents believed themselves to be free and independent they would view their children similarly. Thus, the imposition of Christian marriage also allowed missionaries to access Aboriginal children, whom they described as being without discipline (Anderson 1991).

The state, too, was involved in the legislation of this process. In an attempt to enforce marriage and Western capitalist notions of family and property relations, Aboriginal women and their children came under bureaucratic assault in other ways. A revision to the Indian Act in 1898 stipulated that any woman who bore a child out of wedlock or deserted her family was no longer considered an Indian and would no longer fall under federal responsibility (Statutes of Canada 1898 c. 34). In 1927, an amendment stipulated that any illegitimate child could be excluded from membership of a band by the Superintendent General at any time (Statutes of Canada 1927 c. 98). A 1951 revision required all Aboriginal marriages to submit to provincial marriage legislation (Statutes of Canada 1951 c. 29). Prior to this, the Department of Indian Affairs would simply withhold treaty payments and annuities to any women engaged in what they termed "polygamous" unions (Stevenson 1999). Another example of how this was done was through the imposition of European notions of property inheritance. An 1884 amendment allowing Indians to make wills specified that a widow was entitled to receive one third of her deceased husband's property only if she was "of good moral character and not separated from her husband at the time of his death" (Statutes of Canada 1884 c. 27, s. 5). This was, of course, based on the requirement that Indians accept the institution of Western marriage. These amendments both implicitly and explicitly imposed on Aboriginal women Western notions of family, and by default worked to destroy Aboriginal forms of relating to each other. For an Aboriginal child to be viewed as legitimate and entitled to federal obligations, it must be born within a Christian union. Aboriginal women were placed in a very precarious position. If they desired to continue to receive federal payments and ensure the continuance of status to future generations, they must assimilate. If they chose not to, the federal government would deny responsibility for them. The failure of Aboriginal women to assimilate, then, was at their own peril as both assimilation and a refusal to assimilate served different political economic interests of the Canadian state.

Indian Policy and Health

There is no specific provision in the Indian Act that addresses the health of Aboriginal peoples. However, the argument has been made that access to health care is both an inherent Aboriginal right and a treaty right. The National Aboriginal Health Organization (NAHO) explains that the maintenance of good health has always been integral to Aboriginal peoples as part of their collective societies, and that health and healing practices were in existence prior to the arrival of Europeans. As such, the right to continue these practices is an Aboriginal right, part and parcel of those rights Canada acquired a responsibility to protect in 1867 and which were most recently recognized and affirmed through Section 35(1) of the *Constitution Act*, 1982 (NAHO 2004; 2003; Battiste and Henderson 2000). Although only Treaty 6, stretching from western Alberta through Saskatchewan and into Manitoba and covering fifty First Nations, specifically includes reference to medical care in its written text, the federal government has acknowledged that a similar clause was promised during the negotiations of Treaties 7, 8, 10 and 11 but this was not included in the written treaty text (Canada 1995: 13; Reiter 1995; NAHO 2003: 5, 17–23). From the perspective of Aboriginal peoples, treaties, especially pre-confederation treaties, were negotiated to ensure their survival, sometimes in the midst of suffering from epidemics related to the arrival of Europeans, and these agreements were meant to address essential issues like health and health care. NAHO highlights that there were seven specific references to contagious diseases affecting Mi'kmaq communities as part of treaty discussions between 1611 and 1760 (NAHO 2003: 17–23; NAHO 2004: footnote 152; Morris 1991: 185, 201; Neu and

Therrien 2003: 75–80; Wicken 1993). Despite this, Canada consistently claims that interventions in the health of Aboriginal peoples are provided solely out of a humanitarian concern on the part of government (Canada 2002: 212; Canada 1971: 105; Canada 1965a: 95).

Whether undertaken for the former or latter reason, notions of race have permeated federal efforts to address Indigenous health in Canada. The settling of the West during the late nineteenth and early twentieth centuries, the destruction of the buffalo and the establishment of reserves for Indians caused a rise of disease and hunger in Aboriginal communities. A cursory glance at annual reports from Indian Affairs during this period makes plain the epidemic proportions of poverty, malnutrition and sickness faced by Aboriginal peoples. Concern for the spread of disease from Aboriginal communities to settler populations living in proximity to Indian reserves led Canada to intervene, albeit reticently and with complete financial restraint, in the health of Aboriginal peoples. Despite claims of humanitarianism, fiscal concerns were at the forefront of health policy in Aboriginal communities at this time (Lux 2001; Shewell 2004: 93–133). Working in conjunction with policies of land settlement and resource extraction, the ways in which health policy was implemented often had the effect of aggravating conditions of poverty and ill health.

Aboriginal communities in the late 1800s, most specifically in the West, were rife with high rates of malnutrition, typhus, smallpox, influenza, pneumonia and tuberculosis (Canada 1885–1900). The minimal public health services that were being established in non-native communities, such as proper sewage and waste disposal, potable water and the availability of food sources, were nonexistent on Indian reserves (Satzewich and Wotherspoon 1993). Reserve life was a new phenomenon for Aboriginal communities, who were recently relegated to bounded patches of often infertile land by the federal government, sometimes away from their traditional food sources and access to water. The colonial mission of establishing Western settlement and constructing a Trans Canada railway resulted in the implementation of the *Dominion Lands Act,* which provided newly arrived immigrants with 160 acres of land for agricultural use as Indigenous peoples engaged in treaty signing were being denied access to these lands (Statutes of Canada 1872).

Federal policies aimed to ensure the assimilation of Aboriginal peoples as a marginal class within Canadian society, forced to adopt habits more conducive to the advancement of Western capitalism. As early as 1880, an annual report from Indian Affairs stated, "the system pursued in affording relief to Indians is calculated to accustom them to habits of industry ... under that system all able-bodied Indians are required to work for the food given themselves and their families" (White 1987: 26). Yet Aboriginal peoples were not allowed to provide for their own subsistence in their own ways, but in ways that were beneficial to a capitalist mode of production. Policies were often implemented to deny Aboriginal peoples the ability to carry out their own independent practices and to establish an agricultural and sedentary way of life, something more in keeping with the development of Canadian society. Even when Aboriginal peoples managed to succeed in agricultural pursuits originating from state imposed policies, this success could be undermined by federal officials when it placed them in competition with non-Aboriginal farmers (Carter 1990).

In other instances, the failure of Aboriginal peoples to respond positively to state imposed policies confirmed their biological and racial inferiority. In 1886, Edgar Dewdney, Indian Commissioner since 1879, stated that the death and sickness on Indian reserves was directly due to hereditary disease which had its origins at a time prior to that in which federal responsibility began (Lux 2001: 141). One of their own, Malcolm Cameron, Liberal Member of Parliament from West Huron, criticized this notion by stating that starvation and ill health on reserves was a direct result of a cruel federal policy implemented to weaken Aboriginal peoples into submission (Lux 2001: 141). Government doctor G.T. Orton also laid blame for the increase of disease in Aboriginal populations on the churches and government. He cited the discouragement of Indian medicine and the imposition of a nutritionally lacking diet as primary factors affecting the rates of ill health in Indigenous populations (White 1987: 221). However, again in 1904, Frank Pedley, deputy superintendent of Indian Affairs, when trying to answer why ill health was so pervasive and mortality so high on reserves, blamed the situation on the moral failings of Aboriginal peoples themselves, their much higher birth rate compared to non-natives and some inherent defect on their part, whether that be mental, moral or physical (Canada 1904: 238). Referring specifically to the death rate of Aboriginal peoples from tuberculosis, he expressed concern not for the fact that federal policy had created conditions in which Indians could not survive, but because this epidemic represented a "menace to the white population" (Canada 1904: 238).

Disproportionately high death rates from tuberculosis were also found in residential schools. The death rate of Indian children from tuberculosis in residential schools was a concern for the Canadian government throughout the course of their existence. Explanations for these fatalities were not often looked for in the conditions in which Indian children lived; whether their poverty, malnutrition or poorly ventilated surroundings. These were most often explained as being indicative of a hereditary taint among Aboriginal peoples. In 1896, Dr. S.E. MacAdam, while working at the Battleford Indian residential school, blamed these deaths on the transition from "savagery to civilization," a transition that hastened the innate tendency of some to develop tuberculosis (Lux 2001: 110). If Indians were dying out through the process of civilization, this was simply the result of the evolutionary struggle unfolding as it should (Lux 2001: 153).

In 1904, Dr. Peter Bryce, a medical doctor and former secretary of the Ontario Board of Health, was appointed chief medical officer of the Department of Indian Affairs. In this role, he began investigating the health conditions of Indian children in residential schools. His 1907 *Report on the Indian Schools of Manitoba and the*

Northwest revealed 24 to 33 percent of children who attended residential schools died from tuberculosis (Bryce 1907). He blamed these deaths on poor ventilation, inadequate sanitation and the presence of consumptive pupils. Despite playing a central role in the eugenics movement in Canada, Bryce concluded the high death rate from tuberculosis in residential school was due to a poor diet and the environment in which Indian children were living rather than any hereditary defectiveness. He recommended the schools be reformed, not to change their civilizing purpose, but to establish a greater role for medical practitioners within these federally supported institutions (Lux 2001: 127–33). Bryce also called for an increase in government expenditures to go toward the appointment and training of nurses and sanitary directors, the improvement of school buildings and the establishment of hospitals. What resulted, whether directly or indirectly intended, was an increased role for the medical profession in the assimilation of Aboriginal peoples (Lux 2001: 127–33). More recent work confirms that the involvement of the medical profession in residential schools was not innocent. Historian Ian Mosby tells us that some physicians used their involvement as an opportunity to pursue their own research despite the impact this might have on Indigenous children. For example, after identifying food shortages and malnourishment as problems in the residential school system, nutritional experiments were carried out that included controlled diets being given to children that ended up producing anemia (Mosby 2013). In another instance, Aboriginal children were used as test subjects in experimental trials of the BCG tuberculosis vaccine, during which nearly one-fifth died while the living conditions in schools and on reserves, which contributed so greatly to the high rates of infection, remained unaddressed (Lux 1998).

Aboriginal communities have historically been responsible for their own health and have developed methods as effective as those of any other society prior to the imposition of Western medicine (Kelm 1998: 83–99; Waldram et al. 1995: 107–11). Aboriginal women have also exerted control over their reproductive health and have diverse ways of explaining menstruation, of approaching fertility and childbirth, of inducing abortion and even of causing sterility (Anderson 2011; Kelm 1998; Waldram et al. 1995). Many settlers also made use of Aboriginal medicine in the early years of Canadian expansion (Burnett 2011; Burnett 2010; Malloch 1989; Mitchinson 2002). Steps were taken by the Department of Indian Affairs that made the continuance of these practices difficult by requiring Aboriginal peoples to submit to Western medical practices. Amendments to the Indian Act in 1914 and 1952 compelled Aboriginal peoples to submit to medical treatment while making Aboriginal resistance illegal (Statutes of Canada 1914 c. 35; Statutes of Canada 1952 c. 149, s. 72). Confining Aboriginal peoples to reserves and allotting their lands to settler populations for agricultural purposes also made access to traditional medicines nearly impossible. What resulted was that Aboriginal peoples in general, and Aboriginal women in particular, were made dependent on the Canadian medical system for even their most basic health needs and this allowed, and continues to allow, services to be provided unequally, coercively and abusively.

The expansion of Canada into the West and resultant Indian policy had dramatic effects on Aboriginal peoples, and the high death rates from tuberculosis and other ailments reflect this. Aboriginal women often could not conceive children due to poor health, pregnancy and lactation placed major demands on mothers, and excessive hunger gave rise to low birth weight babies and high infant mortality rates (Lux 2001: 27–70, esp. 45). This effect was in keeping with the purpose of the Indian Act — to reduce the numbers of those to whom the federal government has obligations either through bureaucratic means, or in this case, through manipulation and outright starvation. Rather than consider how recently imposed colonial conditions might impact the ability of Indigenous women to give birth safely, high infant mortality rates were used to justify the increased medicalization of Native bodies (Shaw 2013; Rutherdale 2010).

Historian Mary Jane McCallum shows that doctors readily attributed infant and maternal death in Aboriginal communities to "midwives, self-appointed and untrained," who worked "on the pallets of ... dingy cabins," in "temporary shelters" and "on the trail during migration along the trap-line" (McCallum 2005: 112). In contrast, the modern infirmary offered child delivery technology during birth, the ability to screen babies for disease and the opportunity to provide expert advice to mothers on the care of herself and her infant during her confinement (McCallum 2005; Foulkes 1962). Western medical practitioners saw Indigenous methods as erroneous and incompatible with assimilation, and the colonization of childbirth and criminalization of midwifery became central aspects of Indian health policy (McCallum 2005: 112). In remote and northern areas this resulted in large numbers of women being evacuated from their communities to give birth or to be treated for tuberculosis (Jasen 1997; Kaufert and O'Neil 1990; Moffitt 2004). Scholar Judith Bender Zelmanovits (2003: 169) states, in reference to this imposition of Western medical and birthing practices on northern communities and the transfer of large numbers of Aboriginal women to southern hospitals to give birth, "This is but another aspect of the patriarchal, patronizing and assimilatory policies articulated in the Indian Acts."

For the federal government, interventions in the health of Aboriginal peoples were often implemented in order to protect surrounding settler populations. P.E. Moore, the director of Indian and Northern Health Services, said that, in spite of the fact that the disease did not become a major cause of death among Indigenous peoples until after they had settled on reserves, government interventions to address tuberculosis in Native communities were undertaken because it was in the "selfish interest of the white man, for his own protection" (Moore 1961: 1012–16). The limited extent to which the federal government did intervene in the health of Aboriginal peoples was also carried out in a way that benefited the political economic interests of the Canadian state. Western medicine required Western medical facilities and if Aboriginal peoples were served by these institutions, federal monies provided for Aboriginal peoples could go to these hospitals. In its compulsion to protect the growing non-Native community from disease, the government recognized that strategically funding medical services on or near reserves allowed Indian funds to be used to the benefit of non-Native populations. Lux (2001: 146) states:

> The medical profession's need for work and the non-Native community's need for medical attendance also had a bearing on how and where expenditures were made. Representatives of isolated immigrant communities reckoned that without Indian department work, local doctors could not afford to establish practices in their villages. Thus medical work for the department acted as a guarantee of medical care for the immigrant communities. Physicians received a dependable income from the department that allowed them to establish private practice in immigrant communities. The rapidly increasing number of doctors employed by the department was in part a reflection of the needs of non-Native communities.

In another instance, the Charles Camsell Indian hospital was refurbished with funds allocated for health services to Aboriginal peoples, and control was subsequently passed over to the province for the servicing of mainly non-Native communities.[8] The ultimate goal of health care policy was to turn Aboriginal peoples into citizens to whom the federal government no longer had obligations or responsibilities, and it was hoped that Aboriginal peoples would take fiscal responsibility for their own health care. However, by undermining their ability to continue to practice their own methods of health, healing and childbirth, Aboriginal peoples were not free to choose the type of health services they wished to receive. In effect, they were being asked to pay for their own assimilation and disenfranchisement as Aboriginal peoples (McCallum 2005: 113–14).

Indian Policy, Sexuality and Motherhood

The ways Indian policy has exerted control over and worked to shape the sexual and reproductive lives of Aboriginal women has also been vital to the goals of assimilation and the reduction of federal responsibilities to Aboriginal peoples. The degree of freedom enjoyed by Aboriginal women in their sexual practices has been portrayed since the beginning of colonization as offensive to the Anglo-Saxon Protestant values, threatening to the social and moral health of society and inconsistent with the task of assimilation. Often referred to as sexually promiscuous, Aboriginal women were considered immoral and blamed for prostitution, the spread of venereal disease and alcohol problems, and were generally said to represent a threat to the public. The social and moral reform movement in Canada during the late nineteenth and early twentieth centuries habitually denounced the "traffic" in Indian women near white settlements in the West and considered

Aboriginal women, in their failure to adopt Christian marriage, to blame for prostitution (Valverde 1991: 86). In their attempt to impose notions of Christian social purity, these groups played a central role in restructuring the domestic sphere and reinforcing the private/public divisions that were evident in European societies, with Aboriginal women relegated to the private sphere. Through proper guidance of wives of settlers and Protestant ministers, or teaching sisters in residential schools, Indigenous women could be taught to take on the proper "womanly" role of the industrious settler housewife. Aboriginal women were encouraged to be responsible for the care and maintenance of the house, kitchen and grounds alone, to manufacture family clothing by knitting, sewing and spinning wool, and to cook with foods of European origin (White 1987: 54–143). All of this often took place in conjunction with the enforced discontinuation of Indigenous practices.

The federal government also considered prostitution a problem of Indian women. Former Prime Minister John A. Macdonald is quoted as saying, "The depravity existing among the Indian women ... is greatly to be deplored. They repair, on arriving at years of puberty to the white centres and enter into lives of prostitution" (Valverde 1991: 57). Government implemented various regulations to manage prostitution. The Indian Act of 1879 punished individuals who kept houses of prostitution (NAHO 2006: 16–17; Statutes of Canada 1879). An amendment made a year later, in 1880, specifically prohibited the keeper of any house from allowing Indian women who were believed to be prostitutes onto their premises (Statutes of Canada 1880). Changes to the Indian Act in 1884 explicitly prohibited any Indian woman or man from keeping or frequenting a "disorderly house or wigwam." This legislation remained in effect until 1906, when sections on prostitution introduced into the Criminal Code were deemed sufficient for the control of Indian prostitution (Backhouse 1985). The pass system of 1885 further confined Aboriginal peoples to reserves and restricted their right to move freely, or to access traditional lands (Smith 2009: 60–78). Officials also hoped that through this system, Aboriginal women of "abandoned character" would be prevented from loitering in settlements as they came under increased surveillance from the North West Mounted Police (Carter 1990: 154–55). However, Yvonne Boyer points out that to have enacted the above provisions was to directly target Aboriginal women and is more broadly and directly connected to the hyper-sexualized view of Aboriginal women as "drunken, dirty and easy squaws" (NAHO 2006: 15; Anderson 2000: 99–115).

The policing of the sexual practices of Aboriginal women following the establishment of Canada stands in direct contrast to their exploitation as sexual and political commodities in the early years of colonization. During the fur trade, for example, due to their central position in Aboriginal societies, alliances were sought with Indigenous women in order to infiltrate communities, to establish trade relations and to gain access to Aboriginal lands and resources (Van Kirk 1980). Some traders took full advantage of the flexibility of Indian marital customs at the time by entering into unions with Aboriginal women. Although the degree to which some of these unions were voluntary, or can be said to have arisen out of genuine attraction, is up for debate, it was common practice for fur traders and resident officers at trading posts in the interior of Canada to have sexual relationships with influential Indian women as a means of developing and maintaining trade relations with surrounding Indian groups (Bourgeault 1983). These unions were so common that in 1806, in an attempt to avoid the costs that a wife and children might bring, the Northwest Company passed a resolution forbidding their men from taking Indian women (Brown 1980: 97). Yet, once political and economic control of lands and resources came to rest in the hands of colonizers and this control was cemented through the establishment of Canada as a nation, Aboriginal women were no longer required and their sexuality came to be viewed by colonial officials as an impediment to assimilation (Bourgeault 1983).

Aboriginal women and other marginalized women have been subject to intense state intervention and institutionalization in prisons, reformatories or training schools where it was hoped middle class notions of womanhood could be instilled. The significance of this for Indigenous women is profoundly different, however, as this surveillance occurred within and was shaped by the material, social and cultural context of colonialism (Sangster 2001). Aboriginal women were criminalized for their sexual conduct while at the same time this legal and moral regulation played an integral role in colonization and assimilation (Sangster 1999). The criminalization of Aboriginal women also led to their being labelled "bad mothers" unfit to care for their children. Efforts have been undertaken since the formation of Canada to ensure the assimilation of Aboriginal women by enforcing the adoption of Western mothering practices. Baby clinics and baby shows took place on Aboriginal reserves with this end in mind, and the federal government enforced an educational program by distributing *The Canadian Mother's Book* to parents (White 1987: 54–143). Aboriginal women have been particularly vulnerable to being considered unfit mothers as a direct result of failing to meet middle class expectations (Kline 1993). Disproportionate numbers of Aboriginal children have been and continue to be taken from their communities and placed in foster or state care.

Beyond the policy of residential schooling, this was the case in the 1960s when thousands of Aboriginal children were taken from their homes in what is now referred to as the "Sixties Scoop." In one of the few works on this subject in Canada, scholar Patrick Johnston (1983) has documented how the extension of provincial child welfare programs on reserves was encouraged by the federal government and that Indigenous peoples should be induced to accept these. Financial incentives also influenced the spike in the number of children adopted out from their families. The increasing delegation of responsibility for Aboriginal health, welfare and educational services by the federal government to the provinces in the late 1950s and early 1960s guaranteed provincial child welfare organizations payment for each child apprehended. This led to an enormous spike in the number of Aboriginal children in state care, with rates rising from less than 1 percent in 1955 to more than 40 percent in 1964 (Downey 1999; Blackstock et al. 2004). In other cases children were "sold" to adoption agencies in the United States for a fee of $5,000 to $10,000 for each child (Bennett, Blackstock and De La Ronde 2005).

At present time, the number of Aboriginal children placed in state care remains disproportionately high. Despite Aboriginal peoples representing only 4 percent of the population, the proportion of Aboriginal children being cared for by the state has been placed at 20 to 40 percent, with the rates in some provinces averaging between 70 and 80 percent (Kline 1992: 387). As cited by Cindy Blackstock, Department of Indian Affairs and Northern Development data indicates that the number of on-reserve status Indian children in child welfare has increased by 71.5 percent between 1995 and 2001. In other words, up to three times more Aboriginal children and youth are presently under state care than during the height of the residential school policy (Blackstock et al. 2004: 905). Interventions of this sort further perpetuate assimilative policies, as these children are the least likely to ever return home and are effectively being disconnected from their communities and ways of life.

The child welfare system has been and continues to be involved as an agent in the colonization of Aboriginal peoples (Hudson and McKenzie 1981). Blaming Aboriginal mothers serves to obscure the conditions of poverty in which many women live and that most often lead to the involvement of social service agencies in their lives (Cull 2006; McCormack 1999). It remains more cost effective to criminalize Aboriginal mothers and remove their children from their homes under the pretense of child neglect than to address the effects of "crushing poverty, unsanitary health conditions, poor housing and malnutrition" in the lives of Aboriginal peoples (Blackstock et al. 2004; Johnston 1983: 23; Kline 1992). Most importantly, the criminalization of mothers obfuscates the roots of these conditions in the historical and continuing practices of colonialism and racism, which include land dispossession and the destruction of traditional First Nations economies (Monture 1989).

This brief review of colonial policy in Canada makes clear that Aboriginal women and their children have been targeted in specific ways to further assimilative ends. The undermining of Aboriginal women has also served the political and economic needs of the Canadian state, that is, of gaining access to Indigenous lands and resources and reducing those to whom the federal government has obligations. This focus on the assimilative attack waged through policies and practices, and the consequences it has had for Aboriginal women, should not be misconstrued as implying that Aboriginal peoples are simply victims. Indigenous peoples have absolutely resisted, adapted and survived in the face of all these policies by keeping their own ways alive in spite of legislative or other attempts to extinguish them. In some instances, Aboriginal agency has resulted in the Canadian government being forced to provide services when it would have been more cost effective not to, and in other cases Aboriginal peoples outright resisted Western practices or made use of these while also keeping their own practices alive (Burnett 2011; Jasen 1997; NAHO 2008; O'Brien 2013).

Regardless of how Aboriginal peoples have responded to imposed policies, it is critical to remember that the context out of which this agency is practiced has consistently been one of encroachment and colonialism. Even when government was not able to fully enforce assimilative policies, the threat of enforcement alone had an enormous impact on Aboriginal peoples. Too often, a focus on Native agency has served as "colonialist alibi," diminishing the responsibility of the state for past or present injustices (Brownlie and Kelm 1994). Consequently, this chapter stresses the ways policies and practices have been imposed on Aboriginal peoples, and women in particular, to help us better understand how these have met the political and economic needs of the Canadian state. This historical and material context created the conditions out of which coercive sterilization became a viable public health intervention in Aboriginal communities. This context also helps us to better understand the implications of this practice for Aboriginal women and their peoples, as one of many policies imposed to undermine Indigenous peoples *as peoples*. We now turn a detailed discussion of what is known about the coercive sterilization of Aboriginal women in Canada and the role played by the federal government in allowing the practice to take place.

Notes

1. Aboriginal peoples hold generic and specific rights. Generic rights are collective rights held by all Aboriginal peoples in Canada and include the right to land; to subsistence resources and activities; to self-determination and self-government; to practice one's culture; and the right to enter into treaties. Specific rights are held by individual Aboriginal groups. They may stem from treaties or as a result of a court decision. The right to have these protected has been recognized and affirmed (Slattery 2007: 111–128).
2. The Royal Proclamation set out that only the British Crown could obtain land from Aboriginal peoples through treaty or direct negotiation; that First Nations possessed occupancy rights to all lands not formally surrendered; that no settler could occupy or claim land unless it had first been bought by the Crown and then sold to the settlers. These are just some of its terms. King George III, *Royal Proclamation, No. 1*, 6 October 1973 <originaldocuments.ca/documents/ RoyalProc117630ct7c> and (Borrows 1997: 155–172).
3. In *Re Eskimos*, in 1939, the Supreme Court decided that this jurisdiction extends to Inuit peoples. Some have argued that this, in addition to specific treaties entered into establishing obligations on the part of the Crown, is evidence that confirms these responsibilities. Aboriginal and treaty rights have since been reaffirmed by Section 35(1) of the *Constitution Act, 1982* and other legal decisions (Cumming and Mickenberg 1972; Hogg 1999: 27–34; Kulchyski 1994).
4. The first treaties are often referred to as the Peace and Friendship Treaties and did not involve land surrender, but were meant to cement peaceful coexistence between Indigenous peoples and newcomers. Some treaties were signed between the British

Crown and the Indian nations who served as allies in the wars for control of North America. In exchange for their alliance, Indians were guaranteed protection, support and the assurance of peaceful relations. When treaties, especially later ones, did deal with land, these were, according to the consistent accounts by Aboriginal peoples across the country, solely for its use "to the depth of a plow" (Neu and Therrien 2003: 78; Allen 1993; Morris 1991).

5. Between the time of the report and the formation of Canada, many acts were issued with this purpose in mind, including *An Act for the Better Protection of the Lands and Property of Indians in Lower Canada and Upper Canada* (1850); *The Civilization of Indian Tribes Act* (1857); *An Act for the Gradual Enfranchisement of Indians* (1869).

6. The Indian Act amendment relating to the Potlatch ban went into effect in 1885; the Sundance in 1895. More generally, "Dances and festivals" were banned under a 1927 amendment. In 1951, the revised Indian Act repealed the explicit ban on Aboriginal cultural practices and ceremonies like the Potlatch, or the wearing of traditional "costume" at public dances, exhibitions and stampedes, and allowed Indian women to vote in band elections. These are just some of the amendments made to the Indian Act since its inception.

7. Under the 1876 Act, an Indian was defined as:
    First. Any male of Indian blood reputed to belong to a particular band.
    Second. Any child of such a person.
    Third. Any woman who is or was lawfully married to such a person
    a) Provided that any illegitimate child, unless having shared with the consent of the band in the distribution of moneys of such band for the period exceeding two years, may, at any time, be excluded from the membership thereof by the band, if such proceeding be sanctioned by the Superintendent General.
    b) Provided that any Indian having for five years continuously resided in a foreign country … shall cease to be a member thereof, etc.

8. Provincial Archives of Alberta, Charles Camsell Hospital fonds, 1946-1988, PR1969.0073.

3. Sterilization, Birth Control and Abusive Abortions

Legislation mandating compulsory sterilization was formally enacted in Alberta and British Columbia (Christian 1974; Grekul 2002; McLaren 1990; Nind 2003; van Heeswijk 1994). In Alberta, the *Sexual Sterilization Act* was in effect from 1928 to 1972 (Statutes of Alberta 1928). During this time, the Eugenics Board, which was composed of two medical practitioners nominated from the Senate of the University of Alberta and the Council of the College of Physicians, and two persons appointed by the Lieutenant Governor in Council, was presented with and passed 4739 cases for sterilization. Of these, 2834 sterilization operations were performed (Grekul et al. 2004: 358). According to a study of the patient files from the Eugenic Records Office of Alberta conducted by Timothy Christian, persons most likely to be presented and approved for sterilization occupied socially marginalized positions. Those most likely to fit this categorization and on whom legislation in Alberta was disproportionately applied based on their numerical significance in the general population were Aboriginal peoples (Christian 1974: 90). When opposition to the Act gained momentum and its repeal became more likely, the rate at which Aboriginal peoples were sterilized underwent a terrific increase, representing over 25 percent of those sterilized. Christian says, "It is incredible that between 1969 and 1972, more Indian and Métis persons were sterilized than British, especially when it is considered that Indians or Métis were the least significant racial group, statistically, and British were the most significant" (Christian 1974: 90).

These findings were replicated by Jana Grekul, Harvey Krahn and Dave Odynak, who found the Act tended to be biased toward women, teenagers and young adults, and Aboriginal peoples, who were consistently overrepresented among those sterilized (Grekul et al. 2004). Even though the number of women in the population never surpassed that of men, women constituted 58 percent of those sterilized overall (Grekul 2008: 254; Grekul 2002: 107–08).[1] Teenagers and young adults made up only 20 percent of the population but were 55 percent of those sterilized (Grekul 2002: 110–11). Aboriginal peoples otherwise identified as "Indian," "Métis," "halfbreed," "treaty," and "Eskimo" comprised only 2.5 percent of the population but consisted of over 6 percent of those sterilized overall, for the entire period in which the Act was in operation (Grekul et al. 2004).[2] These rates compare to Eastern Europeans (of Ukrainian, Polish, or Russian descent), who were marginally overrepresented (19 percent of those presented for sterilization, but not more than 17 percent of the population); Western Europeans (of

German, Norwegian, or Italian descent) who were underrepresented (18 percent of presentations to the Board, but 21–28 percent of the provincial population); and Canadian/Anglo Saxons who also underrepresented until the 1960s (Grekul et al. 2004: 374–75, 382).

Amendments to the Act increased the likelihood that Aboriginal peoples would be subject to sterilization. In 1937, under the pretense of the Act being too restrictive and in order to limit the likelihood of patients refusing sterilization, the consent requirement for "mental defectives" was excised.[3] This amendment allowed the Eugenics Board to compel the sterilization of any patient it defined as mentally defective and who was likely to transmit this defectiveness to his/her progeny (Statutes of Alberta 1937 s. 6). IQ testing was a primary method used to establish mental deficiency and this tool provided a certain scientific legitimacy to the diagnosis. Records indicate that patients whom the Board wished to sterilize were often subject to more than one test in hopes that their score would fall within the criteria for mental deficiency (Christian 1974: 172). IQ tests present many problems, particularly when applied to populations for which they are not designed (Chase 1977; Chrisjohn 1999; Gould 1981). As a result, when subjected to tests based on specific Western European knowledge, those who are not part of this group tend to do poorly (Chrisjohn 1999; Kamin 1974; Tucker 1994). In this case one finds that immigrants of non-Western European descent and Aboriginal peoples were most likely to score below the level of sound intelligence and this also influenced a diagnosis as mentally defective. Grekul and her colleagues estimate that 77 percent of Aboriginal patients presented to the Eugenics Board were diagnosed as mentally defective, as compared to 46 percent of Western Europeans and 44 percent of Eastern Europeans (Grekul et al. 2004: 375). Once defined as mentally defective according to the criteria of the Board, a patient no longer had much say in whether they would be sterilized.

There were also difficulties in how consent was obtained from a third party. A primary means of obtaining consent was by sending a letter through the mail to a parent or guardian stating "unless we hear anything from you in the next two weeks, sterilization will go forth on your child" (Grekul 2002: 204). This method presents numerous problems, as many of those institutionalized came from impoverished families, were more apt to move around in search of employment and thus were less likely to receive correspondence. Language barriers, and the social dislocation caused by poverty, or federal policies imposed on Aboriginal peoples, would have made families harder to contact. It also placed the onus on a family member to refuse consent and if no reply was received, this was assumed to represent consent. Even when one family member refused to give consent, the Board sometimes proceeded to another who would acquiesce (Grekul 2002: 142). Neither did the inability to obtain consent mean sterilizations did not take place. The minutes from the Eugenics Board indicate that when a parent could not be located, only the consent of the Minister of Health was required (Grekul 2002: 141). Finally, in

1955, provincial institutions adopted a generic administrative form that was signed upon admittance of a patient and which stipulated that if it was deemed advisable by the Eugenics Board at some point in the future, the sterilization of the patient could take place, thereby canceling out the requirement to obtain consent at a later date (Grekul 2002: 170).

Following these changes, there was an increase in the number of patients presented from the Provincial Training School (PTS) in Red Deer, an institution housing children and young adults declared mentally defective (Grekul 2002: 160). Ninety-nine percent of the cases presented from this institution did not require consent (Grekul et al. 2004: 370). Grekul states, "Business at this institution really increased during these decades, particularly the late 1950s and the early 1960s. Since it seems unlikely that there was a sudden increase in the number of people who were 'defective,' it is more probable that something changed in either the manner in which the institution was run or the way patients were processed by the board" (Grekul 2002: 160). During this period, Aboriginal children increasingly entered provincial institutions as a result of a federal tendency to pass off responsibility for the provision of services to the provinces, and the federal policy which stipulated that mental defectives who were "capable of being trained" were usually to be admitted to a provincial institution for care and training.[4] Did all of this increase the rate at which young Aboriginal women were being institutionalized and possibly sterilized in provincial institutions like the PTS? Without further detailed study it is impossible to know for certain the extent to which federal policy influenced these rates, but whatever the case, we do know the Board patiently worked around consent stipulations in order to obtain the sterilization they wanted done (Grekul 2002: 191). Grekul and her colleagues conclude:

> Aboriginals were the most prominent victims of the Board's attention. They were over-represented among presented cases and among those diagnosed as "mentally defective." Thus they seldom had a chance to say "no" to being sterilized. As a result, 74% of all Aboriginals presented to the Board were eventually sterilized (compared to 60% of all patients presented). (Grekul et al. 2004: 375)

The sterilization of Aboriginal peoples under the Alberta Sterilization Act was recognized as having the potential to cause problems in the future. In correspondence with the Eugenics Board regarding a patient diagnosed as both schizophrenic and mentally defective, the Department of Indian Affairs suggested efforts be made to obtain consent, if at all possible (Grekul 2002: 156–57). It does not appear the Department was necessarily motivated by any humanitarian or legal concern for Aboriginal peoples, but more with avoiding a charge that bears a resemblance to genocide, despite the term not being prominent in international discourse at the time. It wrote in 1937:

The Department has no power to authorize the sterilization of an insane Indian. It has no objections to the operation, and would regard it with approval if carried out in accordance with the laws and regulations of the Province. It cannot, however, agree that any Indian should be sterilized without the consent of his relatives, and of himself as well, if he is mentally competent to understand the results of the operation. *It is not beyond the realm of possibility that Indians might get an impression that there was a conspiracy for the elimination of the race by this means [emphasis added].* While, therefore, the Department can neither authorize nor forbid the operation itself, it is directed that the greatest care be taken that the Indian and his relatives be got to understand the reason for it, and that written consent be obtained before it is proceeded with. (Grekul 2002: 156)

This statement, made the same year as the first amendment to the Sterilization Act, makes clear that while the Department did not object to the sterilization of Indigenous peoples, it refused to make an incriminating declaration on the subject. However, failing to issue a statement condemning the sterilization of Aboriginal peoples is to condone the practice and can be read as an acknowledgment that, at the very least, it knew the practice was taking place. Again in 1942, when the Eugenics Board contacted the Department of Indian Affairs seeking consent to sterilize another Aboriginal patient, it now responded that the department had "no objections to the laws of the province being carried out and any action taken in accordance with Provincial law will not meet disapproval."[5] This same year another amendment to the Act was made that exempted from future civil action any person who took part in a surgical procedure, or any authoritative figure working in a mental institution and who was involved in a recommendation for sterilization (Statutes of Alberta 1942 ss. 7, 8). One wonders what role these amendments and the federal position played in future actions. The proportion of Aboriginal peoples sterilized by the Act rose steadily from 1939 onward, tripling from 1949 to 1959 (Christian 1974: 4–121). Despite the stipulation that consent be obtained, it was only sought in 17 percent of Aboriginal cases overall (Grekul et al. 2004: 375).

At times, the federal government undertook more explicit measures legitimizing the provincial Act while serving its own political and economic interests. In the 1950s, Indian Health Services looked into the care of Indian mental patients in Alberta and made efforts to secure their admission to provincial mental institutions. Although the Department initially considered establishing a separate federal institution to care for Aboriginal cases from across Canada, no such institution materialized. Instead, government invested, through Hospital Construction Grants, in provincially run institutions, with the hope of securing a commitment from provincial governments, in this case the Province of Alberta, for the care of Aboriginal mental patients when required.[6] In 1951, an amendment was also made to the Indian Act that increased the application of provincial laws to Indians

(Statutes of Canada 1951 s. 88). This amendment included the first definition of a mentally incompetent Indian as one defined according to the laws of a province in which "he" resides (Statutes of Canada 1951 s. 1). In other words, a mentally incompetent Indian was whatever a province deemed him or her to be. Therefore, any provincial laws dealing with those defined as mentally incompetent could be applied to Aboriginal peoples. This same amendment also stipulated that the property of any mentally incompetent Indian could be denied to that person (Statutes of Canada 1951 s. 51). In the case of so defined Indians living on reserve, property would pass to the Minister of Indian Affairs to be sold, leased or disposed of in any way deemed fit by the Minister. For Indians living off reserve, property would pass to the province in which that person resided. The increased application of provincial services to Indigenous peoples also by default reduces the services the federal government needs to provide. The material benefits gained by defining Aboriginal peoples as mentally incompetent, and any subsequent sterilization that might take place, would be in keeping with the longstanding policy of acquiring Indian lands and reducing the number of those to whom the federal government has obligations.

British Columbia (B.C.) was the second province to enact a *Sexual Sterilization Act*, in effect from 1933 to 1973 (van Heeswijk 1994; McLaren 1990). This Act permitted the provincial Eugenics Board to sterilize any inmate of a provincial institution deemed "hereditarily unfit," specifically, any inmate of an industrial school or industrial home for girls (Statutes of British Columbia 1933 s. 1). Records concerning sterilizations under this Act, said to have been performed on "only" a few hundred people, are thought to be lost or destroyed. However, in the first study of the *Sexual Sterilization Act* in the province, Gail van Heeswijk reviewed the *Essondale Report*, a document outlining the case histories of sixty-four patients from the Essondale institution who were sterilized under the Act from 1935–43 (van Heeswijk 1994; Wosilius 1995). The Essondale Hospital, subsequently renamed the Riverview Hospital, was one institution in which sterilizations took place. Through her review of this report, van Heeswijk provides a glimpse into the workings of this legislation in B.C., those who were most likely to be sterilized and the reasons given for the operation (van Heeswijk 1994).

Over the course of the eight years discussed in the report, sixty-four people were sterilized at Essondale. Of those, fifty-seven patients were women. The reason given for sterilization in thirty-five cases was the promiscuous behaviour of the women. Further, forty-six of the fifty-seven women sterilized were single, twenty-two had illegitimate pregnancies and another five had their pregnancies terminated prior to or during the sterilization procedure (van Heeswijk 1994: 51). Van Heeswijk draws a number of conclusions from these facts. The fear of feebleminded women reproducing children of their own kind played a role in sterilization decisions. The primary reason for the sexual sterilization of women, according to the author, appears to be due to their non-conformity to socially defined roles (van Heeswijk 1994: 68). Sterilization in B.C. also served a political and economic function and was considered a solution to increased urbanization and the resulting high rates of poverty, crime, unemployment and overcrowding in institutions (van Heeswijk 1994: 51; Wosilius 1995: 76, 105). Angus McLaren states that the primary argument given in defense of sterilization in B.C. was that the prevention of mental deficiency and its accompanying evils was an economic necessity. Sterilization would reduce the institutional costs of caring for the feeble-minded by limiting their reproduction and allowing patients to be released without posing a further threat to society (McLaren 1990: 97).

Neither the report nor van Heeswijk makes any mention of the ethnicity of patients, but some of those sterilized at Essondale were Indigenous. Correspondence from W.S. Barclay, Regional Superintendent, Pacific Region, Indian Health Services, indicates that as of 1956, "The B.C. Provincial Mental Hospital at Essondale have quite a number of Indians under their care."[7] In a subsequent trial dealing with charges brought forward by victims of coercive sterilization at Essondale, the following evidence is cited. This evidence deals with one Aboriginal patient, C.M., and provides insight into the process leading up to sterilization. For this reason, sections of it are quoted at length. It begins with an entry in the "Ward Notes" dated 14 July 1961, by Dr. Tecson, a psychiatrist, which reads as follows:

> This twenty-two year old Indian girl was admitted in 1955 ... She has been a known mental defective with considerable behaviour problems. She responded fairly well to Chlorpromazine and she was discharged on probation in 1958. She managed to stay only a few months having been violent whenever intoxicated. Upon return to the hospital she managed to escape on five different occasions ... It is indicated that she has had a brain abscess following mastoiditis with a possible tuberculoma and also a question of birth injury. It is undetermined on account of the [paucity] of materials as to whether her mental deficiency was subsequent to any or all of these conditions. It would probably be much more logical to simply label her as a case of mental deficiency ...

This report then helped inform the Eugenics Board Summary, prepared by the Supervisor of Social Services at Essondale, which reads in part:

> Patient is a mentally defective Indian girl who has always been incorrigible, wild, undisciplined and promiscuous ... Sterilization is, therefore, strongly recommended to prevent patient from having illegitimate children which the community would have to care for and for whom it would be very difficult to find foster homes.

Following this referral for sterilization, the Superintendent, Dr. Bryson, signed a recommendation for sterilization on 24 March 1965. He then wrote:

> This [now] twenty-six year old woman is a mental defective who has

shown promiscuous sexual behaviour as a component of her erratic and disturbed mental condition ... Rehabilitation plans and her release from hospital without the benefit of an operation for sexual sterilization would undoubtedly result in illegitimate children who would run a grave risk of a mental disorder. (*D.E. (Guardian ad litem) v. British Columbia* 2003: 132–34)

C.M. appeared before the Eugenics Board on 13 April 1965 and it authorized her sterilization, which occurred on 18 May 1965. In this case, the young Aboriginal woman was institutionalized in the provincially run Girls Industrial Home, a training school for delinquent children, and was sent to Essondale for sterilization from there.

Another case cited at trial concerned an Aboriginal woman admitted to Essondale in 1945. Though clinical records are incomplete, they indicate the Superintendent wrote to the Indian Commissioner seeking consent to sterilize this woman. Presenting a summary of her case, the Superintendent stated:

This mentally defective young woman['s] ... social background reveals a history of promiscuity, venereal disease, tuberculosis and one illegitimate pregnancy ... Because of limited intelligence, lack of supportive family supervision and a propensity for illicit sexual behaviour, her rehabilitation through the auspices of the Indian Affairs Department, is most problematical ... it is, therefore, desirable to offer her the protection of sexual sterilization ... While she will undoubtedly continue to be a social problem on discharge from this hospital, sexual sterilization would prevent her from having further children who might become social problems. (*D.E. (Guardian ad litem) v. British Columbia* 2003: 145–46)

It is clear from these two entries that there was an explicit concern that potential illegitimate pregnancies would place an additional social and economic burden on society, and that sterilization would help curb these additional costs.

We also know the federal government was providing financial support for wards at Essondale. Though van Heeswijk states that fees for sterilizations were paid to the performing physician by the institution from which the inmate was referred, the arrangement was such that whenever possible, for Aboriginal charges, a per diem rate was paid to the institution by the federal government (van Heeswijk 1994: 43). Robert Menzies and Ted Palys inform us that the per diem rate was negotiated on a provincial basis and in B.C., $1.00 was paid by the federal Department of Indian Affairs for its wards in provincial care. This rate rose to $1.35 per day in the 1930s (Menzies and Palys 2006: 154). In Ontario, the negotiated rate in 1926 was $7.00 per week, which rose to $2.00 per day in 1953.[8] This was in keeping with federal policy at the time whereby the Department of National Health and Welfare, Directorate of Indian Health Services looked after the medical care of Indians on reserves, and mental defectives were usually admitted to a provincial institution for care and training.[9] When the question of responsibility for the care of mental defectives was discussed at a meeting of the interdepartmental committee of Indian Health Services and Indian Affairs on 13 December 1956, officials agreed Indian and Northern Health Services would continue to assume responsibility for the care and custody of insane Indians. The Indian Affairs Branch would assume responsibility only when the mental condition of the Indian in question was such that they were capable of being "trained."[10]

Additional documents produced as the result of an audit undertaken in 1964 of the Coqualeetza Indian Hospital provide insight into the route followed by other Aboriginal peoples once they entered the system and which would sometimes lead to their sterilization. The documents specify that Indians could be admitted to the Coqualeetza Indian Hospital for assessment prior to referral onward to the Woodlands School, the Health Centre for Children, or other special centres. Mental patients were transferred to the following provincial institutions and payments were made by the Department as follows:

<u>July 1964</u>

Essondale	7466.70
Skeenaview and Valleyview	3398.55
Woodlands	7041.30
Mental Institution Edmonton	170.50
Total	18077.05[11]

We know sterilizations were performed on some of those institutionalized at Woodlands, a provincially run institution housing children abandoned at birth, the disabled and wards of the court, and where some Aboriginal children were sent (McLaren 2002). It remains unclear whether sterilizations took place at Woodlands by way of transfer to the Essondale Hospital or whether they were arranged by family physicians in the community (McCallum 2001: 23–24; Public Guardian 2004: 20). However, children were admitted to this institution with the purpose of sanctioning their sterilization and the Department of National Health and Welfare, Indian Health Services, did pay the per diem rate for Indian wards in its care (McCallum 2001: 23–24; Menzies and Palys 2006: 154).[12]

Other provinces in Canada considered similar sterilization legislation which never came to formal fruition (McConnachie 1987; Normandin 1998; Ross 1981). Historian Kathleen McConnachie (1987: 241) provides insight into efforts to promote sterilization legislation in Ontario. Although the idea was advanced twice, it was defeated both times by opposition led by the Catholic Church. Ontario legislation in the 1930s allowed sterilizations to be performed for medical reasons, with the signature of two doctors. A doctor who performed the operation for other reasons could be liable under Section 39 of the Medical Act. McConnachie (1987:

237) concludes, "What lobbyists for sterilization legislation were striving for in the 1930s was legislative legitimization for the practice already widespread in the province." Due to widespread opposition to an official sterilization Act, doctors lobbied instead for an amendment to the Medical Act to protect them from subsequent legal action if they performed such an operation and this helped ensure the legitimacy of the practice in a roundabout way (McConnachie 1987: 237).

Despite the absence of a sterilization Act in Ontario, sterilizations for eugenic reasons did take place and government was "not unaware" of these actions. Correspondence between Dr. William Hutton, founder of the Eugenics Society of Canada, and the provincial Minister of Health acknowledges that doctors had been performing sterilizations on the "mentally unfit" in Brantford and other areas for years (McConnachie 1987: 237). Commenting on this, McConnachie writes:

> The worsening of social and economic problems of the depression years generated more interest in eugenic sterilization. The mayor of Fort Erie, Ontario, for example, called for the sterilization of all men on relief. The Simcoe County Council passed a resolution calling for all children in provincial institutions for mentally handicapped to be sterilized, then discharged. Dr. W.L. Dales of Newmarket urged the sterilization of all mentally defective children who were in provincial shelters awaiting admission to the Ontario Hospital at Orillia. After Dr. W.H. Hutton, founder of the Eugenics Society of Canada, addressed the annual Convention of Ontario Mayors in 1936, a subcommittee resolution endorsed compulsory predischarge sterilization of all feeble-minded in institutions and the voluntary sterilization of the feeble-minded outside institutions. (McConnachie 1987: 215–16)

Economic conditions played a role in calls for sterilization. As early as 1934, Cora Hodson, then secretary of Britain's Eugenics Society, reported that in Ontario "operations for poor persons are being procured under philanthropic auspices in some areas, where there has been much suffering in recent years, agricultural and economic alike" (Hodson 1934: 39).

It was largely due to the efforts of A.R. Kaufman, the rubber magnate who is often referred to as the father of birth control in Canada, and through his founding of the Parent's Information Bureau, that over one thousand sterilizations were performed in Ontario. In many cases, these were done on a "goodwill" basis by physicians who believed that sterilization was a viable means of preventing or alleviating poverty (McLaren and Tigar McLaren 1986; Revie 2006). Kaufman claimed that from 1930 to 1935, his Bureau funded a number of "sympathetic surgeons" to operate on about four hundred women in hospitals (Revie 2006: 127). Again in 1938, in correspondence with the Canadian National Institute for the Blind Toronto, he wrote:

I can say that my bureau has been responsible for over 500 sterilizations and there has been no legal action up to date ... My opinion is that individuals lack normal health when they are blind or are afflicted with various diseases or mental deficiency ... Co-operative doctors in Canada have sterilized 500 individuals on the request of my bureau, and only in about a dozen cases has there been paid even a small fee.[13]

Kaufman claimed that between 1930 and 1969, one thousand male steriliza-tions were performed in the "sick room" at his rubber plant in Kitchener, Ontario. Following a 1969 PIB advertisement appearing in the *Kitchener Daily Record* and offering free sterilizations to parents on welfare, nearly seven hundred of these procedures were performed (Revie 2006: 128).

More than for economic reasons, sterilizations were politically motivated as well. Kaufman wrote in 1937:

I have said, and still think, we must choose between birth control and revolution. We are raising too large a percentage of dependent classes and I do not blame them if they steal and fight before they starve. I fear that the opportunity will not be so long deferred as some day the Governments are going to lack the cash and perhaps also the patience to keep so many people on relief. Many of these people are not willing to work but I do not criticize them harshly for their lack of ambition when they are the offspring of people no better than themselves. (Dowbiggin 2008: 119)

Through sterilization, the number of impoverished people to whom the govern-ment would need to provide assistance would be reduced, and the potential revolu-tionary tendencies of the masses would also be curtailed (Dowbiggin 2008: 112).

The full extent to which sterilization affected Aboriginal peoples in Ontario is not known. It is known that by 1928 Indigenous peoples were being classified as mentally unfit and this was most often a precursor to sterilization. During this time, Peter Sandiford, a foremost proponent of intelligence testing and a self-proclaimed social Darwinist, conducted a study of Aboriginal children in Ontario (McLaren 1990: 61–63). The results, he said, indicated that Indian children suffered from a greater level of retardation than whites and that IQ seemed to rise with the admixture of white blood (Jamieson and Sandiford 1928). In that same year, in private correspondence to Dr. George L. Wallace at the Wrentham State School in Massachusetts, Clarence Hincks also indicated "Three Canadian provinces are now considering sterilization, and the Ontario government is sanctioning steriliza-tion although we have no legislation" (McConnachie 1987: 226). It is also unclear whether the federal government would have been made aware of sterilizations if they were performed on Aboriginal charges. In 1933, Dr. B.T. McGhie, Director of Hospital Services from the Ontario Department of Health, sent a circular let-ter to all health districts and in this particular case, to Dr. S.J.W. Horne, an intense

advocate of sterilization and Superintendent of the Ontario Hospital School in
Orillia, in which he wrote:

> I note that in the Psychiatric Reports made by some of our physicians
> and submitted to this office that recommendations have been made for
> sterilization. It is often necessary to forward these reports on to the de-
> partments interested, and in view of the fact that sterilization can not be
> legally undertaken except for some physical disability, more care should be
> taken with respect to making that recommendation. Will you, therefore,
> kindly instruct your physicians that this recommendation is to be made
> only where it is known that some physical condition exists that would
> warrant such operative procedure.[14]

Sterilizations were at the very least being recommended as early as 1933.[15] And,
because these reports would need to be forwarded to "interested departments"
for payment, the Director of Hospital Services for Ontario recommended that no
mention be made of sterilizations performed for other than medical reasons.[16] If
performed for other than medical reasons, this information might not have been
made available to the federal government.

However, one can infer that eugenic sterilization was taking place and did not
stop at this time. Five years later, in 1938, R.C. Montgomery, Director of Hospitals
in Ontario, wrote to Dr. Horne to clarify the position of the Ontario Department
of Health on sterilizations and in doing so, acknowledges that operations were
being performed for other than medical reasons. He writes:

> Sterilization operations are performed under three different kinds of
> circumstances, viz., -
> (a) to benefit the health of the person sterilized;
> (b) for eugenic reasons to prevent the birth of defective offspring;
> (c) for economic reasons where the parents cannot afford to maintain
>   additional children.
>
> ...
>
> The best opinion seems to be that eugenic sterilization, that is, steril-
> ization to avoid having defective children, is illegal even with the consent
> of the person sterilized and the consent of the spouse.
>
> In my opinion, sterilization for economic reasons is also illegal even
> with the consent of the patient.[17]

The position of the Ontario Department of Health was consistent with the
general view of Canadian law at this time. Sterilizations for eugenic reasons were
permitted under enacted legislation in B.C. and Alberta, and otherwise, only in
cases where the health of a woman was in question. Sterilizations performed outside of these parameters were legally questionable. Prior to the changes to law in

1969 that decriminalized contraceptive practices, this meant that even requests by women for voluntary sterilization as a permanent form of fertility control were approached with caution by the medical profession out of fear of being held liable. In the case above, despite concerns with liability, it does not appear the province reprimanded those performing sterilizations.

The federal government had its own concerns with liability for sterilizations being performed on those under its charge. In a letter written by P.E. Moore, director of Indian and Northern Health Services, to the Regional Superintendent of the Saskatchewan Region concerning the sterilization of an Aboriginal woman from the Thunderchild Reserve, Battleford Agency, Moore states:

> In the July, 1957 account of Doctor John M. Richards, Turtleford, Saskatchewan, for services to Indians of the Thunderchild Reserve, Battleford Agency, appears an item for [name withheld]. This patient had a caesarean section and bilateral salpingectomy [sterilization by removing or cutting the fallopian tubes]. The diagnosis is given as toxemia of pregnancy.
>
> There are two points in connection with this account which are worth considering:
> 1. While the caesarean section could be considered an emergency, the salpingectomy was most certainly elective and, therefore should have had prior approval.
> 2. Sterilization is a procedure of which Indian Health Services must be very wary and we must be certain that all formalities are scrupulously observed.
>
> In Canada, sterilization can only be legally performed on the grounds that further childbearing would endanger the life of the mother or adversely affect her health. The question of eugenics or economics does not enter into the matter. Before sterilization can be performed it is necessary that at least two practitioners examine the patient separately and give in writing the results of their findings and their reasons for advising sterilization. It is then also necessary that both the patient herself and her husband each give consent for the procedure to be done. This consent should be written and amply witnessed. Any other points required by Provincial law must be observed. The above remarks only apply to primary sterilization and do not apply to necessary surgery which leads to sterilization as a secondary effect. The only type of caesarean section which would do this would be a Porro [a caesarean section followed by hysterectomy] which is very rarely done.
>
> Would you please look into the above case and make sure that all is noted. Inasmuch as it appears that the indication for caesarean section was toxemia and not disproportion it is not obvious that the sterilization was

justified. Before we pay this account (which might imply some liability on our part) it would be best to check this point. In the meantime we will hold this account.[18]

There are a few points to be made regarding this letter. The first is that Indian Health Services was indeed aware that sterilizations were being performed on Aboriginal women by physicians without following the proper legal channels of obtaining consent, that sterilizations were performed for other than medical reasons and that payment for these by Indian Health Services would imply a liability by the federal government. However, if this sterilization had already been performed, which it had, and the medical records were already filled out, which they were, what purpose would withholding payment until such time as records were "checked" serve, unless it was anticipated that changes would be made to official records accordingly? Why would Indian Health Services not simply refuse payment for what appears to be, from this piece of correspondence, an illegally performed sterilization?

The federal government fell short of enacting legislation directly sanctioning the sterilization of Aboriginal peoples, but through its refusal to condemn the practice, by enacting policies and legislation affecting other aspects of Indigenous life that made sterilizations more likely and through its financial support, it allowed sterilizations to be carried out more effectively. In other instances, federal involvement with imposing measures to prevent births in Aboriginal communities was much more direct. For instance, on 30 December 1938, a memorandum was sent by the Deputy Commissioner of Indian Affairs, R.A. Gibson, to K.R. Daly, a senior solicitor from the Department of Mines and Resources, informing him that the Northwest Territories Council would consider enacting legislation for the sterilization of "imbeciles." Suggesting proposed legislation follow that which was already in effect in other provinces, Gibson requested Daly prepare a suitable presentation for the next council meeting.[19] Daly responded with a caution. Owing to the "graveness" of the federal government undertaking to adopt legislation dealing with sterilization, the best way to proceed was to discuss the issue with the Minister of Pensions and National Health.[20] Whether this discussion took place is unclear, but the issue did move forward and a précis was prepared by Daly for the Northwest Territories Council.[21] A proposal was presented on Tuesday, 17 January 1939, at which time it was voted for. However, on Wednesday, 18 January 1939, it was put on hold for further consideration.[22] One must note that those responsible for initiating such proposals were federal representatives from Indian Affairs.[23]

No further correspondence regarding sterilization in the North appears in the records reviewed until 1941. At this time, the issue of sterilization was taken up by Dr. J.A. Bildfell, a medical doctor serving Aboriginal peoples in northern Canada. Bildfell, who worked in the North from 1932 to 1933 and 1940 to 1942, was bewildered by Inuit resistance to Western medicine and pathologized them for this. He wrote:

> The native is little beyond the stage enjoyed by primitive beings, and what is more his environment simple as it is, though severe, has contributed little to hasten his evolvment [sic]. Hence in his attitude towards Medicine I consider him ... half way on the rough highway between instinct and a highly developed intellectual function. (Tester and McNicoll 2006: 94–95)

Bildfell reported to the Director of the Northwest Territories Division of the Department of Mines and Resources on cases of insanity in the area and requested that certain medical cases from Pangnirtung, Baffin Region, be transferred to the South for sterilization. Referring to the medical history of one patient, he wrote:

> It has occurred to me during the year that it might be expedient to provide for compulsory sterilization ... where insanity appears in a younger adult and where there exists a definite history of insanity in the family ... I am of the opinion that sterilization in this case would have been justified and beneficial to the Eskimos generally.[24]

Further to this, Deputy Commissioner Gibson returned a reply to Major D.L. McKeand, a member of the Northwest Territories Council who opposed attempts to sterilize peoples of the North, indicating this question should be brought up at the next Council meeting in consultation with the Department of Pensions and National Health.[25] At the following Council meeting, on 21 November 1941, the issue was tabled again. Mr. Gibson stated that the subject of sterilization continued to be brought up by medical officers and he suggested Council seek the advice of Dr. J.J. Heagerty, medical superintendent for the Northwest Territories. In the view of Dr. Heagerty, sterilization had a twofold purpose: to prevent the reproduction of mental defectives and to stop the dissemination of venereal disease. He cautioned that due to the many problems with establishing that a condition was hereditary and the strong opposition to sterilization by religious bodies, the Northwest Territories Council "should not proceed with sterilization of imbeciles and idiots in the Northwest Territories."[26] The minutes of the Council then indicate that "there would be no possibility of taking any action on the matter in the Northwest Territories at the present time."[27] Although this appears to have settled the issue, in the early 1970s the public would learn that coercive sterilizations were in fact taking place in the North in spite of the lack of legislation.[28]

Controlling Births with Birth Control

Sterilization was not the only means of exerting control over the reproductive lives of Indigenous women. Archival research has uncovered that birth control was employed to limit fertility and the federal government was directly implicated in these actions. In 1965, Commander J. Coulter, a member of the Special Planning Secretariat of the Privy Council, Government of Canada, made a request to H.A. Proctor, Director of Medical Services to Aboriginal peoples, asking him to inquire with each Zone Superintendent and other senior officers on his staff on whether it would be feasible to reduce the size of Indian families through birth control. On 27 August 1965, Proctor sent out a request to all Superintendents, writing:

> In connection with its war on poverty among the Indians, the Special Planning Committee of the Privy Council has studied the desirable size of the Indian home under the present circumstances and has wondered whether the size of the required prototype home could be reduced if birth control techniques were actively advocated among the Indian population.[29]

Stating that the Department was concerned only with the medical aspects of the problem and not with the theological, legal or other aspects, Proctor asked for their opinion on whether birth control could influence the size of Indian families in general, and the size of the requested home for each family in particular. The responses received make clear that prior to the legalization of birth control for contraceptive purposes, it was considered viable to promote their use in Indigenous communities and these were prescribed with the express intent of limiting the number of births within the group.

For instance, on 2 September 1965, C.S. Gamble, Regional Superintendent of the Nanaimo Region, wrote:

> I feel it is feasible to reduce the size of the average Indian family by birth control techniques. The goodwill we have earned through our treatment services puts us in a good position to further the knowledge and practice of birth control.[30]

In one of the few cautious responses, L.R. Hurtle, Zone Superintendent from the Atlantic Zone, pointed out:

> On the other hand, oral contraceptives have not been proven safe ... I do not believe that they should be used routinely until a sufficient period has elapsed to prove the safety of this method ... Obviously, with the high illegitimacy rate amongst our Indians, to exert sufficient control over the sizes of families, it would be necessary to feed the pills to a very

large percentage of the single females, even those in the 14 and 15 year old category.[31]

When not completely in agreement, expressed skepticism was related to the practicality of such a proposal. As M. Savoie, Superintendent of the Quebec Zone, wrote:

> We are skeptical of the feasibility of reducing the size of the average Indian family through birth control techniques. Even if it did succeed, our own feeling is that the actual prototype home is adequate for very small families anyway and we fail to see how it would further be reduced. Our only reserves where there might be a chance of some individual success are the more sophisticated ones of Lorette, Odanak, Oka, Caughnawagga and St. Regis. On the other hand, you will note that on these reserves, families are not large.[32]

In most regions, however, responses were positive and many indicate that birth control was already being distributed. R.D. Thompson, Superintendent of the Pacific Region wrote:

> It is my impression that Miller Bay Zone has been successful in distributing more Enovid than the other Zones and that there has already been an appreciable fall in the birth rate.[33]

Enovid was the first hormonal birth control pill on the market in the U.S. and it contained high dosages of progesterone and estrogen. The drug had recently been tested on Puerto Rican women in the mid 1950s and early 1960s. Many of the women who participated in these unregulated clinical trials were not told of its experimental nature or the harmful effects that could come from taking a drug with hormone levels three times as high as those in the pill in its current form. These trials took place in conjunction with this territory's own state-supported sterilization campaign, in the name of population control, which affected over one third of the female population from the 1930s to the 1970s (Lopez 2008; Ramírez de Arellano and Seipp 1983). These policies occurred in a territory with its own colonial history and were implemented under the same shared assumption that poverty and its associated social problems were caused by overpopulation, not relations of exploitation and dispossession, or the unequal distribution of wealth inherent to colonialism conditions (Ramos and Henderson 1975). Although the social, historical and political context was different for women in Puerto Rico and Indigenous women in Canada, it is hard not to see the similarities in approach by colonial governments to problems caused within the populations they are suppressing.

With respect to Indigenous peoples in Canada, more intrusive measures were also employed when the birth control pill was not considered ideal. For instance, intrauterine devices (IUDs) were recommended by S. Mallick, Zone Superintendent from Sioux Lookout, as a solution to what he considered the "many problems" with contraceptives in pill form, including the fact that some Indigenous women could not be relied on to take the pill every day, that they often did not receive contraceptive shipments on time and that this method was too expensive, at a cost of approximately twenty dollars per year per woman. Mallick suggested that Indian Health Services try the plastic coil method as this had proven successful in other countries, would run at a cost of about five cents per device and would enable the department to carry out its own research on a fairly large number of women in a more scientific way.[34] The representative from the Inuvik Zone wrote that among the Louchoux, or Gwich'in, peoples, there was already a large proportion using contraceptive pills and some of these are being switched to IUDs.[35]

A response from J.D. Galbraith, Regional Superintendent from Sardis, calls into question the degree to which Indigenous women were willful participants. Galbraith wrote:

> Our nurse, Miss M. Stokes, at Mount Currie, reported a total of 34 births in Mount Currie in 1963, and 32 in 1964. The total population has been increasing quite rapidly, so that reduction of two seems small, but at least it didn't increase.
>
> It is our opinion here that there will be a certain percentage of the Indian women who will not take sufficient care and interest in the regular use of birth control pills whom it would be better to use the intrauterine device … with the combined use of the tablet for co-operative women and the use of intrauterine devices for some of the less co-operative women, particularly unmarried mothers who go on to have sizeable families, that the size of Indian families could indeed be considerably reduced in the course of time.[36]

From the above responses it is nearly impossible not to conclude that birth control was being employed for population control ends, with the knowledge of federally employed Indian superintendents and the Director General of Medical Services. The response received from the Regional Superintendent of the Saskatchewan Region also brings up an important question relating to the use of these methods in Aboriginal communities and the degree to which these were being imposed rather than sought voluntarily. He writes:

> I doubt very much that the culture of the Indians of this area would ac-cept the idea of family planning or restriction in number by birth control … there is no incentive such as community status or financial gain in reserve life.[37]

Proctor himself acknowledged that Aboriginal peoples valued children in a way that was at odds with their assimilation into Canadian society, the adoption of Christian marriage and a Western nuclear family unit.[38] Indigenous societies most often view children as gifts, for which the entire community is responsible for nurturing and protecting as the future of a people. However, this awareness of cultural differences did not inhibit attempts by the federal government to limit the size of Indian families through the illegal prescription of birth control to Indigenous women.

M.E. Gordon of the Miller Bay Indian Hospital, who was Zone Superintendent in Prince Rupert, provided a breakdown of the quantity of birth control issued per region from September 1964 to September 1965. Gordon then went on to write that the pills issued by field nurses, although mostly given to cover prescriptions by local doctors, in some instances were prescribed directly by nurses if the husband and priest were in agreement.[39]

Table 1: Birth Control Issued in Prince Rupert Zone, 1964-65

Enovid issued from September 1964:	c-276 Ortho Novum quantity issued since 1964:
Masset field nurse, 1500	Dr. Archibald, Burns Lake, 500
Terrace field nurse, 7000	Dispensary, 2100
Wrinch Memorial Hospital, 7000	Masset field nurse, 3000
Dr. K.H. Christensen, Terrace, 400	Outpatient clinic, 7100
Outpatient clinic, 5800	Port Simpson field nurse, 5300
Dispensary, 2800	Wrinch Memorial Hospital, 1000
Fort Simpson, 6500	Terrace field nurse, 2500
Lower Skeena field nurse, 2500	
Burns Lake field nurse, 1000	
L. Whiteside, Telegraph Creek, 1000	
Dr. Woolacott — Kitimat, 500	

Source — These numbers are drawn from the source listed in footnote 39.

At this point, a few cautious responses received by Proctor regarding the distribution of contraceptives to Aboriginal populations led the Department of National Health and Welfare to issue criteria to Zone Superintendents instructing that only physicians should prescribe or distribute birth control pills and that these should be distributed to individuals on a repeat basis only under the surveillance of a physician:

> whether or not these drugs are prescribed must rest on the judgment of the physician and the conscience of the patient. The department will not become interested as long as the physician uses his best judgment in the light of accepted practice and the patient is fully aware of possible consequences.[40]

Proctor then prepared a formal response for the Special Planning Secretariat and summarized that, in spite of Aboriginal beliefs about premarital sex or the ideal number of children sought by families, the chief intrinsic difficulty in making use of birth control to reduce the birth rate was a lack of motivation on the part of Indians themselves, not the legal status of birth control for non-medical reasons.[41] However, if Aboriginal peoples "lacked motivation" to make use of birth control measures, to what extent was their use at this time voluntary? Proctor concluded that the government "could hardly advocate a more intensive promotion of birth control in light of the present legal situation," yet claims that the prescription of birth control to Indigenous women was increasing began to arise almost immediately.

In a letter written by Kahn Tineta Horn from Caughnwagga (Kahnawake) to R.F. Battle, Director, Indian Affairs Branch, Indian and Northern Affairs, and subsequently forwarded to Proctor, the issue of coercive birth control practices is brought up. Horn writes:

> In conversation, my sister was informed by a nurse in the employ of one of the doctors serving the Indians of Caughnwagga that the doctor for whom she works has been given instruction "to issue birth control pills, contraceptives and other means of birth control to Indians that he takes care of, but not to the Roman Catholic French Canadians who are in his practice." This nurse informed my sister that when she commenced working for this doctor who takes care of Indians, the average number of births in Caughnwagga was over 100 per year, and as a result of the current increase in the number of married couples and adults she estimated it would be around 150 or more per year at the present if it was not for the contraceptive measures being authorized which has reduced it to about 100. My question is this. Can you determine whether the doctors in charge of the Indians in Caughnwagga are treating the Indians in relation to birth control the same or differently from their other patients.[42]

This charge, of birth control being prescribed to reduce the birth rate of Indian women, was not new to Proctor. However, in his reply to Chief Delisle of Caughnwagga (Kahnawake) on 17 February 1966 regarding Horn's letter, he feigned ignorance of the alleged practice and denied any responsibility on the part of his Department:

> I know of no instructions from the Department such as these referred to in Miss Horn's letter. The Department of National Health and Welfare does not wish to force birth control on Canadian Indians who do not wish to practice it nor does the Department wish to deny advice or guidance on birth control to those Indians who wish to have this guidance. The Department expects that each physician treating Indians on behalf of Indian Health Services will apply the same principles and considerations to the provision of birth control advice to his Indian patients that he ap-

plies to his other patients, bearing in mind the religious convictions and personal preferences of each patient.[43]

A month later, concerns regarding the steady increase in the prescription of birth control to Indigenous women for population control ends were again expressed to Proctor, this time by the Regional Director from Saskatchewan, T.J. Orford. He wrote:

> Some concern is felt in this office about steady increase in the prescribing of anovulatory drugs for Indian female patients. It is proving almost impossible to control. The stand which has been taken up to this point has been that we would consider payment for prescriptions or supply from M.S. [Medical Services] stocks placed in retail outlets or supply from our own institutions only when anovulatory preparation was prescribed for a specific gynecologic reason and that we would not consider payment when prescribed for contraceptive purposes only. This ruling has been met with opposition from some of our own medical officers who consider population control should be a factor in our service … With the steady increase of prescribing the drug one can only conclude its use is not confined to treatment purposes.[44]

What was also becoming obvious was the precarious legal position in which the Department found itself, at once denying knowledge of what was a questionable practice, both legally and ethically, while at the same time issuing payment for services provided by its employees to wards under its charge. This led Proctor to respond on 6 April 1966, stating the official position of the Department:

> The Department feels that just because an Indian or Eskimo looks to the Federal Government for assistance in obtaining medical care, that person should not be deprived of advice and assistance which would be available to other Canadians who do not look to the Department for assistance … It has been the policy that so far as our own establishments are concerned, Indian or Eskimo Patients presenting with a request for advice on birth control may receive the same but that our staff are not to attempt to persuade against their will these people to adopt something which may be foreign to their beliefs.[45]

The official position of the Department was that birth control should not be given coercively. Yet one must remember that the use of contraceptives for birth control purposes was illegal at this time. The Department appears unconcerned by this fact. In the face of increasing claims that contraceptives were being prescribed to Indigenous women as a birth control measure, sometimes by nurses and sometimes in a coercive manner, one would expect caution to be exercised or at the very least a warning to be issued. However, if any concern was expressed it was with the possibility of the Department facing blame, not with practices being imposed on Aboriginal women. Proctor continued:

> So far as prescriptions written by non-departmental practitioners are concerned, I do not feel that the department is in any particular danger of criticism if it fills the prescriptions or pays for them, since the anovulatory drugs are, after all, useful for a variety of purposes other than contraception. It is simply not feasible for the department to correspond over every such prescription to make sure it is not being used for non-medical purposes. If any blame is to be attached for the issuing of such prescriptions, it is the professional person who issued the prescription in the first place who would receive the criticism.[46]

In what comes next, the logic standing behind official policy is made plain. Nowhere does a concern with the health and wellbeing of Aboriginal women appear. What becomes clear is a calculated effort by the Department to rationalize illegal and unethical practices in hopes of avoiding potential liability in the future:

> To be practical and to protect ourselves from possible criticism, I would suggest that you prepare a circular letter to designated physicians in your Region emphasizing that the Department expects that private medical practitioners will use the same principles in prescribing anovulatory drugs for Indian patients as they would use in their own private practice for their other patients … it would be wise to emphasize that the Department does not expect and cannot condone the indiscriminate prescription of such drugs to single females for strictly contraceptive reasons. You will note that in this way, the only mention of the word, contraceptive, is in relation to the single female and under circumstances where the Department cannot condone the practice. By asking the physician to use the same principles … we throw onto him entirely the onus to ensure that the legal niceties of the situation are observed while not in any way laying ourselves open to attack on the grounds of attempting to prevent Indian women from receiving drugs which are medically necessary. It does seem likely that the heavy use of such drugs will be apparent in certain areas and your Zone Superintendents could be alerted to such areas and asked to keep an eye on the situation and have a talk with the practitioners prescribing the medication in large quantities. The above is an attempt to take a realistic course of action under present circumstances and one which takes a middle course between supporting the zealots who would restrict the size of all families for that purpose alone and those who would refrain from supplying these preparations under any circumstances whatsoever.[47]

The federal government did not openly condone the prescription of birth control to limit the birth rate, but it was aware that certain "zealots" working under its charge were taking advantage of its failure to condemn the practice and employing these for coercive ends. The failure of the Canadian government to acknowledge or adequately address the alleged and actual illegal and/or unethical practices of its employees is further compounded when one considers that once made aware of wrongdoings, it sought to protect itself from liability rather than protect Aboriginal women from coercion. This trend continued following the legalization of birth control.

To Sell, Advertise and Distribute Openly

Much to the approval of many women who desired increased access to birth control as a means to control their own reproduction and under the banner of "reproductive rights," the sale, advertisement and distribution of contraceptive information and services became legal in 1969 (Statutes of Canada 1969). At the end of that year the federal government still denied any policy of disseminating birth control in Indigenous communities. During deliberations at the Standing Committee on Indian Affairs and Northern Development, the Minister of National Health and Welfare John Munro stated:

> It is not government policy or departmental policy to promote family planning at this time in Canada. We are not going to promote it as policy. We are not going to promote it to any particular group. We do not promote it or encourage it. Our health service has things like pills, for instance, available to the Indian population if the Indian women want to use them, just as pills are made available in any health service, whether it is public or private, for anybody else in the population. (Canada 1969a: 240)

However, a memorandum written ten months earlier by Munro and discussed below demonstrates that a policy was indeed in practice, whether or not it was explicitly stated by government. This memorandum also shows the federal government was concerned with the broader implications of family planning practices in Aboriginal communities and whether these might be construed as genocidal.

Charges that the government was carrying out a policy of "cultural genocide" were lodged by Harold Cardinal in response to the longstanding treatment Aboriginal peoples experienced at the hands of government policy makers and bureaucrats. Cardinal wrote extensively on the attempt by the federal government to implement the White Paper as a "thinly disguised programme of extermination" (Cardinal 1969). This policy document, proposed by the federal government after a series of investigations found Aboriginal peoples to be the "most disadvantaged group among the Canadian population" (Hawthorn 1966–67) sought to eliminate Indian status and abolish the Department of Indian Affairs within five years. It also recommended the Indian Act be repealed, that reserve lands be converted into private property and that a commissioner be appointed to address outstanding land claims (Canada 1969b). For Aboriginal peoples, the White Paper represented yet another attempt at assimilation, or of undermining treaties and reducing federal obligations in order to gain access to their lands and resources (Indian Chiefs of Alberta 2011).

In a meeting with government officials around this time, Cardinal brought up these concerns face to face. In a memorandum written on 12 February 1969 and sent to Dr. J.N. Crawford, Deputy Minister of National Health and Welfare, Munro referred to the "genocide question" and clarified the logic behind plans to legalize birth control. He wrote:

> Your sensitivity to the genocide question — which arose in a certain form when Harry Cardinal was here — I am sure [also] proceeds from your analysis of birth control programs in the United States, so obviously pointed at Negro areas ... I think we can avoid making some of the mistakes the Americans have made. I know our policy for our lay dispensers now is that they will try to prescribe and persuade, but that they don't encourage any public education or information campaigns ... My preliminary thinking goes like this: we might take as our concept the establishment of credibility generally in Canada for discussion of family planning. That is, politicians and experts involved in social development would be free, I think, after the passage of the Omnibus Health Bill, to talk as openly and with as much good taste as possible about this wide field. ... I hope, with trying to move towards this kind of openness, aiming at the *whole* Canadian community, that the message would at least partially get through to sub-groups like our Indians.[48]

In other words, it was federal policy for physicians and health care workers to "persuade" Indigenous women to adopt birth control practices prior to their legalization, but not to advocate their use publicly. The Minister anticipated that changes to the Criminal Code would allow for public education campaigns, under the pretense of their being directed toward the general population, to specifically influence Aboriginal women. Legalizing the sale and advertisement of contraceptives would increase the effectiveness of efforts to reduce the size of the Indian population while allowing government to avoid criticisms that federal policy was genocidal in its application.

A year later, the federal government announced it was initiating a formal family planning program. In a news release from 18 September 1970, Munro declared:

> In adopting this program, the government recognizes and supports the right of Canadians to exercise free individual choice in the practice of family planning. It is our hope, through the program, that family planning information and services will become available to all who want them ...

the use of family planning, is a decision to be taken by the individual citizen. There will be no suggestion of coercion toward anyone; we shall do everything possible to safeguard against that. (Munro 1970)

What exactly the government was prepared to do to safeguard against possible coercion is unclear considering its inactions regarding similar, previously lodged claims. Official government policy now made it more difficult to intervene in coercive practices in Aboriginal communities. It also allowed the federal government to avoid responsibility for these by hiding behind the rhetoric of individual choice and non-interference due to doctor–patient privilege. As J.H. Weibe, Director of Medical Services, commented, "on the surface it [this new policy] would appear to regularize what has been our approach to family planning for many years."[49]

In further correspondence with Maurice Leclair, the Deputy Minister of National Health and Welfare, Wiebe wrote that he was "acutely aware" of the claim of genocide on the part of Indigenous peoples and this was why the current "non-program" was to provide drugs or devices on an individual doctor-patient basis. However, if government wanted to succeed in breaking the cycle of poverty, it would need to consider a more positive, albeit subdued approach to family planning.[50] Wiebe subsequently sent out a letter to regional directors informing them that family planning activities would be expanded on Indian reserves and in northern territories:

> Due to provisions of the criminal code and other legislation Medical Services formerly remained aloof from active advocacy of family planning in the practice of public health on Indian reserves, but the subject was included in the curricula of departmentally directed courses of instruction, such as those for the indoctrination of health workers.[51]

In reference to the above statement, one must ask what role the "indoctrination of health workers" through "departmentally directed courses of instruction" played in the previously noted actions of Indian Superintendents, physicians and nurses relating to the coercive sterilization of Aboriginal women, or the indiscriminate prescription of birth control. Though no "explicit policy" was issued up to this point relating to family planning in Aboriginal communities, one was encouraged through instructions issued by the Department of National Health and Welfare. At the very least, the Department silently accepted the morally, legally and ethically questionable practices it knew were occurring. The objectives of the "new" federal family planning policy were aimed at:

> [The] reduction of abnormally high birth rates in communities where this situation pertains with consequent:
> a) reduction in infant mortality
> b) reduction of incidence of unwanted children

    c) reduction in incidence of child neglect and abuse
    d) reduction of incidence of child abandonment or desertion
    e) improvement in family comfort and nutrition.[52]

The underlying assumption of this federal initiative was that if Indigenous women could be made to have fewer children this would by default reduce other problems in Aboriginal communities like poor nutrition, abuse, neglect and infant mortality. Also implicit in this policy is an assumption that it was Indigenous women, by having "too many children," who were to blame for these problems. What went unaddressed were the conditions that caused these problems to begin with. The federal government overlooked the long-lasting and continuing effects of past and present policies imposed on Aboriginal peoples that stem from relations of colonialism, land theft, the unequal distribution of resources and a program of assimilation. These policies are directly linked to increasing rates of infant mortality and to the disruption of the social fabric of Indigenous communities, something which contributes to issues of abuse and neglect, and levels of family comfort and nutrition (Canada 1996).

It is more cost effective to avoid addressing these historical and material issues, and instead, to intervene in Aboriginal communities by first blaming Aboriginal women. In this case, the solutions provided also tend to be profitable to pharmaceutical companies and the medical profession, and they allow the federal government to evade responsibility for the expropriation of Indigenous lands and resources, and the conditions created by its own policies. It is difficult to view this "new" policy as separate from a long line of those coercively imposed on Aboriginal peoples. In his final instructions to the Deputy Minister of National Health and Welfare, Wiebe wrote "You will note that activities are to remain low key except where local or native support and desirable local and native assistance is given."[53] This indicates, at a minimum, that local or native support for such policies was not always present. And, as we will see next, the indiscriminate prescription of birth control was not the only reproductive abuse being experienced by Aboriginal women at this time. Neither was it the only policy for which the federal government would face scrutiny.

Sterilization and Birth Control in the North

At the same time as Canada announced a formal family planning policy, questions began to arise about the coercive treatment of Aboriginal women in northern Canada. On 9 October 1970, David Lewis, former leader of the New Democratic Party and representative of York South, questioned Jean Chrétien, then Minister of Indian Affairs, on whether he was aware that a program of sterilizing Native women had been introduced in the Holman Island community on Victoria Island.[54] Despite denying knowledge of any such program, Chrétien stated that health services in this area were under the jurisdiction of the Department of National Health and Welfare. Because it was not possible that such a program be implemented without any authorization, Lewis asked that the Minister relay this question to the department in question. The following week, with the Minister of National Health and Welfare absent despite being scheduled to appear, the issue was reintroduced. Chrétien now responded by indicating that sterilizations were performed on "a few women" from the Holman Island community and seven others at Yellowknife, with the approval of two doctors and the consent of each woman and her husband. Yet he insisted there was no sterilization program in the North.[55] Lewis continued to probe. Had it been determined whether these people were approached by someone representing the Department of Health and seeking their consent and if so, would that not represent a program of seeking consent? He also inquired into whether the women in question were spoken to in their own language, and if not, was there an interpreter present?[56] André Fortin, member from Lotbinière, also asked for clarification on whether these sterilizations were performed at the request of Indigenous people. Chrétien stated that it was very difficult to know, that probably the doctors discussed the matter and offered this solution, that the wife and husband would have given consent and that this was not incompatible with the freedom of other individuals to make similar choices. He also indicated that he had made an inquiry on the matter and would inform the House once he received a response.[57] However, no formal action was undertaken and no further response appears to have been issued at this point. The concern that coercive sterilizations were being performed on Aboriginal women continued to reappear.

On 1 April 1973, the Canadian Broadcasting Corporation (CBC) public affairs program *Weekend* aired a news story suggesting there was a calculated attempt to reduce the birth rate of Indian peoples in northern Canada.[58] The program claimed Inuit women were sterilized without their consent in the North and while at the Charles Camsell Hospital in Alberta, and it discussed the linguistic barriers and climate of paternalism that led women to be sterilized "for their own good." It also featured charges that some Inuit children were separated from their families, sometimes never to be seen again after being sent to southern hospitals for medical treatment (Sandiford Grygier 1994). These charges were immediately followed by a letter of protest by the Minister of National Health and Welfare, Marc Lalonde, who attacked the journalistic integrity of the reporters and denied all allegations of coercion.[59] Lalonde responded that two of the women in the news story had numerous children, that written consent for sterilization was provided and to infer that because these women could not communicate in English they were unable to understand the implications of what was happening was incorrect. He stated the hospital guidelines mentioned in the broadcast were from 1970 and these had since been superseded by more stringent ones in 1972, which were followed. He also accused the CBC staff of maligning his Departmental officers and of exploiting Indigenous people for the purpose of sensational journalism.

The program responded to these charges the following week. On 8 April 1973, host Jim Eayrs spoke with Brian Pearson, councilor for the Northwest Territories at Frobisher Bay. Pearson said it was generally known that women were sterilized without being made aware of what the procedure entailed. He granted that perhaps this was not an intentional policy because doctors tended to see the procedure as beneficial to women in the face of their "enormous" families. In reference to claims of Indian children "vanishing" after being sent to southern hospitals for medical treatment, he commented:

> There are tremendous difficulties with names, tremendous difficulties with these kids who in a lot of cases don't speak English, who become sort of out-patient, in-patient kind of people you know. They find foster homes for them. For example, the story goes and I think this has happened many times, perhaps less now than it used to. An Eskimo some three months old that was sent to Southern Canada with TB. The child was eventually returned to her home exactly twelve years later and on arrival at the house, the Social Worker or Community worker, knocks on the door and says to the Eskimo couple who live there and in very primitive conditions … "here is your daughter, we brought her back for you." To which they reply, "we don't have a daughter, never had one." The Community worker said, "yes you did." "That was a long time ago," the Eskimo said, "but she died. The white man took her away and we never heard of her since."[60]

Commenting on the problems of interpreters, Pearson stated:

> One of the interpreters informs me that after he had gone through the lengthy procedure of explaining what it was all about [sterilization], 6 months later [the patient] came back to the Hospital saying "why can't I get Pregnant?" They said, "don't you remember, we cut your plumbing out." "Oh well, Jesus, what did you do that for." A whole question of misunderstanding. [61]

This problem was reconfirmed by Brian Gunn, a former employee of the Department of Indian Affairs and Northern Development and a consultant to the Eskimo Brotherhood, who was also interviewed for this program. He stated:

> The Medical people who are involved have to rely on interpreters and it's not always easy for an interpreter to put the message across or maybe he puts it across in such a way that it is misunderstood and sometimes even the interpreter doesn't understand the consequences himself, this can lead to confusion for the patient and I think perhaps there has been some carelessness, as well.[62]

Dr. Lee Guemple, Chairman of the Department of Anthropology at the University of Western Ontario, who served as interpreter in hospitals in southern Canada, clarified:

> [Eayrs]: Is there an Eskimo word for Sterilization?
>
> Dr. Guemple: I think not, at least not that I am aware of. I suppose one could be made up, a paragraph long sort of word.
>
> [Eayrs]: There isn't an English equivalent?
>
> Dr. Guemple: No, there isn't.[63]

Dr. Guemple was not the typical interpreter either. Gilbert Smith, administrator of the Stanton Yellowknife Hospital, was interviewed regarding its "policy" on interpreters and admitted that a housekeeping staff who spoke one of the dialects had been used as an interpreter, that sometimes other patients were called on, and that the hospital had a list of twenty-three students from Sir John Franklin High School who could be contacted if needed.[64] Surely one cannot say that providing interpretive services for complex medical procedures, or ensuring the informed consent of patients, is part of the job description of any of these individuals and this does not consist of satisfactory policy.

The problem of interpreters was further confirmed shortly after the CBC program aired by an inquiry made by M.L. Webb, Assistant Deputy Minister, Medical Services, regarding the sterilization consent form used at the Frobisher Bay Hospital.[65] In response to a request by Webb to have the translated consent form tested, A.D. Hunt, Assistant Deputy Minister, Northern Affairs Program, indicated:

> A group of Eskimo women, with above average education for the Eastern Arctic, were in Ottawa last week for a conference and we took the opportunity to ask them to look over the form. Out of a total of nine, two thought it meant to have an abortion, five thought it would mean the person would have an operation and then have no more babies, and the remaining two had great difficulty in understanding what the message was about. Under the circumstances, it would seem that the form needs a bit of re-drafting to ensure that people are fully aware of what they are agreeing to.[66]

It appears no such re-drafting took place. The sterilization consent form was subsequently sent by Hunt to the Government of the Northwest Territories Official Corps of Interpreters, who refused to translate it due to the varying dialects on Baffin Island.[67] Despite its obvious problems, the standard form continued to be used after this time.[68] It is apparent from the above discussion that in spite of the assertion from the Minister of National Health and Welfare that government policy ensured Indigenous women were fully informed of the risks and consequences of a sterilization procedure and were able to provide informed consent, this does not appear to be the case.[69]

With respect to the guidelines followed by the Charles Camsell Hospital, as of 1 April 1970, these guidelines were based on the number of children a woman had, and economic concerns and other broad "conditions" were also considered as criteria for sterilization. The guidelines stipulated that:

1. A woman of any age with six children, 25 years of age with five children, 30 years of age with four children and 35 years of age with three children [is a candidate for sterilization]

2. Although age and parity are major guidelines indicating the appropriateness of tubal ligation, it must be recognized that the procedure is designed to preserve the health and welfare of the patient. When the criterion of health and welfare is combined with age and parity formula, it may mean a major medical problem such as psychosis or cardiac failure but will also be interpreted to encompass real but less obvious problems such as maternal exhaustion, fear of pregnancy, marital strife, and economic concerns.[70]

In response to allegations of coercion, more specific guidelines were issued on 10 November 1970, as indicated by Minister Lalonde. These more stringent guidelines required that two doctors agree in writing that there was a legitimate reason for sterilization, that the implications of the procedure be fully explained to both marital partners in the presence of a third party and that a "good" interpreter be used for those who did not fully understand English.[71]

The extent to which these guidelines were followed is not known. Less than a year later, on 28 July 1971, Dr. A.P. Abbott, chairman of the Abortion and Sterilization Committee at the Charles Camsell Hospital, wrote to J. MacDonald, the director of nursing, informing her that the Sterilization Committee was in unanimous agreement that the criteria for sterilization should be relaxed. He wrote:

> It was the unanimous feeling of the Medical Staff that the criteria be relaxed so that anyone over the age of 30 *or* who had more than 4 children should require only one signature in addition to that of the attending doctor on the Application for Sterilization.[72]

On September 20 of that same year the University Hospital in Edmonton, Alberta, dissolved its Tubal Ligation Committee. The hospital required instead that a single consultation be conducted by a doctor wishing to perform the sterilization with another member of the hospital staff supporting this view.[73] On 12 April 1972, a request by the executive director of the Charles Camsell Hospital asking that it also be allowed to institute the same procedure as that followed by the University

Hospital was approved by Dr. O.J. Rath, Regional Director of Medical Services for the Alberta Region, with the sole specification that consent for Aboriginal patients be given in writing.[74] In other words, although new guidelines were issued as Minister Lalonde had indicated, by leaving the decision to perform a sterilization up to the discretion of the doctor rather than a board, with the sole specification that written consent be obtained, these were in fact less stringent guidelines than those previously enacted and they left more power in the hands of individual doctors. More discretionary power in the hands of doctors also provided more opportunities for those who might be inclined to use this power coercively.

There are other inherent problems when it comes to the issue of informed consent. For a patient to be "informed" requires all viable treatment options, and the possible risks and benefits associated with each, be shared before choosing which way to proceed. This principle has been established in Canada through case law, and has generally arisen in response to abuse or negligence experienced by unwitting patients at the hands of medical professionals (e.g., *Reibl v. Hughes* 1980; Colodny 1989). Informed consent, though important, is not enough to ensure freedom from coercion. The focus on individualized choice inherent in the notion of consent also denies the larger context in which decisions are made. It obfuscates the existence of any systematic abuse directed toward certain populations like Aboriginal peoples, and it assumes all women make choices within the same context and that the implications of these choices are the same for all. In other words, one cannot legitimately speak of the consensual nature of a choice when unequal relations of power are at work. As is obvious from the current discussion, unequal relations did and continue to exist between Canada and Aboriginal peoples, or Western medical practitioners and Aboriginal women. We must also consider that many Aboriginal women, most especially some forty years ago, had limited understandings of the language or concepts specific to Western medicine. Considering all of this, even when a documented consent form does exist, the voluntary aspect of the decision must be questioned. This is particularly the case when Indigenous peoples are forced to live under conditions of colonialism and Western medicine is employed to assist in assimilation.

Allegations of coercion are further supported by abortion practices in the North. In 1969, it also became legal for abortions to be performed in cases where the "health" of a woman was deemed "at risk" by a therapeutic abortion committee consisting of three doctors (Statutes of Canada 1969). This amendment to law stipulated that abortions could only be performed in accredited hospitals by licensed physicians; all others would continue to be subject to Criminal Code sanctions. However, because the notion of "health" was left undefined, questions began to arise relating to how much weight abortion committees were placing on economic factors when determining whether the continuation of a pregnancy would endanger the "mental" or "physical" health of a women (Thomas 1977: 966). Jane Jensen, historian of abortion politics in Canada, argues a primary motivation for the 1969 amendment was to clarify the legal liability of doctors who performed abortions and that the amendment actually increased the control of the medical establishment over reproduction by giving physicians more power to decide what should be done to the bodies of women. She writes, "Most simply, if doctors saw any pregnancy as 'unhealthy', they could legally abort it" (Jensen 1992: 19, 18–55). It did not take long for some to claim that while certain women were being denied access to abortion, namely those in better financial situations and whose "mental health" was least likely to be affected by an additional child, others, like Aboriginal women, were being subject to the procedure for economic reasons (Stevens 1974b). Findings from the Badgley Committee, formed in 1975 with the specific purpose of studying the equitable operation of abortion law in Canada, support this view. The committee found that some women were pressured to consent to sterilization while in the vulnerable position of being an applicant for abortion, and based on the opinions of some of the physicians and some of the patients in the national survey, an agreement to be sterilized had been used on occasion as a prerequisite to obtaining an abortion (Badgley 1977: 360; Boldt et al. 1982; Dickens 1985).

Instances of abortions being performed at the Frobisher Bay Hospital, a federally run hospital serving primarily Aboriginal peoples, despite it not being accredited to do so, also came to the attention of government. In correspondence from Maurice Leclair to B.D. Dewar, Assistant Deputy Minister of Medical Services, on 24 May 1974, an illegally performed abortion was blamed on an immigrant physician who had since left the country, making disciplinary action unfeasible.[75] Further correspondence reveals that Medical Services had been made aware of other instances of abortions being performed illegally at this hospital in 1972 and had failed to act.[76] Again in 1974, rather than investigate, Justice Minister Otto Lang issued instructions to all hospitals in the Yukon and the Northwest Territories that abortions were not to be approved on economic or social grounds (Stevens 1974b). However, as journalist Geoffrey Stevens, who covered this story, pointed out, "Anywhere else in Canada, a prosecution would have to be begun by provincial authorities" (Stevens 1974a).

The charges continued. In a study conducted by the Canadian Civil Liberties Association in response to claims that the abortion law worked so erratically that Canadian women were denied equal access under the law, they found that the regulation requiring abortion patients to submit to sterilization was discovered in a hospital in the Maritime provinces and in a Western hospital (Gray 1974). Charges of unnecessary hysterectomies being performed at the Stony Plains Hospital in Edmonton, in 1972 and 1973, were also alleged (*Globe and Mail,* November 16, 1974: 13). Similar accusations, of unnecessary hysterectomies being performed on Indigenous patients, this time at the Whitehorse General Hospital, led Member of Parliament Erik Neilson to formally inquire in the House of Commons on 1 November 1971. When asked how many hysterectomies or similar operations were performed on Indian patients at this hospital from 1969 to 1971, John Munro, now the Minister of National Health and Welfare, indicated that a total of twenty-seven had taken place at this one hospital.[77]

A formal inquiry into abortion practices in the North was eventually commissioned, but not until nearly twenty years later, four years after the much heralded 1988 R. v. Morgentaler decision which left abortion governed by provincial and medical regulations (Brodie 1992: 57–111; Jensen 1992: 18–55). In 1992, investigations began as a result of one woman claiming she was forced to undergo an abortion without anesthesia at the Stanton Yellowknife Hospital (Walsh 1992; Smith 2005a: 96–98). Her story led to over one hundred more complaints received by the Northwest Territories Status of Women Council from other women with similar experiences. Some claimed the doctors carrying out their abortions made abusive remarks (Walsh 1992; Smith 2005a: 96–98). The Stanton Yellowknife Hospital, which serves primarily Inuit women, responded that it provided all women with aspirin as pain relief during the procedure (Lowell 1995: 27). However, Lynn Brooks, executive director of the Status of Women Council, was unable to find any other hospital in Canada where abortion recipients were given only aspirin for pain control (Walsh 1992).

An Abortion Services Review Committee was formed on 15 April 1992 by the Minister of Health to investigate. The mandate of the committee was to review the guidelines and procedures for therapeutic abortions and for dilation and curettage operations in cases of incomplete spontaneous abortions. A medical audit was also conducted of patient records relating to abortion procedures at the Stanton Yellowknife Hospital. The committee found that between 1986 and 1990, 1332 abortions were performed at this hospital, and 795 of these were performed on Inuit, Indian and Métis women. In addition, 656 women traveled to regions outside of the Northwest Territories to procure abortions, with some patients from the Baffin region travelling to Montreal or Ottawa, and others from the Keewatin Region sent to Winnipeg. Some women also came to the hospital from other regions like Fort Smith, Inuvik and Kitikneot (Northwest Territories 1992: 10). The audit confirmed that in a sample of randomly selected patient files, only five out of twenty-eight abortion procedures involved any type of anesthesia (Northwest Territories 1992: 30–32). Other problems identified related to the lack of information, counselling and education given to women both pre- and post-operation, the inadequacy of patient complaint procedures, inconsistent policies on reproductive health services and the lack of cross cultural awareness of the medical caregivers. We should avoid concluding from these findings that all abortions were necessarily performed in a coercive manner, but the medical audit substantiated enough claims to warrant further investigation and the establishment of a clear set of recommendations on how to proceed in the future. No such review of allegations surrounding coercive sterilization has been undertaken.

The discussion thus far has made apparent that reproductive policies and practices have been imposed on Aboriginal women in an unequal, coercive and abusive manner. For Aboriginal women, being made dependent on the Canadian medical system for their most basic reproductive needs is not only potentially harmful in this respect, but it also serves to further their assimilation into Canadian society. When understood in this context, the actual number of Aboriginal women coercively sterilized is not as important as the fact that conditions are such that even one sterilization is allowed to happen. Despite failing to undertake an open and honest inquiry into allegations of coercive sterilization, the federal government was forced to inquire, albeit in a limited manner, into sterilization rates in some Indigenous communities. Though incomplete, for lack of additional sources of documentation, this information represents the beginning of formally calculating the extent to which sterilizations were carried out on Aboriginal women in Canada. This information can be considered in addition to what has already come to light regarding sterilizations under provincial legislation.

Sterilization by Number

Locating exact information on the number of sterilizations performed on Aboriginal women in Canada is not an easy task. Health services for Aboriginal peoples were provided by the Department of Indian Affairs pre-1945, and the Department of National Health and Welfare post-1945. Indian Affairs transferred its records on Indian health services to the Department of National Health and Welfare at this time. Health services for Aboriginal peoples from northern areas were formally provided by Northern Health Services prior to it merging with Indian Health Services once the Medical Services Branch, Department of National Health and Welfare, was created, in 1962. Further, some Aboriginal women might have been sterilized while institutionalized in residential schools, while others would have had the procedure imposed in provincial training schools or mental hospitals. Still others could have been recommended for sterilization after coming into contact with professionals in the child welfare or criminal justice system, or while in federal or provincial hospitals during the course of routine medical treatment or while giving birth. Nor is it obvious whether all sterilizations would have been documented as such. Clearly, all of these factors make a definitive analysis of sterilization next to impossible with records scattered across so many different agencies.

In 1973, Assistant Deputy Minister of Medical Services M.L. Webb indicated that because the Department did not have population figures for some northern areas, and because there were other hospitals in the territories or provinces for which no detailed statistics exist, it was not possible to produce sterilization rates which could then be compared.[78] However, files produced in relation to the delivery of health services to Aboriginal peoples, and information found in the file set entitled "Birth Control" held in Record Group 29, Department of National Health and Welfare, Medical Services, Indian Health Services have yielded information dealing with the sterilization of Aboriginal women. Some of these records appear as attempts to produce official statistics on sterilizations performed in federally operated Indian Health Service hospitals and what one suspects are other, non-federally operated hospitals. This information is summarized here.

Table 2: Sterilizations at Medical Services Hospitals *

	1971		1972		1973		1974		Total
	Indian	Eskimo	Indian	Eskimo	Indian	Eskimo	Indian	Eskimo	
Moose Factory Ontario	10	2	24	15	34	9	44 (1)	9	147 (1)
Sioux Lookout Ontario	14	--	19	--	12	--	16 (4)	--	61 (4)
Norway House Manitoba	3	--	4	--	30	--	17	--	54
Fisher River Manitoba	--	--	--	--	--	--	--	--	--
Percy Moore Manitoba	--	--	--	--	--	--	16 (1)	--	16 (1)
Blackfoot Alberta	--	--	--	--	--	--	--	--	--
Blood Alberta	1	--	1	--	--	--	--	--	2
Charles Camsell Alberta	44	8	67	2	N/A	N/A	4	N/A	125
Frobisher Bay N.W.T.	--	22	--	13	--	21	--	22 (6)	78 (6)
Inuvik N.W.T.	2	8	4	6 (1)	7	3	7 (7)	--	37 (8)
Whitehorse Yukon	6	--	12	--	--	--	8 (8)	--	26 (8)
Mayo Yukon	--	--	--	--	--	--	--	--	--
Fort Qu'Appelle Saskatchewan	1	--	4	--	--	--	9 (1)	--	14 (1)
North Battleford Saskatchewan	7	--	8	--	--	--	5	--	20
Total:	88	40	143	36	83	33	126	31	580 (29)
	128		179		116		157		

Source — These numbers are drawn from the sources listed in footnote 79.
* The figures in brackets represent the number of sterilizations for which the sex is unclear. All other numbers represent sterilizations performed on Aboriginal women.

The first source of information was produced at the request of Dr. Whiteside, a non-physician associated with the National Indian Brotherhood, in response to allegations of coercion in the North. These statistics deal with the number of sterilizations performed at hospitals run by the Department of National Health and Welfare, Medical Services, Indian Health Services from 1971 to 1972.[79] Subsequent information also released by Medical Services provides sterilization rates from 1973 and 1974 at these same hospitals. Table 2 indicates that over the four years in question, at least 580 sterilizations were performed at Indian Health Services hospitals. Of these, at least 551 sterilizations were on Aboriginal women. Based on additional information not included in this table, 46 more sterilizations were performed at the Charles Camsell Hospital in 1970, and 4 sterilizations and 1 vasectomy were performed at the Inuvik General Hospital in that same year.[80]

A second source of information on sterilizations came as the result of a formal parliamentary inquiry conducted in response to charges lodged by a priest, Rev. Robert Lechat. In 1976, Lechat alleged in a series of articles that the federal government was intensifying a sterilization program aimed at Aboriginal peoples in the North. He named six communities in the Keewatin District where he claimed women were sterilized without full knowledge or consent. For example, in Repulse Bay, he alleged that out of twenty two women between thirty and fifty years of age, ten were sterilized, or 45 percent of the childbearing population. In Chesterfield Inlet, out of twenty-three women between thirty and fifty years of age, he alleged six were sterilized, or 26 percent of the childbearing population.[81] In response to these charges, Wally Firth rose in the House of Commons on 25 October 1976 and asked:

> Does this represent government policy? ... If so, how many people have been affected by it? How long has this program been going on, and why is it being carried out? ... I wonder if the government has the guts to undertake an inquiry, find out exactly what is going on and explain to the Canadian people what this is all about. When you couple what is happening with ideas put forward in a training manual for the correctional institute in Yellowknife, a manual which describes the native people as shiftless, lazy and goodness knows what else in unkind terms, you wonder how many sick people, including civil servants, in those parts are making major decisions affecting the people's lives. Therefore, I ask the government to look seriously at that program and let us know exactly what is happening.[82]

Subsequent to this, a notice of a parliamentary inquiry was sent to Charles E. Caron, Assistant Deputy Minister, Medical Services, seeking the number of Native women of childbearing age residing in (a) Repulse Bay (b) Chesterfield Inlet (c) Pelly Bay (d) Gjoa Haven (e) Hall Beach (f) Rankin Inlet and in each case, how many of these women were sterilized between January 1966 and October 1976.[83] A response was submitted by Medical Services on 1 December 1976 and is compiled in Table 3. These numbers came directly from D. Harkness, Assistant Regional Director of Medical Services, N.W.T. Region.[84] They indicate that a total of seventy sterilizations were performed on women from these northern areas over the course of the ten years under consideration. The reason given for all of these sterilizations, with one exception, was multiparity, or having given birth to "two or more children." It remains unclear where these sterilizations were performed, as this is not indicated on the return. Medical facilities were often lacking in some of these very small communities, therefore women might have been sent to the closest northern medical facility with surgical services, or alternatively, they could have been sent to southern hospitals under federal or provincial jurisdiction. For instance, Medical Services implemented a medical travel for birth policy for women in remote northern areas, and although this policy initially applied only to high-risk pregnancies, during the 1970s, all pregnant women were expected to leave home to give birth. The University of Manitoba had a contract to provide physician and obstetrical services to the Keewatin District, and women from this area were transported to facilities in Churchill or Winnipeg, while others would have been sent to the Charles Camsell Hospital in Edmonton, Alberta (Robinson 1991; Kaufert and O'Neil 1990; Moffitt 2004). However, women were not only sterilized while giving birth. Despite the lack of clarity here, and despite governmental insistence that there was no policy of sterilization in the North, these figures confirm those alleged by Lechat.[85]

Table 3: Sterilizations Reported as a Result of Parliamentary Inquiry, 1966–76

Settlement	Population of Childbearing age (15 to 50 years of age)	Number of Sterilizations	Age Span of those Sterilized	Average Age	Diagnosis
Repulse Bay	48	10	21–43	38.1	Multiparity
Chesterfield Inlet	54	10	28–44	33.3	Multiparity
Pelly Bay	40	5	27–43	31.6	Multiparity, one history complicated pregnancies
Gjoa Haven	90	11	28–41	36.1	Multiparity
Hall Beach	64	8	22–37	31.1	Multiparity
Rankin Inlet	146	26	28–44	33.3	Multiparity
Total:	442	70	% of women of childbearing age sterilized:	12–21 %	

Source — These numbers are drawn from the sources listed in footnote 84.

Table 4: Sterilizations on Aboriginal Women in Northern Settlements, 1970–73*

Settlement	Sterilizations				
	1970	1971	1972	1973	Total
Baker Lake	6	-	5	4	15
Bathurst Island/Inlet	-	-	1	1	2
Belcher Islands	-	-	2	1	3
Broughton Island	2	-	2	-	4
Cambridge Bay	3	2	5	3	13
Arctic Bay	1	2	-	3	6
Cape Dorset	1	1	3	1	6
Chesterfield Inlet	1	-	1	1	3 (10)
Clyde River	-	1	2	1	4
Coral Harbour	5	-	1	1	7
Eskimo Point	-	-	2	-	2
Fort Liard	-	-	1	-	1
Frobisher Bay	10	2	-	4	16
Gjoa Haven	1	2	1	3	7 (11)
Grise Fiord	-	-	1	-	1
Hall Beach	-	-	2	-	2 (8)
Holman Island	3	-	2	1	6
Iglookik	2	2	1	3	8
Inuvik	1	-	-	2	3
Lake Harbour	3	-	1	-	4
Pelly Bay	2	2	1	3	8 (5)
Coppermine	10	1	6	4	21
Pond Inlet	1	1	1	1	4
Pangnirtung	2	-	2	-	4
Rankin Inlet	3	-	3	2	8 (26)
Repulse Bay	-	-	-	1	1 (10)
Resolute Bay	3	-	-	1	4
Sachs Harbour	1	-	-	-	1
Spence Bay	4	1	2	2	9
Somerset Isle	1	-	-	-	1
Whale Cove	2	-	1	1	4
Yellowknife	-	-	-	1	1
Portage La Prairie Mental Home	-	-	1	-	1
Total	68	17	50	45	180 (70)

Source — These numbers are drawn from the sources listed in footnote 86.
* The numbers reported by the parliamentary inquiry are included in brackets for contrast purposes.

These settlements were not the only areas in which sterilizations took place. Based on additional information drawn from this same file set from Medical Services, it appears the sterilizations reported through the parliamentary inquiry were only a fraction of those known to have been performed on Aboriginal women. Table 4 represents a third source of information and shows the number of sterilizations performed on Aboriginal women in the North from 1970 to 1973.[86] Based on this information there were 180 sterilizations performed on women from the North in four years alone, and the greatest proportion of these were performed on women from areas other than those discussed by parliament in its inquiry.

To complicate matters further, there is also a fourth number set which reports sterilizations performed on Aboriginal women for the period from 1970 to 1975. Based on this information, the following tables, Table 5, Table 6, Table 7 and Table 8, were produced, which give a breakdown of sterilizations by northern Zone and Region. Table 9 summarizes these numbers by Zone for comparative purposes. Despite encompassing only half the time period covered by the parliamentary inquiry, these alternative numbers reveal consistently higher rates of sterilizations than those reported, with a total of 344 sterilizations performed on Aboriginal women.[87] It is unclear due to the lack of information in this correspondence

Table 5: Sterilizations on Aboriginal Women in Baffin Zone, 1970–75*

Settlement	Sterilizations						
	1970	1971	1972	1973	1974	1975	Total
Arctic Bay	2	1	0	3	2	1	9
Broughton Island	2	2	0	1	0	5	10
Cape Dorset	1	4	5	1	5	0	16
Clyde River	0	3	1	1	2	0	7
Grise Ford	0	0	1	0	0	0	1
Hall Beach	1	1	1	2	1	0	6 (8)
Igloolik	0	2	1	4	2	1	10
Lake Harbour	3	0	0	0	2	0	5
Pond Inlet	1	5	1	1	3	1	12
Pangnirtung	1	0	2	2	5	6	16
Port Burwell	0	0	0	0	0	0	0
Resolute Bay	2	0	0	2	0	0	4
Frobisher Bay	9	5	0	3	1	3	21
Total:	22	23	12	20	23	17	117 (8)

Source — These numbers are drawn from the sources listed in footnote 87.
* The numbers reported by the parliamentary inquiry are included in brackets for contrast purposes.

whether there is overlap between all these number sets or whether they should be considered as separate sources of information. Due to the variations in sterilization rates from one set to another, often with very different numbers reported for the same area in the same year, it does not appear that one set incorporates another.

For instance, Medical Services reports in Table 2 that thirteen sterilizations were performed on Aboriginal women in 1972, at its hospital in Frobisher Bay. Yet if one refers to either Table 4 or 5, in that same year, no sterilizations are indicated under Frobisher Bay. One must assume, based on this information, that thirteen sterilizations were performed on Aboriginal women at the federal hospital in Frobisher Bay. It remains to be seen whether these sterilizations, at this hospital,

Table 6: Sterilizations on Aboriginal Women in MacKenzie Zone, 1970–75*

Settlement	Sterilizations						
	1970	1971	1972	1973	1974	1975	Total
Fort Smith	0	1	1	0	0	1	3
Yellowknife	1	2	0	4	4	4	15
Coppermine	1	0	0	5	0	4	10
Gjoa Haven	0	3	0	3	1	2	9 (11)
Pelly Bay	2	0	0	2	0	1	5 (5)
Rae/Edzo	0	0	2	0	0	3	5
Lac La Martre	0	0	0	0	1	1	2
Hay River	0	0	4	0	2	2	8
Fort Resolution	0	1	1	0	0	2	4
Fort Wrigley	0	0	2	0	0	0	2
Fort Simpson	0	1	4	2	1	1	9
Spence Bay	1	1	0	2	2	0	6
Holman Island	0	0	1	1	1	0	3
Snowdrift	0	0	1	1	0	1	3
Cambridge Bay	2	1	0	1	4	1	9
Fort Laird	1	0	1	1	0	1	4
Fort Providence	0	4	3	2	2	1	12
Bathurst Inlet	0	0	0	0	1	0	1
Rae Lakes	0	0	0	0	1	0	1
Pine Point	0	0	0	0	0	0	0
Kakisa Lake	0	1	0	0	0	0	1
Total	8	15	20	24	20	25	112 (16)

Source — These numbers are drawn from the sources listed in footnote 87.
* The numbers reported by the parliamentary inquiry are included in brackets for contrast purposes.

were performed on women from this settlement or from surrounding areas. However, if no sterilizations were listed in Table 4 and 5, one must conclude that the figures from these tables (4 and 5) do not include sterilizations performed at the Medical Services hospital in Frobisher Bay (figures from Table 2). Nor do they represent overlapping sterilizations, because they list different numbers for the previous years (for 1970 and 1971, Table 4 indicates ten and two sterilizations for these years, and Table 5 indicates nine and five, respectively). It is believed, therefore, that the information in Tables 4 and 5 covers sterilizations performed at institutions other than Medical Services hospitals.

Let us consider another example. Medical Services reported, in Table 2, that at least nine sterilizations were performed on Aboriginal women in their hospital in Inuvik in 1972. Table 4 indicates no sterilizations were performed on women from Inuvik in that year, and Table 7 indicates that five took place. This means that although nine sterilizations were performed on Aboriginal women at the federal hospital in Inuvik, these women did not necessarily reside in this settlement. For one reason or another, five women from Inuvik were sterilized while at another facility. Because no sterilizations were reported from Table 4, and the numbers from Table 7 are not included in the nine listed in Table 2, these sources of information must be taken as non-overlapping.

To make clearer what might not be, a first set of numbers shows that 580 sterilizations were performed at federal Indian hospitals across Canada, and at least 551 of these were on Aboriginal women. It does not specify whether these women came

Table 7: Sterilizations on Aboriginal Women in Inuvik Zone, 1970–75*

Settlement	Sterilizations						
	1970	1971	1972	1973	1974	1975	Total
Aklavik	0	0	0	0	0	0	0
Inuvik	0	1	5	2	0	1	9
Fort Norman	1	0	2	0	0	0	3
Fort McPherson	0	0	1	1	0	0	2
Sachs Harbour	1	0	0	0	1	0	2
Norman Wells	0	0	0	0	0	1	1
Fort Good Hope	0	0	1	0	0	0	1
Tuktoyaktuk	0	0	1	0	1	1	3
Fort Franklin	0	0	2	3	0	1	6
Paulatuk and Cape Perry	0	0	1	0	2	0	3
Total:	2	1	13	6	4	4	30

Source — These numbers are drawn from the sources listed in footnote 87.
* The numbers reported by the parliamentary inquiry are included in brackets for contrast purposes.

from the communities in which the hospitals were located, or from elsewhere. A second set of numbers indicates that 180 sterilizations were performed on women who came from at least thirty-two different settlements, and one woman who was institutionalized at the Portage La Prairie Mental Home, Manitoba. Where these sterilizations took place is not indicated. A third set of numbers tells us that women from fifty-two northern settlements were sterilized, but it does not tell us where these sterilizations took place. Some of the settlements reported here overlap with those from another number set. However, because each set reports quite different numbers, it does not appear there is overlap between them. If one number set encompassed the other, it would not be possible to have the discrepancies discussed in the paragraphs above. Additional information is needed to identify exactly where all these documented sterilizations were performed and the total number of women sterilized, yet this confusion does not affect the fact that the numbers of sterilizations officially reported by the federal government, through its inquiry, were only a fraction of those known to have taken place.

On 17 March 1977, Wally Firth also requested the government release the number of vasectomies performed on Aboriginal men in the Northwest Territories for each year since 1970.[88] Government made these numbers available and they can be viewed in Table 10. However, Minister Lalonde issued a note of caution when considering these numbers, which speaks to the lack of accounting measures implemented by Medical Services to keep track of services as they were provided to Aboriginal peoples. It also indicates that more operations were taking place than were documented here. The caution was:

Table 8: Sterilizations on Aboriginal Women in Keewatin Zone, 1970–75*

Settlement	Sterilizations						
	1970	1971	1972	1973	1974	1975	Total
Baker Lake	4	4	4	1	1	2	16
Belcher Islands	0	1	3	0	6	0	10
Chesterfield Inlet	1	0	1	2	3	2	9 (10)
Coral Harbour	5	1	0	0	2	2	10
Eskimo Point	0	2	1	1	3	1	8
Rankin Inlet	2	2	7	4	4	2	21 (26)
Repulse Bay	0	3	0	1	1	1	6 (10)
Whale Cove	2	1	1	0	1	0	5
Total	14	14	17	9	21	10	85 (46)

Source — These numbers are drawn from the sources listed in footnote 87.
* The numbers reported by the parliamentary inquiry are included in brackets for contrast purposes.

Table 9: Totals, Sterilizations on Aboriginal Women from Northern Zones, 1970–75*

Zone	Sterilizations						Total
	1970	1971	1972	1973	1974	1975	
Baffin	22	23	12	20	23	17	117 (8)
Keewatin	14	14	17	9	21	10	85 (46)
MacKenzie	8	15	20	24	20	25	112 (16)
Inuvik	2	1	13	6	4	4	30
Total	46	53	62	59	68	56	344 (70)

Source — These numbers are drawn from the sources listed in footnote 87.
* The numbers reported by the parliamentary inquiry are included in brackets for contrast purposes.

> For most communities in the North, data on vasectomy procedures is not available. Since the vast majority of vasectomies are performed as out patient procedures in doctors [sic] offices, data exists only in individual patient records maintained in those offices. Moreover, the computer maintained by the Northwest Territories Medicare officials has not been programmed to record or retrieve this vasectomy data. For the reasons outlined above, these statistics relate only to procedures performed on in-patients in some hospitals and probably understate the over all situation in terms of the number of vasectomies performed. Due to the small number of vasectomies performed and the small populations in these northern communities, the rate per hundred thousand, although strictly accurate, can be misleading. (Canada 1977: 4070–71)

This note is similar to that which appeared in 1973, written by M.L. Webb when attempting to compile the number of Aboriginal women sterilized in the North. However, if government was not keeping track of services provided in its name, often by its very own employees, to wards under its charge, who exactly was supposed to be keeping track?

Additional questions arise. Why would the federal government, when purporting to inquire into sterilization rates in the North and the possibility of abuse, limit its inquiry to six very specific and very small areas rather than all northern areas from which women who were being sterilized came? This question becomes even more pertinent when it appears, at least by 1976, that government did have additional information on hand relating to sterilizations performed on Aboriginal women. Why focus on areas with some of the lowest rates of sterilizations in the North unless government was attempting to frame the issue in such a way as to limit public knowledge of the full extent to which Indigenous women had been subject to the procedure? It remains for the government to answer these questions. The public has the right to know and Aboriginal peoples deserve to know exactly how

Table 10: Vasectomies on Aboriginal Men, Northern Region, 1970–75

Community	Year	Number of Vasectomies
Frobisher Bay	1970	2
	1971	2
	1972	6
	1973	7
	1974	7
	1975	3
Inuvik	1970	-
	1971	3
	1972	12
	1973	14
	1974	7
	1975	8
Hay River	1970	3
	1971	2
	1973	8
	1974	2
	1975	3
Yellowknife	1970	-
	1971	1
	1972	-
	1973	2
	1974	1
	1975	5
Pine Point	1970	2
	1971	6
	1972	3
	1973	2
	1974	2
	1975	5
Fort Providence	1972	1
	1973	1
Fort Simpson	1974	1
Fort Smith	1972	1
Total		122

Source — Information drawn from source at footnote 88.

many sterilizations were performed, where these were taking place and under what pretenses. The answers are not obvious from the information gathered through this research. Nor should it be left to individuals to sift through enormous volumes of federal records in order to piece together insights into a practice that took place over many years, in many locations and that affected countless people in such definitive ways. An honest and forthcoming inquiry is not only necessary but could be more productive given the computer capacities now available.

We do know the number of sterilizations performed at one institution surpassed those reported by the federal government through its parliamentary inquiry. Researchers Jamie Cohen and T.F. Baskett studied the rate of sterilizations performed at the Churchill Health Centre, formerly known as the Fort Churchill General Hospital, located in northern Manitoba. This centre provided medical services for the town of Churchill as well as a small group of Indigenous peoples at Tadoule Lake, those on the northern end of the Hudson Bay railway line, and some of the Inuit population from the Keewatin District, Northwest Territories. During an eleven-year period, from 1966 to 1976, 173 tubal ligations were performed. Of these, 104 (60.1 percent) were on Inuit peoples, 52 (30.1 percent) on Caucasians and 17 (9.8 percent) on Indians. The place of residence was the Keewatin District in 59.5 percent of the cases, Churchill in 34.7 percent and 5.8 percent from the Manitoba hinterland. Nearly half (48 percent) of these were performed during the three-year period from 1972 to 1974 (Cohen and Baskett 1978: 222–24).

Over this eleven-year period, nearly 70 percent of tubal ligations performed at this one location were carried out on Aboriginal peoples, and there was an increase in the final years of the study. The authors explain this increase as due to a "back log" of cases arising from specialist resources of the Northern Medical Unit being made fully available (Cohen and Baskett 1978: 222–24). Yet this trend also appeared in the rates of sterilizations performed at other federal hospitals and the increase in the proportion of Aboriginal peoples sterilized under the Alberta Sterilization Act in its final three years of operation. And even though the percentages of sterilizations in their study were in keeping with the proportion of ethnic groups in the population of the area, it can be misleading to examine statistics in such a way. Because Aboriginal populations are often so small, if just one woman of childbearing age is sterilized annually, the proportionate percentages become much larger over time. The authors also point out that these numbers do not represent all patients sterilized from these or other areas. Sterilizations were performed outside of Churchill, at both federally run hospitals serving Aboriginal peoples and in provincial institutions. Further, if one considers these sterilizations in addition to other factors such as abortions, stillbirths, infant deaths and the sometimes indiscriminate prescription of birth control and IUDs, concerns surrounding the sterilization of Aboriginal peoples make much more sense. These factors, in addition to the numerous effects of the previously discussed assimilative policies and practices, and the resulting epidemic rates of poverty, suicide, disease and over-policing which often lead to higher and earlier death rates as compared to the Canadian population, all give greater weight to concerns surrounding the sterilization of Aboriginal women.

The sterilization of Aboriginal women allows the Canadian state to deny responsibility for and avoid doing something about the deplorable conditions in which most Aboriginal communities live, conditions recognized as the direct result of the process of dispossession and colonialism. Wally Firth, the member of the House of Commons who spoke out against the unwitting sterilization of Inuit women, quoted from a newscast on CFFB Frobisher Bay, from 3 September 1974, describing the state of health for many Indigenous women and children at the time. Aboriginal peoples in the North had the lowest nutrition standards and the highest mortality in North America and the situation was getting worse:

> In a random series of tests conducted by Dr. Alex Williams of the Frobisher Bay General Hospital, over 75 per cent of the pregnant Inuit women and young Inuit children examined showed critically low nutrition levels. In a number of cases, said the former chief of medical staff, vitamin A and vitamin C necessary for the prevention of infection and skin disease, simply were not present. The results, he said, were children, if they survived, who at as little as eight days old, had perforated ear drums, systematic infections, skin sores and almost no resistance to disease. Not only that, the IQ level of children born with these vitamin deficiencies was 20 per cent to 40 per cent lower than average.[89]

It is more cost effective to curb the reproductive capacities of Aboriginal women than it is to address the fundamental issues required to improve the living conditions into which Aboriginal children are born. This was in fact the expressed logic standing behind the federal family planning policy announced in 1971.

Some might say it is one thing to refer to eugenic sterilization as shameful and unjust, but that we cannot paint all sterilizations as coercive; to do so is to deny the agency of Aboriginal women to make choices about their own reproduction and continues the paternalism so rampant in past Indian policy. Yet the Committee to End Sterilization Abuse, formed in response to reproductive abuses experienced by marginalized women in the United States in the mid 1970s, once wrote:

> Forced infertility is in no way a substitute for a good job, enough to eat, decent education, daycare, medical services, maternal infant care, housing, clothing, or cultural integrity ... when society does not provide the basic necessities of life for everyone, there can be no such freedom of choice. (Shapiro 1985: 144)

Similarly, it can be said that until such conditions are met, and until conditions of colonialism are ended and the longstanding policies and practices imposed on

Aboriginal peoples by the Canadian state are brought to a halt, and Aboriginal peoples are returned lands, resources and the freedom to provide for their own subsistence in ways they so choose, without stipulations, one cannot speak of freedom of choice.

As indicated at the outset of this work, the sterilization of Aboriginal women and the resulting loss of children is an attack on the sovereignty of nations and yet another means of appropriating Indian lands (Ralstin-Lewis 2005). The ability of Native women to reproduce is necessary in order to ensure the reproduction of the next generation of Aboriginal peoples, and this ability continues to stand in the way of the appropriation of Indigenous lands and the extinguishment of Aboriginal title (Smith 2005a). To quote Robert Lechat speaking of the sterilization of Inuit women in northern Canada:

> Doesn't it happen now and again that a more powerful nation, while pretending to promote the interests of a weaker nation, thinks first of its own interests? After all … there are barely 20,000 Inuit and look at their land claims … In spite of their small number they cost the Federal Treasury a pretty penny. Too many, under present conditions, would cause serious financial problems. (Lechat 1976: 6)

The coercive sterilization of Aboriginal women has indeed represented a cost-effective method allowing the Canadian government to avoid accountability for the theft of Indigenous lands and resources. The effects of the sterilization of Aboriginal women — whether intended or not — are in line with past Indian policy and serve the political and economic interests of Canada. The point needs to be reiterated, then, that whether imposed coercively on one woman or many, it is this entire historical and material context which gives sterilization larger implications when applied to Aboriginal women and which opens the practice to a credible claim of genocide under international law.

The End of the Line

What are we to make of all of this? There have been consistent and longstanding allegations by Aboriginal women of abuse, coercion and wrongdoing at the hands of government officials and medical professionals. Are we to believe these to be fabrications or as resulting from conspiratorial theories? Are we to blindly accept the rhetoric of politicians that "no formal policy" of coercively imposing fertility control methods on Aboriginal women in Canada has existed? At what point do we begin to consider consistent and longstanding practices not as isolated instances of abuse but as policy, whether explicitly and openly stated or not? Despite governmental assurances that its family-planning policies and practices are applied in the same way in both Indigenous and settler populations, it is evident that this has not been the case. There has always been a two-pronged approach in the ways reproductive policies have been employed and the consequences these have had for women from different social locations. Historian Diane Dodd tells us that with respect to contraceptive technologies pursued in the late nineteenth and early twentieth centuries, a desire to control the quantity and quality of the population was just as much a motivating force in the movement for birth control reform as was the desire by some women to secure more control over their fertility, and sometimes economic arguments were emphasized at the expense of the rights of women (Dodd 1985). This two-pronged approach helps us understand why reproductive technologies were employed coercively on some Indigenous women long after eugenic justifications for these fell into disrepute, while at the same time these represented positive gains for other women. A consideration of the larger historical and material context also allows us to understand how and why this coercion has taken place, as well as the implications it has for Indigenous peoples.

The sterilization of Aboriginal women did take place in Canada and was often coupled with other policies or practices relating to the control of births, including coercive abortions and the indiscriminate prescription of contraceptives, and always within the larger historical and material context of colonialism and assimilation. Amid these charges and allegations, and federal actions and inactions surrounding Indigenous health in general, and sterilization in particular, there remain more questions than answers. As Menzies and Palys state in reference to the psychiatric incarceration of Aboriginal peoples over the last hundred years:

> Again and again ... interlocking networks of government and expert scrutiny operated in concert with the activities of missionaries, priests and pastors, nurses, teachers, and increasingly by the 1930s, social workers practicing in the field service of the provincial Welfare Branch ... Sometimes Indian agents would assume primary responsibility ... On other occasions, medical practitioners took the lead. (Menzies and Palys 2006: 161)

A similar point can be made about the circumstances leading up to the coercive sterilization of Aboriginal women. However, in assigning responsibility for wrongdoings and hence, responsibility for rectifying these wrongs, we must look to those who set the initial chain of events in motion for final accountability. This responsibility is found with the federal government, which from all appearances has had as its unwritten purpose the bureaucratic elimination of Aboriginal peoples, by one means or another, since its very inception.

Even though the federal government fell short of enacting legislation directly sanctioning the sterilization of Aboriginal peoples, in its refusal to condemn the practice, by enacting policies and legislation affecting other aspects of Aboriginal life and making sterilization more likely, and through its financial support to provinces, it has allowed these sterilizations to be carried out in its own institutions and those under provincial control. With respect to longstanding allegations of abuse relating to the reproductive lives of Aboriginal women, the federal government has consistently demonstrated, through its actions and inactions, that its primary interest has been with cost saving and avoiding accountability. In some cases, it appears to have made a calculated attempt to rationalize illegal and/or unethical practices in order to avoid potential liability. And by refusing to fully acknowledge, address or rectify abuses, and make certain these stop and do not happen again, the federal government faces the most important responsibility of all. The next chapter examines some of the events that transpired following the repeal of sterilization legislation in Canada, and how the continued actions and inactions of federal and provincial governments worked to ensure many centrally important questions regarding the sterilization of Aboriginal women would not get asked.

Notes

1. With the exception of 1937, 1947, 1954–55, 1957–58, and 1961, more women than men were sterilized, even when more men were presented to the Board. In each decade, more women than men were sterilized.

2. These are averages. The actual proportion of the population that was Indian or Métis fluctuated during the period in which sterilizations were carried out, as did the number of those sterilized.

3. A mentally defective person was one in whom there was "a condition of arrested or incomplete development of mind existing before the age of eighteen years, whether arising from inherent causes or induced by disease or injury" and a diagnosis was usually determined by a psychiatric evaluation coupled with one, or a series of IQ tests (Statutes of Alberta 1937 s. 2 c).

4. Library and Archives Canada [hereafter LAC], RG 29, "Mental Diseases," Volume 2971, File 851-4-300, pt. 1A, Correspondence from C.A. Roberts, M.D., Principal Medical Officer, Mental Health, to Director, Indian Health Services, 28 September 1956.

5. Eugenics Board, Minutes, letter from T.R.L. McInnis, Indian Affairs Branch, Department of Mines and Resources, to the Medical Superintendent, Provincial Mental Hospital, Ponoka 10 September 1942, highlighted in Dyck (2013: 82).

6. LAC, RG 29, "Mental Diseases," Volume 2971, File 851-4-300 pt. 1A, Correspondence from P.E. Moore, Director, Indian Health Services to Deputy Minister of National Health, 3 November, 1953; LAC, RG 29, "Mental Diseases," Volume 2971, File 851-4-300 pt. 1A, Correspondence from C.A. Roberts, M.D., Chief, Mental Health Division, to Director, Health Insurance Studies, 10 November 1953; LAC, RG 29, "Mental Diseases," Volume 2971, File 851-4-300 pt. 1A, Correspondence from Gordon E. Wride, M.D., Assistant Director, Health Insurance Studies, to G.D.W. Cameron, M.D., Deputy Minister of National Health, 14 November 1953.

7. LAC, RG 29, "Mental Diseases," Volume 2971, File 851-4-300, pt. 1A, Correspondence, from W. S. Barclay, Regional Superintendent, Pacific Region, Indian Health Services, to A. L. Henderson, Research Analyst, Hospital for Mental Diseases, Brandon Manitoba, 23 February 1956.

8. Provincial Archives of Ontario [hereafter PAO], RG 10-107, Container 80: "Indian Patients 1926-1949," Files Reference Code RG 10-107-0-516, Correspondence, H.M. Robbins, Deputy Provincial Secretary, to Bursar, Ontario Hospital, Hamilton Ontario, 18 August 1926; PAO, RG 10-107, Container 147: "Dept. of Indian Affairs 1950," File

Reference Code RG 10-107-0-942, Correspondence, T.M. Gourlay, Executive Officer, Ontario Department of Health, to all Superintendents, 25 August 1953.

9. LAC, RG 29, "Mental Diseases," Volume 2971, File 851-4-300, pt. 1A, Correspondence from C.A. Roberts, M.D., Principal Medical Officer, Mental Health, to Director, Indian Health Services, 28 September 1956.

10. LAC, RG 29, "Mental Diseases," Volume 2971, File 851-4-300, pt. 1A, Correspondence from the Department of Indian Affairs to P.E. Moore, Director, Indian and Northern Health Services, Department of National Health and Welfare, 10 January 1957.

11. LAC, RG 58-C-1, Attest Audit Files, "Historical Files From 1974 and Prior Department of Health and Welfare Coqualeetza Indian Hospital — Audit (1964)." Volume 256, File Part 1, 1964, Report by G.P. Anderson, *Audit of Coqualeetza Indian Hospital Report*, Submitted to Mr. Douglas, 28 September 1964.

12. There are claims from an organization called the "Truth Commission into Genocide in Canada" that sterilizations took place at three major centres in British Columbia, namely the Nanaimo Indian Hospital, the King's Daughters Clinic, and the W.R. Large Memorial Hospital. A report produced by this organization contains claims that, according to Dr. George Darby Sr., a practicing doctor in the 1950s, the Department of Indian Affairs paid him additional funds as part of "an actual sterilization program," and another doctor was "paid $300 for each native woman sterilized." This claim and many others contained within the report lack any documented evidence, and the report in which these are made often distorts well known facts in a sensational manner. Though some of the evidence presented is hearsay, to say the least, other information in the report is based on the actual recollected experiences of those who went through residential schools. I do not dismiss these experiences, but it appears the author of the report, namely former reverend Kevin Annett, is making use of these in order to buttress other claims, made by him, relating to sterilizations in the above mentioned Indian hospitals, and "an actual sterilization program" instituted by the federal government. The facts appear to be much less sensational and the evidence, in lesser supply, consisting more of a series of decisions relating to funding and cost saving. This is not to say that no sterilizations took place or that it was not "unofficial" government policy and the federal government is responsible for the outcome of such practices on Aboriginal women nonetheless. However, in an effort to prove these claims, Annett prefers to sensationalize the truth and to cite evidence to buttress his claims that he, in the final, appears unable to produce. See The Truth Commission into Genocide in Canada 2001.

13. LAC, MG 28 I 233, "Prevention of Blindness — Sterilization Project," Volume 21, File 8, 1936-1939, Correspondence from A.R. Kaufman to CNIB, Toronto Chapter, 2 December 1938.

14. PAO, RG 10-6, Correspondence of the Deputy Minister of Health, "Legislation - Sexual Sterilization Act. 1948-1960," File Reference Code RG 10-6-0-1072, Correspondence from B.T. McGhie, M.D. to Dr. S.J.W. Horne, 11 September, 1933.

15. B. T. McGhie was in correspondence with Dr. Horne on at least a couple occasions regarding sterilization. McGhie sent Horne information he requested from the Deputy Minister of Health in Alberta on the work of the Eugenics Board, on one occasion on the 25 May 1933, and again ten years later on 6 December 1943. PAO, Correspondence of the Deputy Minister of Health, "Legislation - Sexual Sterilization Act. 1948-1960," File Reference Code RG 10-6-0-1072.

16. PAO, RG 10-6, Correspondence of the Deputy Minister of Health, "Legislation - Sexual Sterilization Act. 1948-1960," File Reference Code RG 10-6-0-1072, Correspondence from B.T. McGhie, M.D. to Dr. S.J.W. Horne, 11 September, 1933.

17. PAO, RG 10-6 Correspondence of the Deputy Minister of Health, "Legislation - Sexual Sterilization Act. 1948-1960," File Reference Code RG 10-6-0-1072, Correspondence from R.C. Montgomery, M.D. to Dr. S.J.W. Horne, 17 February 1938. As late as 1942, the Children's Aid Society of Brant, Ontario, unanimously passed a resolution subsequently forwarded to the Legislature, requesting that they consider the passage of a sterilization act similar to that in effect in Alberta. PAO, RG 8-5, Correspondence of the Provincial Secretary, "Sterilization [between 1934 and 1943]," Box 115, Correspondence from J.L. Dixon to Honourable H.C. Nixon, Provincial Secretary, 20 March 1942.

18. LAC, RG 29, "Birth Control," Volume 2869, File 851-1-5 pt. 1 A, Correspondence from P.E. Moore to Regional Superintendent, Saskatchewan, 20 August 1957.

19. LAC, RG 85, "Sterilization of Imbeciles," Volume 901, File 10109, Correspondence from Gibson to Daly, 30 December 1938.

20. LAC, RG 85, "Sterilization of Imbeciles," Volume 901, File 10109, Correspondence from Daly to Gibson, 4 January 1939.

21. LAC, RG 85, "Sterilization of Imbeciles," Volume 901, File 10109, Précis, Northwest Territories Council, pp.1-2, 14 January 1939.

22. LAC, RG 85, "Sterilization of Imbeciles," Volume 901, File 10109, Memorandum from Deputy Commissioner Gibson to Major McKeand, member of the Northwest Territories Council, 17 January 1939.

23. Incidentally, this was the same year that the Supreme Court established in Re Eskimos, 1939 S.C.R. 10 that federal jurisdiction and responsibility extended to Inuit peoples.

24. LAC, RG 85, "Sterilization of Imbeciles," Volume 901, File 10109, Correspondence from J.A. Bildfell, M.D. to the Director, Northwest Territories Division of the Department of Mines and Resources, 17 September 1941.

25. LAC, RG 85, "Sterilization of Imbeciles," Volume 901, File 10109, Correspondence, letter returned to D.L. McKeand, from Deputy Commissioner Gibson, 14 November 1941.

26. LAC, RG 85, "Sterilization of Imbeciles," Volume 901, File 10109, Correspondence from J.J. Heagerty, M. D. to R.A. Gibson, 25 November 1941.

27. LAC, RG 85, "Sterilization of Imbeciles," Volume 901, File 10109, Extract from the Minutes of the One Hundred and Thirty-fourth Session of the Northwest Territories Council held on 21 November 1941. It is unclear how a statement by Dr. Heagerty, dated 25 November, appeared in an extract of minutes from 21 November 1941. The author believes the statement from Heagerty was specifically requested post meeting, to be included in Council minutes, based on handwritten notes on the top corner of the document.

28. We also now know that it was at this time, from 1939 until 1963, that government implemented a policy of forced relocation for many Inuit to the eastern Arctic in an effort to deal with social problems in Aboriginal communities that arose as a result of government policy and contact with non-Indigenous people. Unfamiliar with their surroundings and ill-equipped to survive the climate, many Inuit starved to death. Some of the settlements from which women would subsequently be sterilized were formed as a result of this policy (Marcus, 1995; Tester and Kulchyski, 1994).

29. LAC, RG 29, "Birth Control," Volume 2869, File 8851-1-5 pt. 1A, Correspondence from H.A. Proctor to Zone Superintendents, 27 August 1965.
30. LAC, RG 29, "Birth Control," Volume 2869, File 851-1-5, pt. 1A, Correspondence from C.S. Gamble, Superintendent, Nanaimo Region, to Pacific Region Superintendent, 2 September 1965.
31. LAC, RG 29, "Birth Control," Volume 2869, File 851-1-5, pt. 1A, Correspondence from L.R. Hurtle, Superintendent, Atlantic Zone, 20 September 1965.
32. LAC, RG 29, "Birth Control," Volume 2869, File 851-1-5, pt. 1A, Correspondence from M. Savoie, Superintendent, Quebec Zone, to Eastern Region Superintendent, 21 September 1965.
33. LAC, RG 29, "Birth Control," Volume 2869, File 851-1-5, pt. 1A, Correspondence from R.D. Thompson, Superintendent, Pacific Region, to H.A. Proctor, Director General, Medical Services, Department of National Health and Welfare, 13 September 1965.
34. LAC, RG 29, "Birth Control," Volume 2869, File 851-1-5, pt. 1A, Correspondence from S. Mallick, Sioux Lookout Zone Superintendent, to H.A. Proctor, Director General, Medical Services, 15 December 1964. Mallick also quoted an article entitled "Threepenny Answer to Starvation" published in the *Manchester Guardian*, Thursday, 10 December 1964.
35. LAC, RG 29, "Birth Control," Volume 2869, File 851-1-5, pt. 1A, Correspondence from Inuvik Zone Superintendent to Foothills Superintendent, 8 September, 1965.
36. LAC, RG 29, "Birth Control," Volume 2869, File 851-1-5, pt. 1A, Correspondence from J.D. Galbraith, Coqualeetza Hospital, Zone Superintendent, Sardis, to Regional Superintendent, Pacific Region, 8 September 1965.
37. LAC, RG 29, "Birth Control," Volume 2869, File 851-1-5, pt. 1A, Correspondence from Regional Superintendent, Saskatchewan Region, to H.A. Proctor, Director General, Medical Services, 3 September 1965.
38. LAC, RG 29, "Birth Control," Volume 2869, File 851-1-5, pt. 1A, Correspondence from H.A. Proctor, to Commander J. Coulter, Special Planning Secretariat, 1 October 1965.
39. An internal handwritten memo written by Proctor to an unknown recipient indicates concern for such a trend and Proctor asks "What do you think about nurses issuing 'The Pill' apparently without medical supervision?" LAC, RG 29, "Birth Control," Volume 2869, File 851-1-5, pt. 1A, Correspondence from M.E. Gordon, Zone Superintendent, Prince Rupert, to R.D. Thompson, Regional Superintendent, Pacific Region, and forwarded to H.A. Proctor, 24 September 1965; LAC, RG 29, "Birth Control," Volume 2869, File 851-1-5, pt. 1A, Internal handwritten memo written by Proctor, n.d.
40. LAC, RG 29, "Birth Control," Volume 2869, File 851-1-5, pt. 1A, Directives issued by the Department of National Health and Welfare, Medical Services, to Zone Superintendents, 5 April 1965.
41. LAC, RG 29, "Birth Control," Volume 2869, File 851-1-5, pt. 1A, Correspondence from H.A. Proctor, to Commander J. Coulter, Special Planning Secretariat, 1 October 1965.
42. LAC, RG 29, "Birth Control," Volume 2869, File 851-1-5, pt. 1A, Correspondence from Kahn Tineta Horn, to R.F. Battle, Director, Indian Affairs Branch, Indian and Northern Affairs, 28 January 1966.
43. LAC, RG 29, "Birth Control," Volume 2869, File 851-1-5, pt. 1A, Correspondence from H.A. Proctor to Chief Delisle, 17 February 1966.

44. LAC, RG 29, "Birth Control," Volume 2869, File 851-1-5, pt. 1A, Correspondence from T.J. Orford, Regional Director, Saskatchewan, to H.A. Proctor, Director General, Medical Services, 16 March 1966.

45. LAC, RG 29, "Birth Control," Volume 2869, File 851-1-5, pt. 1A, Correspondence from H.A. Proctor, Director General, Medical Services, 6 April 1966.

46. LAC, RG 29, "Birth Control," Volume 2869, File 851-1-5, pt. 1A, Correspondence from H.A. Proctor, Director General, Medical Services, 6 April 1966.

47. LAC, RG 29, "Birth Control," Volume 2869, File 851-1-5, pt. 1A, Correspondence from H.A. Proctor, Director General, Medical Services, 6 April 1966.

48. LAC, RG 29, "Birth Control," Volume 2869, File 851-1-5, pt. 1A, Memorandum from Minister of Health to Dr. J.N. Crawford, Deputy Minister of Health, 12 February 1969.

49. LAC, RG 29, "Birth Control," Volume 2869, File 851-1-5, pt. 1B, Correspondence from J.H. Wiebe, M.D., Director, Medical Services, 2 October 1970.

50. LAC, RG 29, "Birth Control," Volume 2869, File 851-1-5, pt. 1B, Correspondence from J.H. Wiebe, M.D., Director, Medical Services, to Maurice Leclair, M.D., Deputy Minister of National Health, 27 October 1970.

51. LAC, RG 29, "Birth Control," Volume 2869, File 851-1-5, pt. 2, Correspondence from J.H. Wiebe, M.D., Director, Medical Services, to Regional Directors, 8 October 1971.

52. LAC, RG 29, "Birth Control," Volume 2869, File 851-1-5, pt. 2, Correspondence from J.H. Wiebe, M.D., Director, Medical Services, to Regional Directors, 8 October 1971.

53. LAC, RG 29, "Birth Control," Volume 2869, File 851-1-5, pt. 2, Memorandum from J.H. Wiebe, M.D., Director, Medical Services, to Dr. Maurice Leclair, Deputy Minister of Health, 19 October 1971.

54. Canada, *Commons Debates*, 9 October, 1970, 16.

55. Canada, *Commons Debates*, 14 October, 1970, 111.

56. Canada, *Commons Debates*, 14 October, 1970, 111; LAC, RG 29, "Birth Control," Volume 2869, File 851-1-5, pt. 2, Newspaper clipping, "Eskimo Sterilization Inhumane — Lewis," n.d.

57. Canada, *Commons Debates*, 14 October, 1970, 112

58. LAC, RG 29, "Birth Control," Volume 2870, File 851-1-5, pt. 3A, Jim Eayrs, "Sterilization of Eskimos," *Weekend* (1 April 1973) CBC, NWT.

59. LAC, RG 29, "Birth Control," Volume 2870, File 851-1-5, pt. 3A, Correspondence from Marc Lalonde to Laurent Picard, President, CBC, 6 April 1973; reprinted in *The MacKenzie Pilot*, May 3, 1973, pp. 29–30.

60. LAC, RG 29, "Birth Control," Volume 2870, File 851-1-5, pt. 3A, Transcript of interview conducted by Jim Eayrs with Brian Pearson, CBC, *Weekend*, 8 April 1973.

61. LAC, RG 29, "Birth Control," Volume 2870, File 851-1-5, pt. 3A, Transcript of interview conducted by Jim Eayrs with Brian Pearson, CBC, *Weekend*, 8 April 1973.

62. LAC, RG 29, "Birth Control," Volume 2870, File 851-1-5, pt. 3A, Transcript of interview conducted by Jim Eayrs with Brian Gunn, Canadian Broadcasting Corporation program, *Weekend*, 8 April 1973, 8.

63. LAC, RG 29, "Birth Control," Volume 2870, File 851-1-5, pt. 3A, Transcript of interview conducted by Jim Eayrs with Brian Pearson, Canadian Broadcasting Corporation program, *Weekend*, 8 April 1973.

64. LAC, RG 29, "Birth Control," Volume 2870, File 851-1-5, pt. 3A, *News of the North*, Yellowknife, NWT, 11 April 1973.

65. LAC, RG 29, "Birth Control," Volume 2870, File 851-1-5, pt. 3B, C.M.L. Webb, Assistant

Deputy Minister, Medical Services, to A.D. Hunt, Assistant Deputy Minister, Northern Affairs Program, 1 May 1973.

66. LAC, RG 29, "Birth Control," Volume 2870, File 851-1-5, pt. 3B, A.D. Hunt, Assistant Deputy Minister, Northern Affairs Program, 1 June 1973.

67. The letter states that Port Burwell has its own unique dialect, with another in Lake Harbour, Pangnirtung, Cape Dorset, and a third in Broughton Island.

68. LAC, RG 29, "Birth Control," Volume 2870, File 851-1-5, pt. 3B, Correspondence from F.J. Covill, Regional Director, Medical Services, Northwest Territories Region, to Director General, Program Management, Medical Services Branch, 11 June 1974; LAC, RG 29, "Birth Control," Volume 2870, File 851-1-5, pt. 3B, Correspondence from V.L. Urbanoski, Zone Director to F.J. Covill, Regional Director, Medical Services, Northwest Territories Region.

69. Canada, *Commons Debates*, 2 April 1973, 2854-2858.

70. LAC, RG 29, "Birth Control," Volume 2870, File 851-1-5, pt. 3A, Guidelines for Tubal Ligation issued to Regional Director, Northern Region from O.J. Rath, Regional Director, Alberta Region, 1 April 1970.

71. LAC, RG 29, "Birth Control," Volume 2870, File 851-1-5, pt. 3A, Correspondence from Regional Director, Medical Services, Northern Region, Guidelines for Approval of Sterilization Procedures, 10 November 1970.

72. LAC, RG 29, "Birth Control," Volume 2869, File 851-1-5, pt. 2, Correspondence from A.P. Abbott, to J. MacDonald, 28 July 1971.

73. LAC, RG 29, "Birth Control," Volume 2870, File 851-1-5, pt. 3A, Memorandum from R.P. Beck, M.D. Professor and Chairman of the Department of Obstetrics and Gynaecology from the University of Alberta, to Attending staff and nurses, 20 September 1971.

74. Correspondence, from R.R.M. Croome, M.D. Executive Director, Charles Camsell Hospital, to Dr. O.J. Rath, Regional Director, Alberta Region, 24 February 1972, requesting permission to initiate the same procedures regarding sterilization as those followed by the University Hospital and the Royal Alexandra Hospital. LAC, RG 29, "Birth Control," Volume 2870, File 851-1-5, pt. 3A, Correspondence from R.R.M. Croome, M.D. Executive Director, Charles Camsell Hospital, to Dr. O.J. Rath, Regional Director, Alberta Region, 24 February 1972; Correspondence, from M.L. Webb, Assistant Deputy Minister, Medical Services, to Dr. O.J. Rath, Regional Director, Alberta Region, 12 April 1972, indicating that the outlined procedures met with the full approval of Medical Services, with the specification that the consent of the patient be given in writing. LAC, RG 29, "Birth Control," Volume 2870, File 851-1-5, pt. 3A, Correspondence from M.L. Webb, Assistant Deputy Minister, Medical Services, to Dr. O.J. Rath, Regional Director, Alberta Region, 12 April 1972.

75. LAC, RG 29, "Birth Control," Volume 2870, File 851-1-5, pt. 3B, Correspondence from Maurice Leclair to B.D. Dewar, Assistant Deputy Minister of Medical Services on 24 May 1974.

76. LAC, RG 29, "Birth Control," Volume 2870, File 851-1-5, pt. 3B, Correspondence from M.L. Webb, M.D., Assistant Deputy Minister, Medical Services, to the Regional Director, Northern Region, Therapeutic Abortions at the Frobisher Bay General Hospital, 7 April 1972.

77. Canada, *Commons Debates*, 1 November 1971, 9194. There are other allegations. In a letter dated 19 December 1974, Minister Lalonde was asked by a "Mr. Bell"

whether he was still "permitting the pill to be passed off as a vitamin pill to the Indians, Métis and Inuit?" LAC, RG 29, "Birth Control," Volume 2870, File 851-1-5, pt. 3B, Correspondence from Mr. Bell to Minister Lalonde, 19 December 1974. Or, at St. Anne's Hospital in Fort Smith, NWT, Dr. Roy Cazabon's hospital privileges were rescinded following an inquiry into allegations of malpractice. After the federal government refused to look into the matter despite Commissioner S.M. Hodgson being "gravely concerned," a medical audit was conducted. Among other problems, the audit found an unacceptably high incidence of normal tissue in surgeries for appendicitis; between 70 and 80 percent of the tissues removed by Dr. Cazabon were in fact normal. The Committee stated "a large number of people were operated on unnecessarily." Knowing what we do about sterilizations and the trend of performing appendectomies in the same instance as sterilizations, one must view these instances with suspicion. Why would a supposedly competent doctor perform unnecessary medical surgery on otherwise healthy tissue? Canada, *Commons Debates*, 11 January 1974, 9272; "Commissioner "Gravely Concerned" Over Doctors," *The Pilot*, 13 December 1973, 1; "Board Mum," *The Pilot*, 24 January 1974, 1; "Dr. Cazabon Loses Appeal," *The Pilot*, 31 January 1974, 1; "Commissioner Replies to Committee," *The Pilot*, 7 February 1974, 2.

78. LAC, RG 29, "Birth Control," Volume 2870, File 851-1-5, pt. 3A, Correspondence from M.L. Webb, Assistant Deputy Minister, Medical Services, to Dr. Maurice Leclair, Deputy Minister of National Health, 5 April 1973.

79. LAC, RG 29, "Birth Control," Volume 2870, File 851-1-5, pt. 3A, Correspondence from M.L. Webb, Assistant Deputy Minister, Medical Services, to Dr. Maurice Leclair, Deputy Minister of National Health, 13 April 1973. This document includes a table drawn up by Webb based on requests for information from the above listed hospitals, sent to Deputy Minister Leclair and subsequently forwarded to Dr. Whiteside. It was compiled from information drawn from the following sources: LAC, RG 29, "Birth Control," Volume 2870, File 851-1-5, pt. 3B, Correspondence, "Sterilizations — Minister's Briefing Book," from Zone Director, Inuvik Zone, to Director General, Medical Services Branch, 28 February 1974; Correspondence, "Sterilizations — Minister's Briefing Book," from M.P.D. Waldron, acting Regional Director, Alberta Region, to Director General, Medical Services Branch, 12 February 1974; Correspondence, "Sterilizations — Minister's Briefing Book," from W.G. Goldthorpe, Zone Director, Sioux Lookout, to Director General, Medical Services Branch, 6 February 1974; Correspondence, "Sterilizations — Minister's Briefing Book," from A. Schwartz, Regional Director, Manitoba Region, to Dr. L. Black, Director General, Medical Services Branch, 5 February 1974; Correspondence, "Sterilizations — Minister's Briefing Book," from N.L. Fraser, Zone Director, Ontario, to Director General, Medical Services, n.d.; Correspondence, "Sterilizations — Minister's Briefing Book," from Hospital Administrator, Frobisher Bay Hospital, N.W.T. to Director General, Medical Services Branch, 31 January 1974; LAC, RG 29, "Birth Control," Volume 2870, File 851-1-5, pt. 3C, Abortions and Sterilizations, 1974, at Medical Services Branch Hospitals.

80. Information is also missing on the total number of sterilizations performed at the Charles Camsell Hospital in 1973 and 1974, perhaps as a result of this hospital becoming a general treatment hospital. LAC, RG 29, "Birth Control," Volume 2870, File 851-1-5, pt. 3A, Appendix P "Charles Camsell Hospital, Sterilization by Means of

Tubal Ligation and Cauterization."

81.. *Akwesasne Notes*, "Killing our Future: Sterilization and Experiments," (Early Spring, 1977): 5; *Globe and Mail*, "Many Inuit Sterilized, RC Says," 9 October 1976, 16; Robert Lechat, "Intensive Sterilization for the Inuit," *Eskimo* (Fall/Winter 1976): 5; LAC, RG 29, Volume 2870, File 851-1-5, pt. 3C, Robert Lechat, "Sterilization of Inuit is Exposed as National Scandal," *Sunday Express*, 4 pps.

82. Canada, *Commons Debates*, 25 October 1976, 414.

83. LAC, RG 29, "Birth Control," Volume 2870, File 851-1-5, pt. 4, Correspondence from Parliamentary Returns Division, to Mr. Charles Caron, Assistant Deputy Minister, Medical Services, regarding question No. 765, 25 October 1976.

84. Information compiled from response received from Harkness and subsequently submitted by the Acting Assistant Deputy Minister, Medical Services Branch, Lyall M. Black, to Christine Brydon, Parliamentary Returns Officer, on 1 December 1976. LAC, RG 29, "Birth Control," Volume 2870, File 851-1-5, pt. 4, Information Release, Parliamentary Returns Officer, 1 December 1976.

85. These numbers were also reported to Parliament by the Minister of National Health and Welfare, Marc Lalonde, on 25 February 1977. Canada, *Commons Debates*, 25 February 1977, 3430.

86. The parliamentary inquiry covered a ten year span, from 1966 to 1976. LAC, RG 29, "Birth Control," Volume 2870, File 851-1-5, pt. 4, Information compiled in tables entitled "Eastern Eskimos -1970"; "Western Eskimos -1970"; "Eastern Eskimos -1971": "Western Eskimos -1971"; "Eastern Eskimos -1972"; "Western Eskimos -1972"; "Eastern Eskimos -1973"; "Western Eskimos -1973."

87. See LAC, RG 29, "Birth Control," Volume 2870, File 851-1-5 pt.4, "Sterilization Operations."

88. Question no. 1 244, Number of vasectomies performed in the Northwest Territories. Canada, *Commons Debates*, 17 March 1977, 4070-4071.

89. Canada, *Commons Debates*, 10 October 1974, reprinted in *The Mackenzie Pilot*, 24 October 1974, 3.

4. Settling the Past

Steps toward the repeal of the Alberta Sterilization Act did not begin until 1969, when Dr. James Goodwin, a practicing physician at the University Hospital, came forward saying he had personally come into contact with ten women who were sterilized without their informed consent (Christian 1974: 30). In an exclusive interview with the Edmonton *Journal* (March 31, 1969), Goodwin claimed these women, who were sterilized between the ages of thirteen and sixteen, came to him with "surprisingly articulate requests" to have their fertility restored. These allegations were followed by an article in the *Globe and Mail* (April 12, 1969) which told the story of a girl who, after being declared mentally defective by the Eugenics Board and subsequently sterilized, went on to successfully complete her grade twelve examinations. These pieces of bad press were supported by the analysis from geneticists Kennedy McWhirter and Jan Weijer, who undermined the scientific basis of sterilization legislation when they claimed that many of the conditions the Alberta Sterilization Act meant to address were not properly defined as medical syndromes, that IQ testing was an unreliable method of determining mental deficiency and there were many genetic preconditions that could lead to this diagnosis. As such, if mental deficiency was caused by genetic rather than social factors, it was impossible to predict its transmission from parent to progeny (McWhirter and Weijer 1969: 426–29). They concluded:

> Apart from the objection that the act permits gross violations of human rights, its structure includes dangerous pitfalls for anyone, however well-meaning, who operates it … From the legal, social, and scientific standpoints the act is a disgrace to the whole of Canada. Its legal defects, coupled with its scientific 'nonsense-clauses,' should ensure that it … will be consigned to the rubbish heap. It is highly desirable that a politically independent body be formed in Alberta to clean up this and other abuses and to re-establish respect for the rule of law. (McWhirter and Weijer 1969: 430)

In this same year, the provincial government created a commission to study mental health services in Alberta. A matter considered by W.R.N. Blair, head of the Blair Commission and former member of the Eugenics Board from 1967 to 1968, was the status and future of the Sterilization Act. Similar to the conclusions reached by McWhirter and Weijer, the commission found that when genetic justifications for sterilization were employed by the Board, evidence of a hereditary predisposition was not always adequate. There were also questions about whether the depressed

IQ ratings used to justify sterilization could be ameliorated, and these ratings appeared to have cultural factors associated with them that led some groups, like Native and Métis peoples, to be disproportionately targeted (Blair 1969: 268). In other words, the causal evidence available to the Eugenics Board when deciding whether to recommend sterilization was limited at best. However, the commission fell short of recommending the repeal of the Act (Gibson 1974: 61). Instead, Blair recommended that the legislation be revised to specify appointment qualifications for those nominated to the Eugenics Board, that complete documentation on candidates for sterilization be presented to the Board a reasonable time before it convened to give members the opportunity to review it accordingly and that an executive secretary be appointed to coordinate this flow of information (Blair 1969: 269).

Notwithstanding his recommendations, the Alberta Sterilization Act was repealed. Pressure for repeal came largely from a concern that involuntary sterilization and the "no-consent clause" in the Act were violations of human rights (Gibson 1974: 60–61). Human rights had become part of international discourse by this time and their importance was enshrined through the 1948 *Universal Declaration on Human Rights* (U.N. General Assembly 1948a). Years later, the struggles waged at home by groups who experienced human rights abuses of their own had finally pushed the federal government to act (Lamberton 2005; MacLennan 2003).[1] In 1960, the *Canadian Bill of Rights* was passed, and this represented the first successful federal attempt to enshrine human rights protections in domestic law (Statutes of Canada 1960). As the Law Reform Commission of Canada stated:

> The Canadian Bill of Rights ensures that all persons shall be treated equally before the law ... In consideration of international obligations and the arguments advanced ... [referring to the dangers of non-consensual sterilization], it is arguable that a valid public interest for sterilization of the mentally handicapped could not be proven. (Law Reform Commission of Canada 1979: 52–55)

Due to the absence of clarification in law on whether those most likely to be sterilized could provide informed consent for such an operation, it was questionable whether the sterilization of individuals defined as mentally defective could legally take place anywhere in Canada.

Timothy Christian credits much of the effort toward repeal to David King, first as a research assistant to the Progressive Conservative (PC) opposition leader, Peter Lougheed, then as MLA for the Edmonton-Highlands constituency (Christian 1974). Between 1969 and 1971, King examined legislation in Alberta that was inconsistent with the soon to be elected PC Party's proposal to overhaul human rights legislation. Alberta had enacted its own *Human Rights Act* in 1966, which fell in line with the federal bill of rights, yet the office mandated with enforcing it was staffed with a sole administrator (Statutes of Alberta 1966). Once elected in 1971, following the defeat of the Social Credit government, the PC Party proposed to formally endorse the *Canadian Bill of Rights* by enacting its own legislation renamed the *Individual Rights Protection Act*, by creating a Human Rights Commission and by hiring full staff to administer it (Statutes of Alberta 1972a). In his investigations, King also found the "no consent" clause for the sterilization of mental defectives to be a violation of the right to autonomy and security of the person, and argued the exemption of physicians who performed the operation from civil liability was without legal foundation and was unjustifiable from a policy point of view (Christian 1974: 30, 33).

A legal opinion received by the provincial government also indicated that the protection from civil liability that s. 9 of the Alberta Sterilization Act purported to confer to those who recommended or performed the procedure was probably ineffective (*Muir v. Alberta* 1996: appendix A). This exemption from liability did not have precedent in law; nor did responsibility for sterilizations performed under this legislation lie solely with medical practitioners (Christian 1974: 33). This meant that not only were physicians at risk, but so were members of the Eugenics Board, institutional employees and the provincial government, which was ultimately responsible for the passage of this legislation in the first place. These concerns were strong enough to cause the head of the provincially funded Blair Commission to formally retract his proposed recommendations by way of a letter tabled during these discussions in the Alberta legislature.[2] As Lougheed stated:

> The bill in its present form is most offensive with regard to the Bill of Rights ... It is a very distrurbing [sic] bill as far as I am concerned personally, and we feel strongly about it.[3]

King then introduced a motion and on 31 May 1972 the Alberta Sterilization Act was repealed (Statutes of Alberta 1972b).

In British Columbia (B.C.), legislative repeal of the Sterilization Act came nearly a year later, also following the replacement of the Social Credit government with one led by Dave Barrett, a New Democrat. B.C. faced its own bad press after a nurse went public with allegations of systemic physical and sexual abuse, and the overmedication of children at the Woodlands School, the provincially run institution housing children abandoned at birth, the disabled and wards of the court. On 29 December 1972, just a few months prior to the introduction of legislation to repeal the sterilization statute, Health Minister Dennis Cocke asked for an investigation into this facility. The inquiry revealed that abuse was rampant, that unexplained and uninvestigated deaths had occurred and that children were admitted to the institution with the purpose of sanctioning their sterilization (Gregory 2006; McCallum 2001: 23, 34; Wahlsten 1997). Some children were also routinely experimented on by researchers like Dr. Bluma Tischler, who published almost three dozen research papers on such experiments in scientific journals (e.g., Ellis, Tischler, and Lirenman 1970; McGeer and Tischler 1959; Perry et al. 1967).

The sale and advertisement of birth control also became legal in Canada in 1969. Gail van Heeswijk tells us that birth control for welfare recipients was already being paid for by the B.C. Medical Service Plan since 1965, and research from the previous chapter tells us that birth control was also being promoted in Indigenous communities at this time (van Heeswijk 1994: 86). To what extent did the legalization of birth control and the lower cost associated with pharmaceutical methods of ensuring sterility affect the decision to move away from involuntary surgical sterilization for those deemed "unfit"? Dr. Bryson, director of the Riverview (Essondale) Hospital, acknowledged the decline in sterilizations performed under the Act as being at least partly due to "modern treatment techniques" (*Vancouver Sun*, November 19, 1968: 9). Yet, as late as 1971, and similar to the recommendations made by the Blair Commission in Alberta, the B.C. Ministry of Health considered a proposal not to repeal the Act, but to enlarge its power to allow for the sterilization of all wards of the state (*D.E. (Guardian ad litem) v. British Columbia* 2005: 10). Van Heeswijk notes that the scientific basis of eugenic sterilization was being questioned, and as in Alberta, the legality of sterilization was of central concern. These factors ultimately won out and led to the repeal of the statute (van Heeswijk 1994: 77–88).

If not attributable solely to a shift in policy direction or the falling into disrepute of eugenic theory, a concern with the liability of those involved in performing both voluntary and involuntary sterilizations was a driving force behind the repeal of this legislation. The *Manitoba Bar News* reported:

> It appears to be almost universally accepted that eugenic sterilization is illegal, and that the surgeon who performs the operation is liable to criminal proceedings from the patient. Sterilization, even when voluntary, is frowned upon as there is a large weight of learned opinion to the effect that voluntary sterilization of the healthy is unlawful. (van Heeswijk 1994: 80–81)

Increasing requests by couples asking to be sterilized voluntarily as a birth control measure featured in discussions surrounding liability (Canadian Medical Protective Association 1970: 211; 1971: 527–28). Section 45 of the Criminal Code outlined that a surgical operation would not be subject to criminal liability if performed for the benefit of an individual, with care and skill, and if this was reasonable based on the circumstance (Law Reform Commission 1979: 58; Criminal Code s 45). Despite the fact that medical practitioners often relied on this section to justify sterilizations on request, the rationale being that "an individual's benefit" was up for interpretation, the legal status of voluntary sterilization was not clearly established and doctors feared being held liable, even as contraceptives were decriminalized in 1969. This concern led the Canadian Medical Protective Association to advise doctors to make decisions regarding sterilization on a case by case basis, and to ensure that both the patient and spouse sign a consent form (Canadian Medical Protective Association 1970: 211).

The lack of clarity regarding liability led John Munro, speaking on behalf of the Government of Canada, to clarify the position of the Minister of Justice on 2 April 1973. That is, sterilization was a matter of medical discretion and if the operation was performed by a qualified medical practitioner at the request of a patient this would not engage the criminal responsibility of the practitioner. Therefore, no action was required on the part of the federal government to clarify criminal law with respect to sterilization.[4] With this clarification, or lack thereof, came an inability to ignore that, without question, a statute allowing the involuntary sterilization of individuals was out of line with the federal position, the Criminal Code and medical opinion, in addition to human rights legislation, especially considering the government of B.C. planned to pass its own *Human Rights Code* later that year to bring the province in line with the federal bill of rights (Statutes of British Columbia 1973a). As the Law Reform Commission of Canada put it:

> In summary, widespread sterilization of mentally handicapped persons has been opposed on the grounds that it discriminates against certain classes and races because the criteria for determining mental retardation and mental illness differentiate between classes and races; that it is difficult to determine equitably who should be sterilized because of imperfections of intelligence tests and lack of knowledge concerning the role of cultural deprivation in individual and familial deprivation; that there is doubt that anyone is qualified to make decisions about who should be sterilized; that sterilization will be used putatively; that sterilization is immoral and that individual rights and dignity have priority, in any case, over the societal benefits that would be derived from such a policy. (Law Reform Commission 1979: 55)

For all of these reasons, the *B.C. Sterilization Act* was repealed on 18 April 1973.

Alberta and British Columbia were not the only provinces where coercive sterilizations took place, nor did they end completely with the repeal of these statutes. We have seen that calls for a government inquiry were made in response to allegations that many Inuit women had been unwittingly sterilized, and these calls continued until a limited investigation was carried out in 1976.[5] In that same year, a study conducted in Ontario indicated that 686 sterilizations were performed in that province in one year alone on persons who were unable to give consent (Evans 1980: 1069). Of these, 308 were on children; 50 boys and the balance girls; and 109 of these were more radical hysterectomies (Bowker 1980: 975; Evans 1980: 1069). Due to the lack of a legal basis for these operations, by 1978, the Ontario Minister of Health Dennis Timbrell placed a moratorium on the sterilization of persons under the age of sixteen and appointed an inter-ministerial committee consisting of representatives from the Ministries of Health, Community and Social Services and the Attorney General whose task was to examine all aspects of consent to health care services (National Institute on Mental Retardation 1979: v).

This committee published an omnibus report on issues relating to consent for medical treatment, and another which recommended draft legislation (Ontario 1979a; 1979b). Rather than tighten regulations surrounding consent, the committee proposed the province adopt legislation permitting minors less than sixteen years of age to give consent for abortion, to be treated for sexually transmitted diseases and to receive birth control counselling and surgery without parental consent. This legislation would also have authorized human experimentation for the purpose of advancing medical science, sterilization as a contraceptive measure, organ transplants and psychosurgery as a form of behaviour control for mentally incompetent persons without their consent (Ontario 1979b: 58). The draft bill met with immediate resistance from some like Donald W. Campbell, Executive Director of the South Huron and District Association for the Mentally Retarded, who sent a letter of opposition to the committee pointing out that "attitudes similar to those during the time of Hitler towards persecuting the handicapped, and developing a master race are not at all removed from your suppositions."[6] Disapprovals like this one led to the subsequent dropping of the draft bill.[7]

Despite claims that the disrepute of eugenic ideology led to the repeal of "archaic" legislation, in the cases discussed above, calls for the strengthening of sterilization legislation immediately preceded the shift to "modern treatment techniques." This fact requires us to question more deeply what other political and economic interests might have caused this shift in policy. Was it a case of new governments purging themselves of legislation based on a "pseudo-scientific" ideology? Perhaps, but what part did the newfound ability to reach the same ends by different means play in all of this? Or, how did a simple and self-interested concern with liability on the part of government factor into these decisions? Did the increased prominence of insurance companies and the need for the medical profession to protect itself from legal responsibility influence discussions (Magnet 1981: 1066–67)? There are some who claim that eugenics never went away and that it continues to influence policy and practice (Black 2003; Kevles 1985; Kühl 1994; Lewis 1995; Paul 1998; Volscho 2010a, 2010b). For all these reasons, it is important to examine these questions in all their complexity rather than simply attribute past injustices to the "mores of the time."

Settling the Past: Courts, Cash and Compensation?

It was not until 12 June 1995 that eugenically motivated legislation was put on trial in Canada. The case against the government of Alberta began in 1989 when Leilani Muir alleged she had been inaccurately deemed a moron and was then subsequently sterilized at the hands of the Alberta Eugenics Board on 18 January 1959. The province, when faced with charges of wrongful confinement and wrongful sterilization, opted to avoid a full trial by admitting liability from the outset. It conceded Muir was wrongfully sterilized due to inadequate IQ testing prior to the fact (*Muir v. Alberta* 1996: 727). This left only damages to be decided before the court (Daisley 1996: 1–3; *Muir v. Alberta* 1996: 695–762). Justice Joanne Viet found that by wrongfully sterilizing Muir, the province was liable for the pain and suffering that resulted from the sterilization and the aggravating damage inflicted by being wrongfully stigmatized as a moron (*Muir v. Alberta* 1996: 697). Justice Viet also ruled that Muir was wrongfully confined and awarded her damages for loss of liberty, pain and suffering and the loss of enjoyment of life and other normal developmental experiences while she was institutionalized. In total, Muir was awarded $740,780 for her experience plus $230,000 in legal costs. The court fell short of awarding punitive damages despite abundant proof that the Alberta government had allowed the deliberate misapplication of the sterilization statute, that it consistently ignored established standards about when sterilizations were to be performed and that it was negligent and intentional in its actions, which made the sterilization of Muir an assault and battery. The province was able to avoid punitive damages by showing a commitment to human rights through its implementation of the *Individual Rights Protection Act* in 1972 (Statutes of Alberta 1972a). By doing so, Justice Viet argued the province had acknowledged that sterilization legislation "struck at the very heart of individual rights in our society" (*Muir v. Alberta* 1996: 733).

Despite the fact that government had stalled the Muir case for seven years prior, it willingly waived its right to claim that the charges it faced fell outside of the statute of limitations. Although the amount of time to begin a legal action varies by province and by offence, in Alberta this generally consists of a two-year period that can be extended to ten years if a judgment is made to this effect (Statutes of Alberta 1980). In cases that deal with injuries that took place when an individual was a dependant or minor, the limitations period can be "tolled," or suspended for a period of time. This limitation period also does not generally apply in cases of a sexual nature. There are other factors that can influence this "tolling" period, including when a person can reasonably be expected to have discovered a wrong-doing or have come to know all the facts related to an incident. These issues would have needed to be settled in the Muir case if the province had claimed the offences were time barred, and contrary to the opinion of Justice Viet, the outcome would not have been obvious. Yet Justice Viet ruled that the refusal of the province to employ such a litigation strategy was "more than equivalent to an apology" (*Muir v. Alberta* 1996: 697).

A case against the province was brought forward earlier, in 1987, by another victim of involuntary sterilization. A woman with cerebral palsy was diagnosed by the Alberta Eugenics Board as "high grade defective — brain damage[d]" when she was fourteen years of age. In 1964, she was transported from her foster home to the Provincial Training School in Red Deer for an appendix operation. During this operation she was also sterilized with the consent of the Department of Child Welfare, despite its consent not being required (*D.L.W. v. Alberta* 1992). She subsequently went on to graduate from college with honours. When she filed a motion to sue, government moved to have the cased dismissed, and argued that because the consent of the Department had not been required for her sterilization under the Act, there was no breach of fiduciary duty. In this case, government lawyers also argued the claim was time barred. A summary judgment was granted to dismiss the case as having been filed outside the two-year limitation period, but this decision was reversed on appeal (*D.L.W. v. Alberta* 1992: 5). On appeal, the court ruled that because Eugenics Board documents submitted by the province in its defense had only just come to the attention of the victim, there was a triable issue as to the applicability of the *Limitations Act* and the case should proceed, to be determined on the basis of full evidence (*D.L.W. v. Alberta* 1992: 9). In light of this judgment, one needs to consider the refusal to employ the limitation of action defense in the Muir case together with the fact that liability was admitted from the outset. This allowed the province to avoid a full trial and the possibility of a precedent-setting judgment related to the *Limitations Act* should the court rule similarly in the Muir case. The decision to admit liability and proceed to damages could be viewed as a cautious and strategic attempt to "try its hand" with the goal of determining the maximum financial loss it might face for abuses perpetrated on Muir, but also the many other victims of the Act, rather than an apology.

This point becomes more applicable considering the Muir case did indeed set a precedent for other claimants who, in 1996, began actions against the provincial government for charges ranging from breach of fiduciary duty, wrongful confinement or sterilization and wrongful diagnosis of mental deficiency, to physical abuse, unnecessary drug treatment, loss of liberty and forced work (*Lytton v. Alberta; Barrett v. Alberta; Busch v. Alberta* 1996). In response, the province initially rejected apologies and offers of compensation, and insisted each case be tried separately despite the specific request by claimants to have their cases amalgamated as one class action suit. Lead counsel for the province argued that eugenic legislation was "consistent with the social morals of the time" and that the province had in fact provided a "stable, loving environment" to these victims (*Economist*, September 11, 1996: 47). However, by 9 March 1998, the number of claimants had quickly risen to more than seven hundred requesting over $700 million in damages (Kondro 1998: 892).[8] In an attempt to avoid court and the enormous costs faced if found liable, the province introduced the *Institutional Confinement and Sexual Sterilization Compensation Act*, or Bill 26.[9] Bill 26 allowed the province to limit compensation to $150,000 and denied victims the ability to challenge this rule by suing the government in court. The bill relied on a notwithstanding clause, shielding government from the legal challenge that sterilization was a violation of the fundamental rights guaranteed under the *Charter of Rights and Freedoms* and the *Individual Rights Protection Act*, the very legislation, ironically, which allowed it to avoid punitive damages in the Muir case (Johansen and Rosen 2008; Lougheed 1998; Statutes of Canada 1982; Statutes of Alberta 1972a).[10] Following immediate public outcry and criticism from within and outside the legislature, the bill was dropped and government began settlement negotiations (Kondro 1998: 892; *MacLean's* March 23, 1998: 29).

The settlement of cases would proceed using a standardized payment formula. The settlement board would not deal with actions commenced by sterilization victims 180 days after the date on which it was established; no damages would be awarded based on vicarious liability, meaning the provincial government would not be held accountable for any act or abuse carried out by one of its employees, whether or not these took place in the process of carrying out their jobs; and no interest would be applied on damages.[11] If a claim was resolved, claimants would receive $75,000 at the time of settlement and an additional $25,000 after three years if they were living outside an institution. In June 1998, nearly 500 individuals, or two thirds of the claimants, accepted a settlement that totaled $48 million (*CBC News Online* June 5, 1998). By October of that year, 40 more claimants received identical settlement packages of $100,000 each (Wittmeier 1999: 13). A total of 635 claims were settled by November 1999 for the sum of $60 million (Shea 1999: 5). At this point, the remaining 246 individuals continued suit against the province.

With a trial date for the first group of remaining claimants set for September 1999, the province filed a motion to have portions of its statement made during the attempted passage of Bill 26 struck from pretrial documents (*Lytton v. Alberta* 1999). Incriminating admissions were made by Premier Ralph Klein and his Minister of Justice in the legislature and in a news release during the attempted passage of Bill 26, and these were included in documents filed on behalf of the plaintiffs as evidence of the government admitting liability. In these rhetorical statements, the province expressed "profound regret on behalf of the Defendant [the provincial government] to those individuals who have suffered as a result of being sterilized under the Defendant's Sexual Sterilization Act" and indicated "that the Defendant was accepting responsibility to provide compensation to Albertans who had been wrongfully sterilized and wrongfully confined" (*Lytton v. Alberta* 1999: 2). When facing the possibility of a court of law, the province quickly distanced itself from these words and asked for them to be struck, arguing there was a great deal of doubt whether statements made by elected officials in their capacity as a government employees were admissible at trial (*Lytton v. Alberta* 1999: 4). Justice Wachowich agreed in part by indicating these statements did constitute evidence and should be struck at this preliminary point, but this did not preclude their being used by the plaintiffs during trial as evidence of admitted liability. Against the concerns of government, Justice Wachowich recommended the case proceed to trial, at which point the weight given to these admissions of liability could be decided. From the outset the odds were not stacked in favour of the province.

As the case proceeded, the legal firms engaged on behalf of the claimants contracted the Population Research Laboratory at the University of Alberta to systematically analyze all the Eugenics Board records made available by the provincial government prior to trial. This information was compiled in an electronic database and prepared as a report to be submitted as evidence (Grekul et al. 2004: 364). When faced with the likelihood of having this potentially damaging information made fully public and with increasing evidence based on past judgments that the court might be sympathetic to sterilization victims, the province set aside previously mandated compensation limits and resumed settlement negotiations. In June 1999, the province retained Joseph Stratton as counsel to negotiate a settlement with a committee of lawyers acting on behalf of the remaining claimants. On 31 October 1999, the province reached an agreement consisting of $82 million in compensation for 246 victims, or an average of $300,000 for each individual (Shea 1999: 6). This announcement led to the discontinuance of the trials scheduled to begin the following month.

In conjunction with this announcement, on 2 November 1999, Justice Minister Dave Hancock issued an "Expression of Regret" on behalf of the province: "We are profoundly sorry that this chapter happened in Alberta's history. The compensation can never fully deal with the trauma suffered by these victims."[12] However, Premier Ralph Klein offered his words much more begrudgingly. In his statement, Klein said, "I guess we extend regrets for the actions of another government in another period of time. It's unfortunate. I won't say criminal — it was the law at that particular time and unfortunately it was a bad law" (*Lethbridge Herald,* November 3, 1999: 4). The meaningfulness of this gesture needs to be questioned, considering the province initially refused to apologize and then offered an apology only after the majority of claims were settled. Also telling is the fact that not two years later, the door was already closing on the willingness of government to entertain new claims by individuals alleging wrongful sterilization (CBC *News Online* January 23, 2001).

How, then, should the actions of the Alberta government be viewed? Should the willingness of the province to settle be viewed as an instance of goodwill, as Klein claimed in the legislature during the attempted passage of Bill 26? Klein also argued this bill was an attempt to save taxpayers money.[13] Yet this same government initially insisted cases proceed as individual claims rather than a class action suit and then bogged down the system in numerous instances with procedural affairs. It was not until the Muir case, when facing the possibility of being held liable for enormous financial damages if other suits were decided similarly, that the province "reviewed the situation" and proposed settlement negotiations. Allan Garber, lawyer to some of the claimants, indicated that up to the time of attempted passage of Bill 26 government lawyers simply refused to negotiate, and "If they'd just talked to the [victims] themselves, they wouldn't have had to resort to lawyers" (Woodward 1998: 12). Social critics like Joe Woodward (1998: 12) have questioned what motives stood behind the temporizing of government and point out that in the two years after the Muir case was settled, 20 of the original 723 claimants died. This was one of many tactics employed by the federal government in its dealings with residential school claimants; as critics of this process have pointed out, every day the government put off dealing fairly with allegations of abuse in residential schools, five residential school survivors passed away (Hagen 2005). We also need to consider whether monetary compensation is sufficient recompense for the violation of bodily integrity and the denial of the ability to bear children. Can it fully repair these wrongs, or do we also need to take a serious look at the system that created such institutions and allowed such legislation to come into existence? The negotiation of settlements ensures this look is not taken and that the details of this historical injustice are never fully brought to light for the public to judge. Additional problems also began to arise. Many victims were said to have been charged too much by their lawyers for services provided. Victor Henning, a Calgary businessman, estimated that lawyers took approximately $25 million from the $82 million awarded in the last compensation package, and some victims returned to court to challenge these fees (*CBC News Online* April 8, 1999; September 22, 2000). As Howard Sapers, member of the legislative assembly for Edmonton-Glenora, pointed out:

> Muir's benchmark case eliminated the risk that other claims would not be settled. Therefore … there was no need for the victims to agree to hefty legal contingency fees (under this arrangement, lawyers collect their fees only if they win a settlement or court award). Claimants … [paid] contingency fees of 30%. (Wittmeier 1999: 13)

Because of the lump sum payment many of the victims also lost their monthly Assured Income for Severely Handicapped of $850. One must ask, as Sapers did, what other reasons motivated government to compensate sterilization victims in this way?

After the Act: British Columbia

At the same time as the Alberta government was closing the door on discussions of compensation, claims of wrongful sterilization were beginning to arise in B.C. Though documents relating to eugenic sterilizations in the province were always thought to be lost or destroyed, records located in 2001 from a psychiatric hospital allowed the first suit to be launched for sterilizations carried out under the *B.C. Sterilization Act* (*D.E. (Guardian ad litem) v. British Columbia* 2003). Proceedings began on 9 January 2001, originally on behalf of thirteen women sterilized at the Riverview (Essondale) Hospital between 1940 and 1968. By the time this case proceeded to trial, in March of 2003, the suit consisted of eighteen women and one man, all sterilized at Essondale while under the care of the province (*CBC News Online* February 7, 2003). In this case, the plaintiffs charged that, in spite of the inherent problems with the *B.C. Sterilization Act*, the medical superintendent at Essondale had failed to adhere to the eugenic principles as laid out in this legisla- tion, and that he had abused his statutory power by basing his recommendations for sterilization on social or clinical factors, rather than biological or genetic factors (*D.E. (Guardian ad litem) v. British Columbia* 2003: para. 205–08). According to hospital notes, the primary reasons given for sterilization were promiscuity, amoral behaviour and unfitness for motherhood based on low intelligence (CBC *News Online* December 22, 2005). Victims alleged breach of fiduciary duty and negligence and battery, and claimed their involuntary sterilizations constituted sexual assaults, which meant their claims were not time barred under the statute of limitations (Statutes of British Columbia 1996). On 27 June 2003, Justice Wedge rejected these arguments and dismissed the case. However, in 2005, this decision was reversed on appeal in nine of the eighteen individual suits, and a new trial was scheduled for the spring (*D.E. (Guardian ad litem) v. British Columbia* 2005: para. 3–5). When facing the prospect of a new trial, the province began settlement negotiations. In December 2005, the court approved a settlement of $450,000 for the nine women complainants and each received between $25,000 and $100,000 plus legal costs (Reynolds 2005).

This case was not the only litigation facing the province at the time. In July 2001, a report prepared by B.C. Ombudsman Dulcie McCallum on behalf of the Ministry of Children and Family Development was released. This report consisted of a review of the Woodlands School, and it made public its findings of systemic physical and sexual abuse, including sexual sterilizations, of children and other vulnerable people while they were institutionalized between 1975 and 1992 (McCallum 2001).[14] This report prompted the launching of two mirror class action suits against the province by former residents of Woodlands, which, at the time, totaled approximately fifteen hundred people. In April 2003, Justice Morrison appointed Poyner Baxter as lead counsel, stayed the second suit, and both suits proceeded as one case (*Richard v. British Columbia* 2003: para. 63; *Richard v. British Columbia* 2004: para. 7–11, 20).

On 30 May 2003, with the province facing legal action, the Minister of Children and Family Development issued an apology to former residents of Woodlands and three other special care institutions under provincial control (Lavoie 2003: A1). In an open cabinet meeting, Gordon Hogg, then Minister of Children and Family Development, apologized for any mistreatment experienced by vulnerable people while institutionalized. Yet, rather than acknowledge the systemic nature of abuse as confirmed by the provincially commissioned report, Hogg blamed these instances on "past policies and priorities" and the "flawed and depersonalized" environment of institutional life.[15] In a purported attempt to heal past wrongs, the province established a $2 million B.C. Institutional Legacy Trust Fund to provide access to counselling services for former residents and their family members. Hogg indicated that neither the apology nor the trust fund was aimed at limiting liability in court, but that these arose out of a moral responsibility on the part of government and its desire to "do the right thing" (Pemberton 2003: A1). However, these statements amount more to rhetoric than substance if one considers the lengthy legal battles and consistent denials of liability that followed, and the fact that the monies promised by the government had yet to be dispersed two years later.

On 1 March 2005, Woodlands survivors involved in what became known as the "Richard action" were present in the legislature when the province was questioned on its refusal to enter into non-adversarial negotiations and deal fairly with victims of abuse. Jenny Kwan, NDP member from the Vancouver-Mount Pleasant riding, argued that there was ample evidence for the government to sit down and negotiate in situations like this and that the main desire of Woodlands survivors was to be able to avoid pursuing reparations through the courts. Kwan reminded the government that it had a moral responsibility to at least meet with survivors to see if a negotiated settlement could be reached and pointed out that the relatively small package provided to victims through the trust fund, which amounted to approximately $400 in compensation to each victim, was inadequate and paled in comparison to the hundreds of thousands of dollars it was spending fighting Woodland survivors in court.[16] Then Minister of Children and Family Development, Stan Hagen, responded:

> I think where we have a disagreement is that our government disagrees with your statement that there was systemic abuse ... I would like to repeat on the record that the government does disagree with the finding that there was systemic abuse.[17]

In its refusal to acknowledge the systemic aspect of the abuse faced by residents at Woodlands, or to negotiate a fair settlement, the province was facing increased criticism. However, there was another lawsuit playing out in the courts at this time that had implications for the Woodlands suit. The case of *Arishenkoff v. British Columbia* (2002) dealt with charges of sexual and physical abuse experienced by Doukhobor children while under custody of the state. These children had been forcibly apprehended and confined to the New Denver facility between 1953 and 1959. The plaintiffs in this case charged that they were unlawfully confined when the province apprehended them, separated them from their parents and placed them in the provincial facility. They alleged abuse of statutory authority, breach of fiduciary duty and negligence on the part of the province, in addition to the physical and sexual abuse many experienced (*Arishenkoff v. British Columbia* 2002: para. 7–9). By the time the "Richard action" finally proceeded to court, this case, as decided on appeal, set an important precedent related to the discussion at hand.

The main issue in *Arishenkoff v. British Columbia* was in the applicability of the *Crown Proceedings Act* (Statutes of British Columbia 1974). This Act, which originally came into existence in 1974, effected changes to the rule that no civil or criminal proceeding could be brought against the Crown. Prior to 1974, common law worked on the principle that the "sovereign could do no wrong," or rather the Crown could not be said to have authorized an unlawful act nor could it be sued in its own court. The *Crown Proceedings Act* put an end to Crown immunity, yet this legislation only applied to crimes committed after its passage. In other words, although the Crown could now be held accountable for its actions, it could not be held liable for anything that happened before 1974. In *Arishenkoff v. British Columbia*, Justice Kirkpatrick initially declared that based on case law, the Crown could in fact be held liable for acts committed before the *Crown Proceedings Act* came into effect if the plaintiff had only discovered the relationship between the wrongdoing and harm at some point after 1974 (*Arishenkoff v. British Columbia* 2002: para. 24–32). However, this decision was subsequently reversed on appeal, and in what became known as "Arishenkoff no. 2," the court ruled that despite any potential wrongdoing, the Crown could not be held accountable for actions which took place prior to the entry into force of the *Crown Proceedings Act* on 1 August 1974 (*Arishenkoff v. British Columbia* 2005). With reference to the "Richard action," this meant the ability of Woodland residents who were victimized prior to this date to receive compensation was threatened.

During this same time additional steps were taken which in their outcome, if not in their intention, allowed for full responsibility for past wrongdoings to be avoided. On 18 May 2006, B.C. became the first province to pass legislation related to the issuing of apologies for past wrongs. The *Apology Act*, actively promoted by Attorney General Wally Oppal, allowed apologies to be issued without them having any influence on civil litigation (Statutes of British Columbia 2006).[18] An amendment to the proposed bill made just prior to its third reading qualified that while an apology would not be admissible in the determination of liability, it could be used in the process of assessing damages.[19] Oppal stated that the last-minute amendment was meant to clarify that:

> It is the intent of the act that an apology is only inadmissible in court as evidence of fault or liability. The law continues with respect to the admissibility of an apology in determination of damages. For example, the Libel and Slander Act specifically allows for an apology made before the commencement of the action or at the earliest opportunity afterwards to be considered by a court in assessing the quantum of damages.[20]

The passage of this Act enabled the province to ensure that its apology to the victims of Woodlands for abuses experienced while under institutional care would be inadmissible in court. At the same time, this statement of apology could be safely employed to the benefit of the province in settlement proceedings. Protection from liability was also ensured if the province wished to apologize and mitigate damages in other suits it was facing at this time.[21] The act of apologizing, though purported to be an act of goodwill, was explicitly described as having the potential to reduce the number of claimants in any given case by almost 40 percent, thereby reducing the number of suits and court costs.[22]

Immediately following the implementation of this protective measure, and faced with the precedent-setting influence of Arishenkoff no. 2, in June 2006 a settlement proposal was finally offered to claimants in the Woodlands suit. In keeping with Arishenkoff no. 2, compensation was offered only to post-1974 victims. To receive compensation, these victims would need to appear before an arbitrator who was responsible for determining the amount due to each individual based on proof of injury or abuse calculated on a "point system." As one commentator explained:

> The points system would establish differing rates of compensation based on whether abuse involved, for instance, anal or oral sexual acts as opposed to rape or physical torment. The survivors, who were children when they were abused, would have to prove their abuse. (Gregory 2007b)[23]

Counsel for the Woodlands claimants was ordered to reject the offer, which many described as "degrading and dehumanizing" and an attempt to create a "hierarchy of oppression" (Gregory 2007a).

Some Woodlands survivors responded by proposing an alternative settlement. If the province matched the $18 million it received from the sale of the Woodlands School and created a settlement fund of $36 million, this would allow a common experience payment of $15,000 for both pre- and post-1974 residents, would eliminate the need for a lengthy legal battle in court and would also spare former residents from being re-victimized by the point system. However, former Woodlands resident Greg Schiller stated that both Premier Gordon Campbell and Attorney General Oppal refused to discuss matters further with the case before the courts (Gregory 2007a; Gregory 2007b). The claimants' own lawyer, Poyner Baxter, responded to this proposal by stating "It's not fair and there's no basis for it ... Under the law, the government can't compensate the pre-1974 victims" (Gregory 2007a). There was in fact considerable precedent for compensating victims in spite of arbitrary cutoff dates like that imposed by the *Crown Proceedings Act*, one of which was the compensation offered to those sterilized under Alberta's sterilization legislation (Doran 2010).[24]

In June 2007, leading up to trial and in keeping with Arishenkoff no. 2, the province obtained a motion to exclude from legal proceedings individuals who resided at Woodlands prior to the 1974 *Crown Proceedings Act* coming into effect (*Richard v. British Columbia* 2008). This motion cancelled out the claims of over one third of the claimants. As the B.C. Coalition of People with Disabilities put it, the implications of this decision meant the "'oldest, sickest and most vulnerable' have been cast aside" (B.C. Coalition of People with Disabilities, n.d.; *Richard v. British Columbia* 2009).[25] In 2008, when questioned in the legislature by Nicholas Simons, representative from Powell River-Sunshine Coast, about the extensive litigation surrounding this case and the inability of government to negotiate a fair settlement for all victims, Attorney General Oppal insisted he was most sympathetic to those who had suffered abuse and that government was willing to negotiate, but the difficulty rested with the victims who had lawyers.[26] However, on at least one occasion, Oppal reiterated that government "d[id] not acknowledge that there was widespread abuse at Woodlands, or that Woodlands staff committed atrocities" (Gregory 2007a).

Settlement negotiations did not resume until just prior to trial, scheduled to begin in early 2010. Facing increasingly diminishing prospects of obtaining compensation, 1100 former Woodlands residents accepted a settlement on 19 December 2009.[27] Those who suffered physical, psychological and sexual abuse by Woodlands staff after 1 August 1974 had fourteen months to apply for compensation.[28] Compensation depended on the level of abuse each person suffered, as calculated based on the previously criticized point system. Monetary awards ranged from $3,000 to $150,000 each. In other words, what was offered in the form of reparations was available only to a portion of those victimized while under provincial care, applied only to certain acts of abuse and was only a portion of what other victims received in similar suits (*J.H. v. British Columbia* 1998; *Beadle v. British Columbia* 1996; *K.L.B. v. British Columbia* 2003). Despite calls from victims who fell short of the 1974 cutoff date for the government to "do the right and moral thing" and provide compensation to all victims who suffered at Woodlands, in July 2010, the B.C. Supreme Court approved the settlement agreement (*Vancouver Sun*, July 9, 2010; *Richard v. British Columbia* 2010). Commenting on these events, Beverly Doran (2010) wrote, "With a convenient stroke of a pen, the B.C. government has effectively ripped away the rights of 500 people, many of them aged and suffering chronic conditions as a result of their treatment at Woodlands."

Compensation and Aboriginal Women

The discussion thus far has made apparent the extensive struggle faced by victims of sterilization when seeking reparations from responsible governments. With its power to enact legislation limiting the ability of victims to pursue charges through the courts, and if they are successful in doing so nonetheless, to extend this litigation unendingly, government has made justice difficult if not impossible to achieve. Up to this point, the discussion has also been silent on the implications of reparations for Aboriginal peoples. Some of the claimants involved in the above mentioned litigation might very well have been Aboriginal peoples, but they do not exist *as Aboriginal peoples* within these discussions. Pursuing redress through an adversarial and individualized court process shapes the parameters of how the issue of coercive sterilization is understood — as an individual crime with only individual perpetrators and victims. This allows governments to avoid discussing the systemic aspect of crimes committed against people under its care, or having to acknowledge when certain groups are disproportionately targeted by policies or practices. This silence in our discussion thus far also perpetuates an understanding that the motivations for and implications of coercive sterilization are the same for all those targeted. While directly beneficial to the state, by failing to understand the coercive sterilization of Aboriginal women within its larger context, this continues to deny justice to Aboriginal peoples.

There is one instance where an acknowledgement was made that the sterilization of Aboriginal peoples could have transpired. In 1998, the Government of the Northwest Territories made a rather feeble attempt to offer assistance to Indigenous women from northern areas that might have been sterilized under eugenic legislation in Alberta. Shortly after settlement of the Muir case and with the province of Alberta facing its large class action suit, it occurred to at least one government official that because many Aboriginal women from northern areas were sent to Alberta to receive health services, some might also have been subject to coercive sterilizations while in the province. Roy Erasmus, member of the Legislative Assembly from Yellowknife North, brought up this issue. He stated:

> We know our native people have been sent to the Charles Camsell Hospital for years and years and many still are. Some of those women were sterilized. It seems native women were sterilized even if they were not sick or retarded or in any other dangerous situation. I have been informed that in the 1960s and 70s, women from Dettah asked their local priest why they did not have any children for the past three or four years. They had found out later that they had been sent to and delivered their children at the Charles Camsell Hospital and were sterilized afterwards ... These women found out that they had been sterilized at the Charles Camsell Hospital and in 1996, a woman sued the Alberta government for this very same thing and she won close to $1 million. Since then, the Alberta government has been dealing with such people on a case-by-case basis ... Mr. Speaker, the question is, will NWT women who were sterilized without their consent also be compensated.[29]

The Minister of Health and Social Services Kelvin Ng responded that although he was aware of the situation in Alberta, no sterilizations performed on northern Aboriginal women were known to him, and therefore he had not taken any action on this issue to date. He said:

> Mr. Speaker, we are not, in respect to this issue, doing anything proactively. I am not aware of any cases of individuals from the Northwest Territories ... we can certainly check our files to see if there were any individuals who might have been out in Alberta for any extended period of time that might have been impacted. We will try to figure out some way to give the issue some profile.[30]

However, by the end of the month government had failed to act. When questioned on whether any women had filed a claim for involuntary sterilization, Ng indicated that none had come forward but the Department of Health was planning a public campaign to bring awareness to the issue. A press release would be issued the following day making a telephone number in the department available for people to contact if they had concerns. In an attempt to broaden awareness, correspondence would also be sent to health boards in the area with information that could be distributed to women (Colbourne 1998). No further information has been located on the outcome of this "awareness campaign."

An article appearing in *Windspeaker* magazine at this time reiterated that the Northwest Territories government would offer support for Aboriginal women who believed they were wrongfully sterilized and wanted to inquire into such claims. Joan Irwin, executive assistant to Ng, stated:

> If a woman who suspects she has been wrongfully sterilized comes forward, the government will provide her with help in gathering information about her situation and how her consent should have been given before she was sterilized. The inquiries will be dealt with on the merits of each case. (Whyatt 1998: 5)

Irwin indicated that the program, as established, was purposefully designed to allow women to contact government rather than have government attempt to find victims (Whyatt 1998: 5). However, we need to consider that not only were records documenting the sterilization of Aboriginal women from the North incomplete but many of these women might not have been sterilized in Alberta. They could have been sterilized in a northern hospital, a federally run Indian hospital, or another hospital, in another province. Considering that the federal government previously claimed its Department of National Health and Welfare was not keeping track of these sterilizations, this documentation would be quite difficult to locate.

To complicate matters further, in the case of Aboriginal peoples, did liability rest with the province under whose direction sterilizations were carried out, or was the federal government ultimately responsible for what happened to wards under its charge? Taking into account what we know about the conditions under which sterilizations took place, even if consent was given, the context in which it was offered must also be questioned. And some women were possibly not even aware that they were sterilized. Roy Erasmus pointed out that many of those affected lived in remote settlements and might not be able to read, or might not pay attention to the news.[31] Yet this government strategy placed the complete onus on women to seek reparations, and it assumed these women would be comfortable approaching government officials to begin this process. It is no surprise that as of August 1998 only one woman had sent an inquiry to government regarding sterilization (Whyatt 1998: 5).

For Aboriginal women, being coercively sterilized is a continuation of the long and unhappy history between Canada and Aboriginal peoples. In seeking justice for this crime, Aboriginal women — if they have been mentioned at all — have been allowed few options other than seeking individual redress through financial compensation within an alien court belonging to a larger system that has sought to assimilate Aboriginal peoples by one means or another since the founding of

Canada. This option presents numerous problems for Aboriginal women who were sterilized, and must then turn to this same system to seek compensation by suing those involved for personal damages and placing themselves at the discretion of the court. Legal scholar Patricia Monture explains, "By agreeing to the litigation process to resolve a claim, Aboriginal Peoples agree implicitly to the terms on which the non-Aboriginal dispute resolution system is based, regardless of the consequences or biases that process affirms" (Monture-Angus 1999: 65). Though the possibility of receiving even a meagre compensatory payment is not insignificant for people who often live in dire conditions of poverty, the onus is placed on victims to pursue charges and prove they have in fact been victimized, and this avenue has proven to be less than just (CBC News Online April 23, 2005; Donovan 2006; Hagen 2005).[32]

A case in point is that of a Rae Edzo woman sterilized in 1986, at the age of 15, at the Stanton Regional Hospital in the Northwest Territories. It was not until 1995, through a conversation with her sister, that she realized she was incapable of bearing children. Though she applied for legal aid in July of that year, it was not until 27 December 1997 that she filed a motion to sue. This woman brought a $1.25 million lawsuit against the Stanton Regional Hospital, the Health Board and the two doctors who performed the procedure. She argued that the defendants had breached their required standard of care and were liable for negligence, that the sterilization constituted an action of battery because it was performed without her consent or that of her guardian, and that the defendants breached their fiduciary duty in failing to protect her. The case, which took nearly ten years to be finalized, was dismissed in part in 2006. The judge ruled the lawsuit was filed outside the two-year statute of limitations on negligence and battery (*Base v. Hadley et al.* 2006; CBC *News Online* February 8, 2004; February 20, 2006).

Another case from December 2002 is that of M.S.Z., who was sterilized without her consent at the Whitehorse General Hospital after giving birth by caesarean section. This woman argued that because her sterilization was done without consent, this medical battery constituted a sexual assault and was therefore not subject to the limitation period of two years (*M.S.Z. v M.* 2008). Her case was dismissed by Justice Gower, who ruled that sexual sterilization did not constitute sexual assault and as such, the charges were filed outside the two-year statute of limitations. Although the argument that sexual sterilization constitutes sexual assault was held in nine cases of involuntary sterilization from B.C., Justice Gower chose not to follow the precedent of *D.E. (Guardian ad litem) v. British Columbia*, stating that:

> While decisions of the British Columbia Court of Appeal are of great persuasive value in the Yukon, as the members of that Court also sit on the Yukon Court of Appeal, strictly speaking, its decisions are not binding upon this Court. Consequently, with great respect, I choose not to follow the majority in D.E. (*M.S.Z. v M.* 2008: para. 23)

What forces influence when or if a law or legal precedent is overlooked or a past judgment is overruled in the process of determination by a court? What role do other political, economic or social factors play in a legal judgment? Has the consistent unwillingness of governments to acknowledge or address harms suffered by Aboriginal peoples, including the sterilization of Aboriginal women, influenced legal judgments? Can it be reasonably expected that the Canadian legal system, which has been imposed on Aboriginal peoples, be at the very same time a source of redress for Aboriginal women?

Monture argues that despite claims of judicial neutrality and objectivity, this legal principle is more one of convenience than fact. Canadian law was and remains a central tool in delivering oppression and perpetuating colonialism for Indigenous peoples (Monture-Angus 1999: 52). Scholar Karilyn Toovey also states:

> Law is not a value free enterprise, devoid of culture. Quite the opposite is true; law cannot be separated from culture and law operates to perpetuate culture. In the case of Canada, the law operates to perpetuate a colonial culture. Therefore, when we speak of Indigenous peoples emancipating themselves through the use of a foreign and imposed law, we are asking Indigenous peoples to adopt the very culture that created their oppression in the first place. (Toovey 2005: 4)

The pursuance of compensation has indeed been limited to individuals who, often for lack of other options, are willing and able to engage in the rules of play of a foreign court system. By doing so, the systemic aspect of a crime against Aboriginal women is turned into an individual one, and this limited quest for justice is turned into a profit-making venture for the legal profession. Framing involuntary sterilization as an individually perpetrated crime limits how the sterilization of Aboriginal women can be viewed, what the consequences of this crime are, who should be held responsible and what should be done in response.

From this perspective, the sterilization of Aboriginal women was an unfortunate consequence of their mental or physical inferiority. Any woman sterilized against her will was simply a victim of the racist biases or negligence of certain physicians, superintendents or Eugenics Board members, to whom is owed financial compensation for the harms she experienced. The systemic aspects of the crime are ignored, and the ability to conceptualize this practice as one of many imposed on Aboriginal peoples historically is rendered nearly impossible. The result is that an emphasis on "justice" for individuals is prioritized to the exclusion of justice for Indigenous communities (Corntassel and Holder 2008). The political and economic ends achieved by the coercive sterilization of Aboriginal women are not addressed, and the historical and material relations between Canada and Aboriginal peoples are allowed to continue unabated.

It has been consistently demonstrated here that the sterilization of Aboriginal women has taken place within the larger context of colonialism and has been employed as one of many policies separating Aboriginal peoples from their lands and resources while allowing for their expropriation. This practice also reduces the number of Aboriginal women able to claim Aboriginal title to these lands and resources and allows the federal government to evade its obligations to Aboriginal peoples by avoiding effective and far reaching solutions to public health problems in Indian communities. Canadian courts, grounded in the liberal framework of individual rights, cannot understand the sterilization of Aboriginal women within this larger context. To do so would undermine the very relations upon which Canada and its provinces base their legitimacy, relations which the legal system has been entrusted to protect. However, this is in fact what is necessary to ensure the just resolution of Aboriginal claims (Monture-Angus 1999: 52).

The silence in litigation and discussions on reparations about the fact that Aboriginal women, too, were coercively sterilized is not an accidental oversight. Paulette Regan, scholar and former residential school claims manager, states:

> Indigenous peoples, whose collective and individual rights have been circumscribed, challenge the very legitimacy of liberal democracies built on the promise to protect rights and ensure equal justice for all ... When the focus is on colonizers as individual "perpetrators" the number of victims is smaller. However, when colonizers are understood as "beneficiaries" of a system created and perpetuated by inequality and inequities, then the number of victims harmed increases exponentially. Dealing with claims based on the actions of individual perpetrators is a matter of criminal or civil justice. But when the benefits, privileges and wealth that colonizers have reaped from Indigenous lands and resources are factored in, the stakes become much higher. (Regan 2006: 23)

If the sterilization of Aboriginal women is understood as one of many policies allowing relations of colonialism to continue, and as having the effect of reducing the number of those to whom the federal government has obligations, the stakes do become much higher indeed. Scholar Roland Chrisjohn goes on to ask:

> Who has benefited from the theft of Aboriginal lands and the destruction of Aboriginal ways of life? ... everyone but Aboriginal Peoples. Individual Eurocanadians grew prosperous as "hewers of wood and drawers of water," but it was neither their wood nor their water. Who will benefit from keeping the facts of these crimes away from the Canadian public? Again, everyone but Aboriginal Peoples. But these benefits are purchased at the cost of Canadians abandoning any pretense of morality, any right to judge, or any claim to knowing right from wrong. (Chrisjohn and Young 2006: 37)

A legitimate attempt to repair the harms committed against Aboriginal women who were sterilized needs to include a consideration that coercive sterilization did not take place in isolation. It was one of many policies and practices imposed on Aboriginal peoples since the founding of Canada. Reparations must include an acknowledgment of the larger relations allowed to continue as a result of such acts — relations of exploitation, subjugation and assimilation — and the continued theft of Indigenous lands and resources and the denial of Aboriginal peoples' access to their means of subsistence. These are not addressed by rhetorical expressions of apology or by offers of financial compensation alone.

A sincere effort to rectify these wrongs must include an attempt to address the larger relations of colonialism. These relations have consistently given rise to the need to control and subvert the ability of Aboriginal women to reproduce. Failing to address these relations in a meaningful way means Aboriginal peoples will continue to be denied the ability to live on their own terms and will remain vulnerable to coercively imposed state policies. Legal scholar William Bradford agues:

> Compensation and apologies, gestures potentially part of an amicable settlement, are not germane to the resolution of Indian claims for injustices that cannot be remedied save by reinvestiture of lands and sovereignty in self-determining Indian tribes. (Bradford 2002: 17)

Apologies and compensation have been offered in such a way that they have ensured the critique and possible transformation of these larger relations cannot happen (Barta 2008a; Bradford 2006; Corntassel and Holder 2008; Glauner 2002; Silver 2004; Torpey 2003).

For Indigenous peoples, apologies have consistently allowed the state to claim forgiveness for past wrongs while avoiding legal responsibility for effective reparations (Barta 2008a; Bradford 2002; Chrisjohn and Wasacase 2009; Corntassel and Holder 2008). Apologies have often been employed as a political manoeuvre aimed at closing a chapter in history and allowing the state to "move on" from the past while at the same time being able to charge those who continue to "complain" with unjustified anger or hostility (Barta 2008a; Silver 2004).[33] Researcher Johanna Schoen, who was granted unique access to the North Carolina Eugenics Board records in the United States, has commented when speaking of apologies offered to sterilization victims there:

> The expectation of the apology-absolution sequence made it tempting to rush through the prescribed rituals without really coming to terms with the history — in fact, without even finding out much about the people supposedly receiving the apology. (Schoen 2006: 19)

In Canada, neither the federal government nor the provinces have taken any steps to acknowledge let alone investigate the true extent to which sterilization was imposed on Aboriginal women. Considering this, how is one supposed to view efforts at "repairing the past" and "moving on" if the wrongs committed against a group prominently targeted for coercive sterilization in Canada have yet to be recognized?

An important implication of the failure of the Canadian government to fully acknowledge the extent that Aboriginal women were targeted by this practice is that to do so might drastically change the nature of the conversation. The United Nations *Convention on the Prevention and Punishment of the Crime of Genocide* states that the imposition of measures to prevent births within a group constitutes an act of genocide when carried out with the intent to destroy a group in whole or in part.[34] If the coercive sterilization of Aboriginal women is considered within its historical and material context and in conjunction with other practices relating to birth control and abortions in Indigenous communities, it becomes increasingly difficult to deny that the overarching goal of government has been to destroy Aboriginal peoples, in whole or in part. At the very least, Indian policy has sought to destroy the ability of Aboriginal peoples to exist in the ways they choose. However, as long as the sterilization of Aboriginal women is only understood as an individual crime, committed by individual perpetrators on their victims, any systemic nature or larger context is avoided and issues related to lands, resources and sovereignty, all necessary components of effective reparations for Aboriginal peoples, remain off the table (Alfred 2009a). This constitutes a great incentive on the part of the Canadian government and its provinces to avoid acknowledging their role in the coercive sterilization of Aboriginal women in Canada.

For the victims of involuntary sterilization, law has been a weapon used to carry out injustice. For those seeking reparations for past abuse, it has also been applied in such a way as to limit liability and has often inflicted further injustice on its victims. By examining litigation surrounding involuntary sterilization, we have seen a series of actions which, taken in their entirety, have sought to limit, defend and/or deny responsibility for the actions of governments and their servants. With governments able to enact legislation limiting the ability of victims to pursue charges through the courts, and if they are able to do so nonetheless, then to extend this litigation unendingly, the call for justice through this route has proven difficult if not impossible. The omission of Aboriginal women, as victims, from these discussions promotes the view that the implications of this victimization are the same for all. Though equally unjust for all those victimized by this practice, the coercive sterilization of Aboriginal women as it has taken place within the larger context of colonialism and assimilation can be considered as part of a genocide against Aboriginal peoples. The next chapter turns to a discussion of this concept as it came to exist under international law and examines the actions taken by the federal government that have allowed it to avoid being held accountable for this charge in relation to its treatment of Aboriginal women and their peoples.

Notes

1. The suppression of "communists" and related propaganda, the internment of Japanese and Ukrainian Canadians, the forced removal and institutionalization of Doukhobor children, and the longstanding treatment of Aboriginal peoples are some examples of human rights violations perpetrated by the state by this time.
2. Alberta, *Hansard*, 31 May 1972, 58-35.
3. Alberta, *Hansard*, 14 April 1972.
4. John Munro, Minister of Labour, in Canada, *Commons Debates*, 2 April 1973, 2817.
5. LAC, "Birth Control," RG 29, Volume 2870, File 851-1-5, pt. 4; Parliamentary Returns Officer, 1 December 1976; Robert Lechat, "Sterilization of Inuit is Exposed as National Scandal," *Sunday Express*, 4 pps.
6. PAO, RG 10-1, "Correspondence of Dennis R. Timbrell, Minister of Health, 1979-1981," File 10-1-3, Correspondence from Donald W. Campbell, Executive Director of the South Huron and District Association for the Mentally Retarded, to Dr. W. Gifford-Jones, Interministerial Committee, 16 March 1979.
7. Other letters of opposition were received from L'Association française des Conseils scolaires de l'Ontario, and the Hamilton Physicians for Life. PAO, RG 10-1, "Correspondence of Dennis R. Timbrell, Minister of Health, 1979-1981," File 10-1-3, Correspondence from Gérard Houle, Executive Director of l'Association française des Conseils scolaires de l'Ontario to the Minister of Health, Dennis Timbrell, 14 July 1980; PAO, RG 10-1, "Correspondence of Dennis R. Timbrell, Minister of Health, 1979-1981," File 10-1-3, Correspondence from Hamilton Physicians for Life to Minister of Health, Dennis Timbrell, 12 August 1980.
8. Alberta, *Hansard*, 9 March 1998, 729.
9. For a discussion of Bill 26 at second reading, see Alberta, *Hansard*, 10 March 1998; for discussions on its withdrawal, see Alberta, *Hansard*, 11 March 1998.
10. Alberta, *Hansard*, 10 March 1998, 780–781.
11. Alberta, *Hansard*, 11 March 1998, 815–816.
12. Government of Alberta News Release, 2 November 1999, <gov.ab. ca/ acn/199911/8353.html>.
13. Alberta, *Hansard*, 10 and 11 March, 1999.
14. Summing up the abuse of Woodlands, McCallum reported that the physical abuse found in the records include hitting, kicking, smacking, slapping, striking, restraining, isolating, grabbing by the hair or limbs, dragging, pushing onto table, kicking and shoving, very cold showers and very hot baths resulting in burns to the skin, verbal abuse including swearing, bullying and belittling, inappropriate conduct such as isolation, wearing shackles and belt-leash with documented evidence of the injuries including bruising, scratches, broken limbs, black eyes and swollen face. Few abuse cases were reviewed by police or other agencies and deaths at Woodlands were poorly documented. Almost three thousand people who died while at Woodlands and whose bodies went unclaimed were buried there. In 1977, following provincial directives, eighteen hundred of these headstones were pulled up and the area was redesignated as a park. McCallum found that some of these headstones were subsequently used to build a staff patio and stairs. Unclaimed bodies were sent to University of British Columbia to be used as cadavers. Some children were also experimented on while at Woodlands. This is just some of the information made public as a result of the McCallum report.

15. Gordon Hogg, "Woodlands Apology," transcript of the open cabinet meeting, 30 May 2003, Province of British Columbia, Executive Council. <corporate.gov.bc.ca/open_cabinet/down/tran/open_cabinet_meeting_may_30_2003.htm>.
16. Jenny Wai Ching Kwan, British Columbia, *Hansard*, 1 March 2005, 12207; British Columbia, *Hansard*, 24 November 2005, 2199-2201.
17. British Columbia, *Hansard*, 24 November 2005, 2200.
18. This legislation was said to be his "personal hobby horse." Wally Oppal would go on to be the Commissioner of the Missing Women Inquiry, established to investigate the increasing numbers of missing or murdered women from the Downtown Eastside in Vancouver. This inquiry was viewed as a sham by many Aboriginal peoples, sex workers and frontline organizations who were shut out of the process because the province denied them funding for research and representation. Meanwhile, all three levels of government and the Vancouver police department were given access to an "army of lawyers" at taxpayers' expense (Cole 2001; Fournier 2011).
19. British Columbia, *Hansard*, 25 April 2006, 4000.
20. Wally Oppal in British Columbia, *Hansard*, 25 April 2006, 4000.
21. In addition to the Richard action, the government also faced the Arishenkoff suit, and the Jericho Hill suit, dealing with deaf children who were institutionalized at a Jericho Hill facility and abused while under the care of the province. See *Arishenkoff v British Columbia*, 2002 BCSC 951; *L. R. v British Columbia*, 1999 BCCA 698; *Rumley v British Columbia*, 2002 BCSC 1300. All these cases were brought up in discussions on the *Apology Act*. British Columbia, *Hansard*, 29 March, 6 April, and 25 April, 2006.
22. British Columbia, *Hansard*, 29 March 2006, 3456–3467.
23. This "point system" was in fact the standard used to settle Indian residential school abuse claims, with the exception that these settlements also included a "common experience payment."
24. Others include the compensation of victims of residential schooling and that offered to victims of the tainted blood affair.
25. The province also attempted to avoid full disclosure of documents, specifically relating to sterilizations, and forced the plaintiffs to obtain a court order mandating they be turned over. It then sought leave to appeal the motion. This appeal was dismissed and the province was again ordered to turn over documentation. *Richard v British Columbia*, 2008 BCSC 1274; *Richard v British Columbia*, 2008 BCCA 549.
26. British Columbia, *Hansard*, 6 March 2008, 10289–10290.
27. The terms of the settlement can be read on the Poyner Baxter website: <poynerbaxter.com /Woodlands.htm>.
28. A copy of the Woodlands Claim Form that victims needed to fill out to receive compensation can be found here: <kleinlyons.com/class/woodlands/woodlands-claim-form-sep.pdf>.
29. Roy Erasmus, Northwest Territories, *Hansard*, 4 June 1998, 9.
30. Roy Erasmus, Northwest Territories, *Hansard*, 4 June 1998, 18.
31. Roy Erasmus, Northwest Territories, *Hansard*, 4 June 1998, 9.
32. In the case of residential schools litigation alone, Aboriginal peoples have been forced into this adversarial process and required to relive the abuses experienced while institutionalized in order to receive compensation, the amount of which is determined by the "point system." For some, after having gone through this process, their claim has been dismissed, or the meagre settlement was challenged by government lawyers. In

one instance, an award of $1500 was challenged, with government spending more than what was initially awarded to fight the claim. With respect to the alternative dispute resolution process put in place as an alternative to litigation, according to government documents released in 2005, while $1 million had been paid out to residential schools survivors, $34 million had been spent on administration.

33. Dave Hancock, Minister of Justice and Attorney General, when issuing the "expression of regret" to those sterilized under the Alberta Sterilization Act, said, "It is important that this very sad chapter of Alberta history is now closed for the hundreds of victims. The compensation can never fully deal with the trauma suffered by these individuals." See Government of Alberta Press Release, *Expression of Regret*, 2 November 1999 <gov.ab.ca/acn/199911/8353.html>.

34. See Article II (d) of the United Nations *Convention on the Prevention and Punishment of the Crime of Genocide*, adopted by Resolution 260 (III) A of the United Nations General Assembly on 9 December 1948, Assembly, *United Nations Treaty Series*, 1021, 78 (1951), 277.

5. Canada, Genocide and Aboriginal Peoples

Article II of the United Nations *Convention for the Prevention and Punishment of the Crime of Genocide* defines genocide as any of the following acts committed with the intent to destroy in whole or in part a national, ethnic, racial, or religious group as such:

> a) Killing members of the group;
> b) Causing serious bodily or mental harm to members of the group;
> c) Deliberately inflicting on the group conditions of life calculated to bring about its physical destruction in whole or in part;
> d) Imposing measures to prevent births within the group;
> e) Forcibly transferring children from one group to another.[1]

Carrying out any one or all of these acts or policies against individuals of a group can potentially constitute genocide under international law. There are also two elements which must be present for the crime of genocide to have taken place: the physical element, which includes the committal of one or more of the enumerated acts; and the mental element, which requires that the committed acts were carried out with the intent to destroy, in whole or in part, a national, ethnic, racial or religious group "as such" (Mitchell 2000: 18). There is no requirement that an entire group be targeted in order for genocide to have taken place, nor is premeditation a requisite element of the crime (Lippman 1985; 1998).

The intent requirement has been met with much debate and continues to generate controversy. On one hand, scholars argue that in order for an act to constitute genocide a specific intent must be established on the part of the perpetrators (Chalk and Jonassohn 1990; Horowitz 1976; Leblanc 1984; Lewy 2005). In its absence, whatever mistreatment or ill effects a group member experiences at the hands of an individual or someone working on behalf of the state, this should be considered something other than an act of genocide (Kuper 1981: 32–35; Schabas 2000: 206–56). In the case of Aboriginal peoples, whatever destruction of Indigenous ways of life might have taken place through colonization, or whatever deaths might have resulted from direct action or negligence, these fall short of genocide because the specific intent to destroy the group "as such" has not been proven. For example, Blanca Tovias has considered whether the attempt to eradicate the Blackfoot Sun Dance by the Department of Indian Affairs constituted genocide, or if it was a case of cultural adaptation through non-violent assimilation. She concluded the latter because policy was hardly "surgical in its execution" and allowed plenty of room for Blackfoot agency (Tovias 2008: 271–95). On the other hand, some argue for a broader understanding of intent because specific intent is almost impossible to establish (Barta 2008b; Davis and Zannis 1973; Greenwalt 1999; Lippman 1998; Alonzo-Maizlish 2002). There are many difficulties with a strict, judicial criterion of intent when considering whether a particular case is genocidal, the most obvious of which is that intentions can be disguised by the perpetrators of atrocities to escape responsibility. For this reason, scholars like Tony Barta argue that historical practice and the foreseeable outcomes of policies also need to be considered when deciding whether a particular act constitutes genocide (Barta 1987; Barta 2008b). In reference to colonial practices, Barta points out:

> Perpetrators and judicial authorities [are] able to disguise genocidal intentions from others most effectively where they [are] also disguised from themselves - by appeal to the exigencies of self-defence, by reference to the larger aims of colonization, and to explicit measures asserting benign intentions towards the Indigenous peoples who nevertheless continued to "disappear"... it is beyond question that the colonial project of taking land inevitably [means] taking lives. (Barta 2008b: 112, 115)

Similarly, philosopher Jean-Paul Sartre observed during the Russell Tribunal that the "proof" of genocide lay in the results of policy, not in the intentions by which these may have been undertaken and as such, negative intentions do not need to be proven (Churchill 1995: 88; Sartre 1968: 615, 623).[2] The results of colonialism for Indigenous peoples in the Americas were immediately visible to the likes of Charles Darwin when he commented, "We can see that the cultivation of the land will be fatal in many ways to savages, for they cannot, or will not, change their habits" (Darwin 1871: 238). Scholar Dirk Moses argues in the Australian context that colonial powers knew very well the outcomes of their settlement projects on Aboriginal peoples and were prepared to countenance their consequences. With respect to Indigenous peoples in Canada we could argue similarly to Moses, that even where genocide was not consciously willed it was implicitly intended "in the sense of the silent condoning, sometimes agonized acceptance, of a chain of events for which [colonists, bureaucrats and settlers] were co-responsible and were not prepared to rupture" (Moses 2004: 29).

Increasingly, the argument is being made that Canada is guilty of some if not all of the acts falling under Article II of the Genocide Convention. Dean Neu and Richard Therrien highlight that the federal government has consistently pursued the bureaucratic, if not physical, elimination of Indigenous peoples in an attempt to secure access to lands and resources that proved critical to the founding of Canada (Neu and Therrien 2003). This bureaucratic elimination could also include defining a group in such a way that births are construed as occurring outside the group, as historical provisions in the Indian Act have done, whereby women marrying outside the group were deemed non-Indian, as were their children; or the revised definition of an Indian in the current Act which, through its status provisions, continues to rely on notions of blood quantum in order to restrict and limit births within a group without any sort of physical interference.[3] Roland Chrisjohn makes the case that residential school policy was clearly an instance of transferring children from one group to another with the intent to destroy Aboriginal peoples and their ways of life (Chrisjohn and Young 2006). Others, like Robert Davis and Mark Zannis, argue that the "pacification of the North" and its subsequent ill effects have caused serious bodily and mental harm to Indigenous populations (Davis and Zannis 1973). The sterilization of Aboriginal women can be said to fall under Article II (d) of the Genocide Convention, imposing measures to prevent births within a group, and many other policies in the areas of health, welfare and education, implemented within the context of stripping Aboriginal peoples of their lands and reducing the number of those to whom the federal government has obligations, could fall under the list of enumerated acts of genocide. Yet, short of being lodged by a relatively few marginalized voices in society, genocide is not generally a term used to describe the treatment of Aboriginal peoples in Canada (Churchill 1994; Tennant and Turpel 1990; Westra 2008). This section discusses why this is the case.

Raphaël Lemkin and the Crime Without a Name

In his 1944 work entitled *Axis Rule in Occupied Europe*, Raphaël Lemkin first defined the crime of genocide that would be considered by the international community with the goal of establishing a treaty that would prohibit destructive acts against various groups, even during times of peace.[4] Though often mistakenly said to refer solely to the events of the Holocaust, Lemkin had been compiling evidence of what he meant by genocide since as early as 1933 (McDonnell and Moses 2005; Lemkin 1933). And despite often being equated with direct killing, his original definition of genocide was much broader. Lemkin wrote:

> Generally speaking, genocide does not necessarily mean the immediate destruction of a nation, except when accomplished by mass killings of all members of a nation. It is intended rather to signify a coordinated plan of different actions aiming at the destruction of essential foundations of the life of national groups, with the aim of annihilating the groups themselves. The objectives of such a plan would be the disintegration of the political and social institutions of culture, language, national feelings, religion and the personal security, liberty, health, dignity and even the lives of the individuals belonging to such groups. Genocide is directed against the national groups as an entity, and the actions involved are directed against individuals, not in their individual capacity, but as members of the national group. (Lemkin 1944: 79)

In other words, genocide is not simply a singular event directed against individuals, but a process by which the ability of a group to exist is undermined through acts directed against members of a group because of their common group status (Leblanc 1991: 37). Inherent to this notion is the idea that human groups have an existence with properties which go beyond those of the individuals that comprise them, and that the existence of a group is separate from and more than the life of its individual members (Davis and Zannis 1973: 18). Lemkin (1944: 79–95) stressed that genocide went beyond the physical destruction of individuals to also include attacks on the social, political, economic, cultural, biological, religious and moral life of the group. He stated:

> Genocide has two phases: one, destruction of the national pattern of the oppressed group; the other, the imposition of the national pattern of the oppressor. This imposition, in turn, may be made upon the oppressed population which is allowed to remain or upon the territory alone, after removal of the population and the colonization by the oppressor's own nationals. (Lemkin 1944: 79)

Implicit in this formulation is the genocidal nature of colonialism. Many are now uncovering how centrally important this point was to Lemkin's conception of genocide (Cooper 2008: Docker 2004; McDonnell and Moses 2005; Moses 2008). Moses, for example, contends that in his writings, Lemkin hints at the fact that colonialism was intrinsically genocidal and therefore, settler colonialism was even more so. The basis of the latter conclusion stems from the aim of the colonizer to supplant the original inhabitants of the land (Moses 2004: 27). Indeed, Lemkin noted that:

> If the majority cannot be absorbed by the ruling minority and is considered a threat to the minority's power, genocide is sometimes the result (i.e. the American Indian) ... economic conditions have most frequently played a dominant role in ... genocide. (Cooper 2008: 238–39)

Lemkin was aware of the effects of colonialism on Indigenous peoples of North America and included these within his conception of genocide. It has been consistently argued here that land was and continues to be a material underpinning of federal Indian policy in Canada. The goal of colonization for the Canadian state has been twofold: to gain access to lands and attendant resources it does not own and to reduce federal obligations to Aboriginal peoples by reducing the number of those considered Indian, either through bureaucratic means or other assimilative methods. Correspondingly, if one refers to the original definition of the term, the results of the entirety of Indian policy have also been genocidal because its goal has consistently been to undermine the ability of Indigenous peoples to exist *as Indigenous peoples*. However, the formal definition of genocide produced under the aegis of the United Nations is limited to acts aimed at destroying certain physical or biological aspects of the existence of a group, with a sole reference to its cultural existence. How did it come about that many aspects of Lemkin's work which were central to his conception of the term were left out of the definition of genocide under international law?

From Draft to Convention: A Compromise with Consequences

Two years after the term genocide first appeared in *Axis of Rule*, within the context of the atrocities of World War II coming to light and partly due to Lemkin's lobbying efforts, the United Nations began considering a formal definition of genocide. On 11 December 1946, a draft resolution which became Resolution 96(I) of the General Assembly was adopted unanimously and without debate. The General Assembly declared genocide a crime under international law, invited Member States to enact the necessary legislation for its prevention and punishment and requested the Economic and Social Council (ECOSOC) draw up a draft Convention for consideration at the next regular session.[5] The ECOSOC subsequently instructed the Secretary General to formulate a draft statute (Robinson 1960: 121–22). The draft produced under these circumstances declared genocide a crime directed against racial, national, linguistic, religious, or political groups. In keeping with the definition advanced by Lemkin, it detailed at considerable length what were referred to as the biological, physical and cultural dimensions of genocide, or three of the seven aspects expanded upon by Lemkin in his previous writings. The category of physical genocide outlined mass extermination and slow death measures (i.e., subjection to conditions of life which, owing to lack of proper housing, clothing, food, hygiene and medical care, or excessive work or physical exertion are likely to result in the debilitation or death of individuals; mutilations and biological experiments imposed for other than curative purposes; deprivation of all means of livelihood by confiscation of property, looting, curtailment of work and the denial of housing and of supplies otherwise available to other inhabitants of the territory concerned); biological genocide consisted of the restriction of births in the group (sterilization or compulsory abortion, segregation of the sexes and obstacles to marriage); and finally, cultural genocide was defined as the destruction of the specific characteristics of a group (forced transfer of children from one group to another, prohibition of the use of the national language, destruction or dispersion of documents and objects of historical, artistic, or religious value and of objects used in religious worship) (Lippman 1998: 11).

The so called Secretariat Draft was used as the starting point in producing the draft Genocide Convention that was eventually transmitted to the Sixth Committee (Legal) of the General Assembly.[6] This draft was then considered by delegates, and modifications were made to the protected classes covered under the Convention. The Sixth Committee omitted the inclusion of political and linguistic groups, and later added ethnic groups to the list of protected classes (Lippman 1998; Van der

Vyver 1999). Members agreed it was not necessary for an entire group to be targeted in order for genocide to take place even though the number of victims could be of evidentiary value; and the acts listed as constituting genocide were determined to be restrictive rather than illustrative, meaning acts considered genocidal would be limited to those listed, rather than those listed serving as demonstrative examples (Thornberry 1991: 70; Robinson 1960: 57).[7] Killing members of a group was limited to the intentional and direct commission of individual and mass murder, as well as a series of separate but related executions; the infliction of serious bodily harm entailed mutilation or torture as well forms of violence which might lead to death; the phrase "mental harm" was inserted to prohibit acts of genocide committed through narcotics, or intentionally causing mental suffering through methods that did not impair physical health; the deliberate infliction of conditions of life calculated to bring about the physical destruction of a group, in whole or in part, prohibited the imposition of conditions which were likely to result in death; the prevention of births encompassed castration, compulsory abortion, sterilization and the segregation of sexes; and the forced transfer of children to environments where they would be instilled with alien customs, languages, religions and values was considered the corollary to the prevention of births and tantamount to the eradication of the next generation (Lippman 1998: 456–57).

The forced transfer of children, though expunged from the ECOSOC draft, was adopted by the Sixth Committee of the General Assembly on the urging of the Greek representative. This aspect was said to refer to the abduction of thousands of Greek children and their transfer to communist countries in Eastern Europe at the close of World War II; and the Nazi "Lebensborn" program under which German officials kidnapped nearly a quarter million children judged to be "racially valuable" from Poland, Russia, Yugoslavia and other Eastern European countries in an effort to Germanize them (Hillel and Henry 1976). The provision, agreed to despite a lack of enthusiasm, is understood to be the sole reference to cultural genocide in the Convention (Leblanc 1991: 14). After persistent and prolonged debate, the General Assembly omitted the entire Article III on cultural genocide, keeping only the act listed above despite this article appearing in all previous drafts, and despite the central importance of the cultural existence of groups to the original conception of the term.

The main argument for the inclusion of such an article in the Convention was that cultural genocide often preceded physical or biological genocide (Morsink 1999: 1029). The Byelorussian representative argued that "acts aimed at the destruction of the language, religion or culture of a group … were always a feature of persecutions having as their object the destruction of the group — as the crimes perpetrated under Hitler showed" (Morsink 1999: 1030). Political scholar Johannes Morsink quotes Mr. Zourek, representative from Czechoslovakia, who:

> drew the [c]ommittee's attention to the fact that a group might disappear

either as the result of the physical extermination of its members or as a result of forcible destruction of its distinctive and permanent characteristics ... He quoted numerous instances of cultural genocide of which the Czech and Slovak had been victims during the Nazi occupation. Those acts were designed [he said] to pave the way for the systematic disappearance of the Czechoslovak nation as an independent and national entity. Such Nazi activity had been accompanied by a thorough attempt to destroy everything which might remind the people of its national past and to prepare the way for complete germanification ... All those acts of cultural genocide had been inspired by the same motives as those of physical genocide: they had the same object, the destruction of racial, national or religious groups. (Morsink 1999: 1030)

In final deliberations, the General Assembly rejected a last effort by the Soviet Union to reinstate a provision on cultural genocide (Sunga 1997: 109). A majority expressed fears that because the concept was not clearly defined, to include it in the Convention would provide this legally binding instrument more political rhetoric than substance, and would leave governments unable to adequately safeguard themselves from such charges (Rehman 2000: 56–57).

The Soviet delegate argued that the failure to include a prohibition against cultural genocide "might be utilized by those who wished to carry out discrimination against national, cultural, and racial minorities" (Lippman 1985: 59). The delegate from Pakistan, Begum Ikramullah, echoed this concern stating the "mere physical existence of a group deprived of the living springs of the spirit was only a body without a soul, unable to make any contribution to the world's heritage" and that the "forcible and systematic suppression of a national culture" could not be justified by "the euphemistic term of assimilation" (Lippman 1985: 59). Ikramullah appears to have touched on the fear shared by the United States, Canada and the United Kingdom that including cultural genocide within a convention prohibiting genocide would outlaw implicitly and explicitly stated assimilatory practices and policies imposed on Indigenous and minority populations.

The United States, Canada and the United Kingdom opposed the provision and were ultimately successful in leading the drive to delete any explicit reference to cultural genocide in the Convention (Churchill 2000; Sunga 1997: 109). The United States argued that however unpardonable the cultural destruction of a group was, this fell in an entirely different category from physical genocide and should be dealt with in connection with the protection of minorities (Lippman 1985: 59; Morsink 1999: 1024). The United Kingdom similarly stated that acts covered under this notion were a matter of human rights and that genocide should be confined strictly to the physical extermination of human groups (Lippman 1985: 59; Lippman 1998: 449). Canada shared both of these views and argued the inclusion of cultural genocide in the Convention was neither within the Council's terms of reference nor properly included in a convention designed to protect human life (Canada 1948a: 191).

During the general debate at the ECOSOC and again during the Sixth Committee of the General Assembly, Canadian delegates reserved the right to move the deletion of Article III on cultural genocide at the third session of the General Assembly (Lippman 1985: 37). In discussions of the draft convention at the Sixth Committee, Canadian representative Hugues Lapointe contended that:

> The people of his country were deeply attached to their heritage, which was made up mainly of a combination of Anglo Saxon and French elements and they would strongly oppose any attempt to undermine the influence of those two cultures in Canada ... [His delegation] felt that the idea of genocide should be limited to the mass physical destruction of human groups ... For that reason he would support the proposal made by the French delegation ... that the attention of the Third Committee should be drawn to the need for the protection of language, religion and culture within the framework of the international declaration of human rights. (Morsink 1999: 1042)

Morsink discusses this comment as a promissory note by Canada to include an article on cultural genocide within the *Universal Declaration on Human Rights*, the drafting of which overlapped in a significant manner with the Genocide Convention (Morsink 1999: 1009–60). The Declaration was the preferred route to be pursued by the United States and the United Kingdom as well. Morsink argues that Western powers understood clearly the connection between cultural genocide and physical genocide, but because they were committed to their respective policies of assimilation they opposed such a provision in a convention aimed at preventing genocide. If the cultural aspects of a group were to be protected at all, they agreed this would happen within the Declaration (Morsink 1999: 1009–10). However, the above promissory note never came to formal fruition and a provision protecting the cultural rights of minorities was ultimately voted down by the Commission for Human Rights as well (Morsink 1999: 1049).

What led Canada and other Western powers to renege on this promissory note? Conversations on whether to include a provision on cultural genocide in either the Convention or the Declaration overlapped substantially (Morsink 1999: 1022). Ralph Maybank, Member of Parliament and head of the Canadian delegation at debates on the Declaration, spoke several times in the Third Committee of the General Assembly (Schabas 1998: 423). In a contradictory fashion to the previous position articulated by Lapointe while deliberating Article III of the Genocide Convention, Maybank objected to the inclusion of a clause protecting the cultural rights of minorities in the Declaration on the premise that Canada had no problems in that area:

Some attempt has been in the [c]ommittee, to define the word "minority," and thus give its proper context in these resolutions. It has been stated that the problem of minorities may arise as the result of the arrival in a country of new settlers from a foreign country, or it may arise from the unfavorable circumstances in which certain Indigenous national groups may find themselves. I can say quite confidently that for Canada the problem of minorities, regarded in *either* of these two ways, does not exist; that is to say it is not pre-set in the sense that there is discontent. In the first place, Canada is a country made up of English speaking and French speaking Canadians, and I trust by the very use of these words I am making clear that neither of these groups falls in the category of a "minority" referred to in these draft resolutions. These two peoples, who comprise the greatest number of Canadian citizens, carry on their lives and activities with complete amity one towards the other, and each has its own language and makes use of its own educational facilities and contributes its own cultural tradition to our country. (Schabas 1998: 423)

Although he completely ignored the existence of Aboriginal peoples in Canada, he said of immigrants:

There were many European and non-European immigrants in Canada. They were free to worship as they pleased and to speak their own language. The Government's policy was one of voluntary assimilation, looking forward to the day when the immigrant would regard himself as a Canadian citizen. While Canadians were free to use whatever language they wanted, the question of education remained within the jurisdiction of each province and the Federal Government neither wished nor was able to interfere in that connection. (Schabas 1998: 423)

The position taken by Canada that it had no problems with minorities was questionable considering the extensive discussions of the issue which took place at home, a year before any of the above statements were made.

In May 1947, a Special Joint Committee of the Senate and the House of Commons on Human Rights and Fundamental Freedoms was formed by Canadian Parliament (Canada 1948b). The committee considered the preparatory materials that would later inform initial international discussions on the Declaration, and that were produced by Canadian John Humphrey, the Director of the Division of Human Rights. The committee sought to clarify what steps would need to be taken in order to ensure respect for human rights and fundamental freedoms at home (Schabas 1998: 411). International legal scholar William Schabas provides us a general outline of the deliberations that took place and demonstrates the nervousness with which much of the Canadian political elite approached the question of adopting a Declaration. By this time, Canada had already established its own reputation as a repressive society. Schabas cites examples of authoritarian activities such as the enactment of legislation to suppress political activity within Canadian borders; the internment of more than twenty thousand "enemy aliens" in camps across the country; the secret interrogation of those suspected of being involved in "spy activity" and the suspension of their right to legal counsel; and the ordered removal of Japanese Canadians from the Pacific coast (Schabas 1998: 410–11; Lamberton 2005; MacLennan 2003). To this we could also add the discrimination against women and the surveillance of queer people in the public service (Kinsman and Gentile 2010) as well as the longstanding mistreatment of Aboriginal peoples through the denial and suppression of their individual and collective rights. Many of these instances appear as concerns which shaped conversations on whether to adopt the proposed Declaration in its current form. The chair of the committee, James L. Ilsley, highlighted:

> Somewhere in these articles there is the right of movement of citizens within their own country, and if you wish to have a law preventing a movement of the Japanese from one part of the country to the other which we have at present time it could well be argued it is contrary to this declaration. (Schabas 1998: 416)

With respect to Aboriginal Peoples, it was questioned whether the provision on democratic rights in the Declaration might entitle them to vote, something Indigenous peoples could not do until 1960 without becoming enfranchised, to which Senator Léon Gouin responded that "they have the right to choose to be wards of the state and not vote, or to vote and have freedom" (Schabas 1998: 414). Concerns were also expressed on whether the right to life provision would interfere with capital punishment or whether the right to rest and leisure would make vacation compulsory (Schabas 1998: 410–11; 415). In its final report, the committee recommended the Declaration be shortened and that articles which appeared to define the duties of the state be left out (Schabas 1998: 416).

The Department of External Affairs then issued a cable of instruction to its delegation, now in Paris and participating in debates on the Declaration in the Third Committee as noted above, stating that although it did not want to be on record as opposing a declaration on human rights, it had apprehensions that by supporting the Declaration, this would open government to criticism on legal and political grounds (Schabas 1998: 426–27). In final deliberations, all members of the international community present voted for the Declaration with the exception of Canada and the Soviet Union, who abstained (Schabas 1998: 403–41). Three days later, on 10 December 1948, when the Declaration was put to a vote before the General Assembly as a whole, Canada changed its position and voted in favour. This change, partly motivated by concerns of self-image, was also fueled by a fear that by voting against the Declaration, Canada would isolate itself from the

United States, who wanted it passed (Schabas 1998: 417–18). It would also have opened the door to the possibility of a private member introducing a resolution in parliament seeking to incorporate the full text of the Declaration, and this would put "every member in the position of having to take a stand on individual human rights" (Schabas 1998: 433–34).

However, a declaration on human rights does not hold the same weight as a convention to prevent genocide. Lemkin consistently expressed fears that the movement for the Genocide Convention was being infiltrated by human rights activists, and he was distressed by what he saw as a trend of confusing genocide, or the collective right to existence of a group, with individual human rights (Cooper 2008: 173, 193). Genocide dealt with the attempt to destroy a group "as such," whereas the Declaration, without an explicit article aiming to protect the collective rights of people, focused on preventing discrimination and ensuring equality rights of individuals within a given state (Morsink 1999: 1057). Morsink makes the point that people are rarely discriminated against simply because of the individuals that they are, and the expression of culture, language or religion is by nature a group activity (Morsink 1999: 1057). Failing to include a provision on cultural genocide in either the Convention or the Declaration made it so the focus rested solely on protecting the rights of individuals rather than explicitly protecting the collective rights of groups (Rehman 2003: 81–82).[8]

This point also proves important when we distinguish between the rights of minorities and Indigenous peoples. Though what constitutes a minority has proven difficult to define, a generally agreed upon definition is a:

> group numerically inferior to the rest of the population of a State, in a non-dominant position, whose members — being nationals of the State — possess ethnic, religious or linguistic characteristics differing from those of the rest of the population and show, if only implicitly, a sense of solidarity, directed towards preserving their culture, traditions, religion or language. (Rehman 2003: 298)

The rights of minorities have a collective dimension and some overlapping concerns are shared by minorities and Indigenous peoples. However, there is a prominent view that Indigenous peoples belong in their own distinct category (Rehman 2003: 297–343). That is:

> Indigenous communities, peoples and nations are those which, having continuity with pre-invasion and pre-colonial societies that developed on their territories, consider themselves distinct from other sectors of the societies now prevailing in those territories, or parts of them. They form at present non-dominant sectors of society and are determined to preserve, develop and transmit to future generations their ancestral territories and their ethnic identity, as the basis of their continued existence as peoples,

in accordance with their own cultural patterns, social institutions and legal systems. (Rehman 2003: 332)

Alternatively, as James Anaya, the U.N. Special Rapporteur on the Rights of Indigenous Peoples, writes:

> The term Indigenous refers broadly to the living descendants of pre-invasion inhabitants of lands now dominated by others. Indigenous peoples, nations or communities are culturally distinctive groups that find themselves engulfed by settler societies born of the forces of empire and conquest. (Anaya 2004: 3)

Indigenous claims are more substantial than minority rights in that they can include claims of collective property rights to lands and resources because of a historical association with, occupation and use of these, in addition to the collective right to self-determination, which can include a possible right to secession and the ability to define their own nations (Rehman 2003: 332–33).

The protection of minorities through human rights legislation does not consider the material basis that makes Indigenous claims unique, and many states are in fact keen on the issue of non-discrimination because this concept implies the flattening of differences between groups and promotes assimilation, invariably to the credit of the dominant majority (Rehman 2000: 119). Because individual human rights norms cannot readily accommodate important aspects of Indigenous claims, like the right to a collective existence as a people, these become fragmented and decontextualized in both national and international jurisdictions (Tennant and Turpel 1990: 291–92). Scholar Ronald Niezen further clarifies:

> The promotion of exclusively individual human rights has dangerous implications because many nation-states have vested interests in controlling and usurping the collective rights (including the collective human rights) of Indigenous peoples. Individual human rights are insufficient to protect collective treaty rights. Emphasizing exclusively individual human rights leaves states with an opening to interfere in group identity, to provide only those cultural choices that weaken both Indigenous societies and the distinct collective (principally treaty) rights that are part of their relationship, as sovereign entities, with states. To do otherwise than to recognize Indigenous rights of self-determination is to invite the continued repression and marginalization of Indigenous societies. (Niezen 2003: 133)

A focus solely on individual human rights is consistent with the longstanding policy of assimilating Aboriginal peoples, of denying their status as sovereign peoples and of ensuring unimpeded exploitation of lands and resources, and concessions by the state which recognize only certain cultural rights of groups within the current system, without also respecting political and legal rights of self-determination, should be viewed with caution.

Lemkin also questioned the effectiveness of including a provision on cultural genocide within the Declaration, which lacked enforceability. As Cooper observes, "Lemkin remained perplexed" that the Declaration "with no legal enforcement could actually trump the legal precedents of the Genocide Convention" (Cooper 2008: 226). A convention brings with it at least a modicum of enforcement machinery and it imposes clear legal obligations upon states, whereas declarations do not. Although courts are not precluded from relying on declarations in legal judgments, this does not often occur (Hartley, Joffe and Preston 2010: 85–94). Despite these difficulties, the *Convention on the Prevention and Punishment of the Crime of Genocide* was unanimously adopted by the United Nations General Assembly on 9 December 1948 and was submitted to individual member states for ratification. Canada ratified the Convention on 21 May 1952, and deposited it with the United Nations Secretariat on 3 September 1952. The *Universal Declaration on Human Rights* was also adopted a day later, on 10 December 1948 and went on to inform the principle human rights treaties relied on today.[9]

Canada and the Genocide Convention

Under Article V of the Genocide Convention, individual states incurred the obligation to enact statutes designed to prevent and punish genocide within their respective domestic laws, but no uniform legislation was required. That is, the enactment of domestic legislation was only necessary where existing law was deemed insufficient in covering the acts made punishable under the Convention (Robinson 1960: 74–79). Despite the straightforward appearance of this article, Canada opted to parse the meaning of the word "necessary" in order to skirt its obligations in fulfilling the Convention altogether. During debates in the House of Commons as part of the ratification of the Genocide Convention, Lester Pearson, then Secretary of State for External Affairs, argued Canada should support the widest possible application of the Genocide Convention. However, he argued that no legislation was required for Canada to meet its obligations as a signatory. Pearson based his claim on the "expert opinion" of the Deputy Minister of Justice W.F. Varcoe, who was of the view that no legislation was required by Canada:

> I would direct your attention to the wording of article V of the Convention. I do not think any legislation is "necessary," inasmuch as I cannot conceive of any acts of commission or omission occurring in Canada as falling within the definition of the crime of genocide contained in article II of the convention, that would not be covered by the relevant section in the criminal code.[10]

This legal opinion, requested prior to Canada signing the Convention, begs the question of whether the act of signing was ever intended as anything more than a public relations gesture allowing Canada to cultivate an enlightened and progressive image on the international stage.[11]

The failure to enact legislation dealing with genocide meant that the only avenue available to individuals seeking to bring a charge in Canada was to do so under existing statutes pertaining to murder or its equivalent. Prosecution for "genocide" was simply not possible through Canadian courts unless it consisted of the outright killing of individuals because of their group membership, a shortcoming that did not go unnoticed by some members of parliament.[12] When questioned on whether the Convention could be applied to acts directed against minorities which fall short of literal extermination, Canada reiterated its position that genocide was to be equated solely with physical destruction rather than also encompass attacks against the cultural or social lives of members of a group. Describing the latter acts as "discrimination," Secretary Pearson stated that, although he did not condone the destruction of the cultural and social lives of members of a group, he thought the Convention went too far exactly because it could be interpreted as applying to this type of "discrimination."[13] Having thus (re)defined the crime of genocide in such a way as to nullify its actions, the Secretary offered a concluding remark:

> May I say that the possibility of the crime of genocide being committed in Canada seems to me to be extremely remote ... In approving this Convention unanimously ... we will be proclaiming throughout the world that genocide is considered by us to be a monstrous crime. We will be doing something to make it more difficult for *any other country [emphasis added]* to commit that crime.[14]

In light of subsequent events, this framing also poses the intriguing possibility that beyond whatever intrinsic propaganda value it may have yielded, the early signing of the Convention was intended to establish a ready pretext for military interventions abroad, either in the guise of peacekeeping or the protection of human rights. Be that as it may, the implications of government actions become clearer still when we consider the extremely limited definition of genocide Canada eventually did enshrine in its statutory code and how this came to pass.

Genocide and the Canadian Criminal Code

On 20 February 20 1964, Bill C-21, *An Act Respecting Genocide*, a Private Members' Bill was passed through its first reading in the House of Commons (Cohen 1966: appendix iv). Despite the previous assurance by Pearson that no legislation was required for Canada to meet its obligations as signatory to the Convention, the stated purpose of this bill was to give the Convention effect as it was ratified by parliament in 1952 (Cohen 1966: appendix iv). Though it did not make it past second reading, this bill proposed its own definition of genocide and outlined punishment under Canadian law for various acts. Genocide here consisted of the acts enumerated under Article II (a), (b) and (c) of the Genocide Convention. A specific article was also included dealing with the publication and dissemination of hate propaganda, and another relating to the advocacy of genocide (Lippman 1998: 458).

On 23 October 1964, Bill C-21 was referred to the Standing Committee on External Affairs, together with Bill C-43, *An Act to Amend the Post Office Act (Hate Literature)*, a bill intended to prevent the use of "her Majesty's" mails to disseminate hate literature (Canada 1964: 1677–83). This committee considered these two bills together with the stated intent of going beyond genocide and refocusing on issues of group libel, or the promotion of racial or group hatred, and of providing for legislation dealing with the newly adopted *Declaration on the Elimination of All Forms of Racial Discrimination*.[15] As Marcel Cadieux, Under-Secretary of State for External Affairs, stated:

> Bill No. C-21 does not in fact restrict itself to the terms of the convention and, in its third clause, it appears to go beyond them since this Section clearly refers to group libel rather than genocide. As you are also all no doubt aware, this provision, which is an attempt to deal with racial or group hatred, raises very directly the fundamental issue of free expression in Canada ... Bill No. C-21 also deals with the subjects covered by the declaration on the elimination of all forms of racial discrimination which was adopted unanimously by the United Nations general assembly of 1963. (Canada 1965b: 1794)

At this preliminary stage, by considering legislation relating to genocide under another pretense, genocide was ensured not to be the central focus of forthcoming debates. This is confirmed by the response given by Mr. Cadieux to a question referring to the past legal position expounded by Lester Pearson in 1952, that no implementing legislation was necessary to fulfil obligations arising from Canada becoming signatory to the Convention:

> With regard to the implementation domestically of the genocide convention there have been recent exchanges of correspondence with the justice department and I understand it is still the Canadian government's position, in respect of the implementation of the genocide convention, that it is still not necessary to provide legislation, and that the scope of our existing criminal legislation is adequate to implement it. But, I hasten to add, this is the position with regard to the genocide convention. What we have in prospect now is a number of conventions that will be adopted, and I really cannot say what the position will be in regard to these that are more directly related to the question of discrimination. The position

really is very limited to genocide itself, that is extermination, incitement
to destruction, not discrimination. (Canada 1965b: 1797)

If the role of this committee was not to consider legislation to fulfil obligations arising as a signatory to the Genocide Convention, why include genocide in
these discussions at all? According to the committee, genocide rarely transpired
spontaneously but was most often preceded by its advocacy in the form of hate
propaganda and hence, this is where the focus of preventative legislation should
lay. The Standing Committee on External Affairs met a total of seven times.[16] It
called witnesses and heard testimony from "experts" in the field in an attempt to
further understand the problem of hate propaganda in Canada. Deliberations
concluded on 24 March 1965, when the committee recommended that more time
was needed to consider this bill and for this reason it would not be able to complete
its study. Following the dissolution of parliament, Bill C-21 died and no further
consideration materialized (Brewin 1967: 235–38).

Concurrently, a special committee was appointed to advise the Minister of
Justice, Guy Favreau, on the need for legislative action to "suppress or control the
advocacy of genocide and the dissemination of hate propaganda" in Canada.[17] The
Cohen Committee, named after its chair Maxwell Cohen, took the contradictory
position that legislation against the advocacy of genocide was necessary to fulfil
international obligations as signatory to the Genocide Convention. Despite stating there can be no misunderstanding as to what is meant by "genocide" because
it is "defined precisely — as the Convention has done — in a manner that leaves
no room for uncertainty" (Cohen 1966: 62–63) the committee recommended
the alteration of international law for Canadian purposes. Although the role of
the Cohen Committee was advisory only, it chose to overlook the internationally
accepted definition and proposed a narrower definition of genocide:

> For purposes of Canadian law, we believe that the definition of genocide
> should be drawn somewhat more narrowly than in the international
> Convention so as to include only killing and its substantial equivalents
> … The other components of the international definition, viz., causing
> serious bodily or mental harm to members of a group and forcibly trans-
> ferring children of one group to another group with the intent to destroy
> the group we deem inadvisable for Canada — the former because it is
> considerably less than a substantial equivalent of killing in our existing
> legal framework, the latter because it seems to have been intended to cover
> certain historical incidents in Europe that have little essential relevance to
> Canada where mass transfers of children to another group are unknown.
> (Cohen 1966: 62–63)

Despite this suggestion, when Senator John Connolly tabled Bill S-49, *An Act
to Amend the Criminal Code (Hate Propaganda)* on 6 November 1966, as a second

attempt to introduce legislation dealing with hate propaganda, the definition of genocide included in this bill was in line with that of the Convention and included all five enumerated acts of genocide.[18] This bill also died after second reading, following the prorogation of parliament on 8 May 1967.

One day later, parliament was reconstituted. On 9 May 1967, Senator Jean-Paul Deschatelets reintroduced *An Act to Amend the Criminal Code (Hate Propaganda)*, now referred to as Bill S-5.[19] Following its second reading on 21 November 1967, the Senate referred the subject matter of the bill to a Special Senate Committee on the Criminal Code (Hate Propaganda). This committee met three times, on 14 and 29 February and 7 March 1968 (Canada 1968). On 23 April 1968, parliament was dissolved and the work of the committee came to an abrupt end.[20] During the debates of this Special Senate Committee, Maxwell Cohen, chair of the Cohen Committee, was called as a witness. When questioned as to why the Cohen Committee recommended a departure from the internationally accepted definition of genocide as it appeared in the Convention and the present draft bill, Cohen clarified:

> The reason we left out (b) and (e) was that we thought they were not relevant to Canadian life and factual needs. We thought that "causing serious bodily or mental harm to members of a group" raised all sorts of subtle and various sophisticated problems which we did not want to see or could see ourselves engaged in. (Canada 1968: 58)

Senator Daniel A. Lang asked Mr. Cohen, if genocide referred solely to murder and its equivalent, why one could not replace the word "destroy" as it appeared in the Convention and the present bill with the word "kill." By doing so, Senator Lang indirectly highlighted that the Genocide Convention was meant to encompass acts much broader than what Canada was willing to concede (Canada 1968: 59). However, Mr. Cohen reiterated, the proposed legislation was not meant to address genocide per se, but its advocacy. In doing so, he made plain the logical sophistry standing behind the incorporation of the advocacy of genocide into the Criminal Code:

> Had the genocide convention become part of the law of Canada, then no doubt the statute which implemented the genocide convention would possibly have read in such a way that it not merely made the crime of genocide as an item in the schedule but also the advocacy of genocide ... The point I wish to make here, of course, is that although Canada has not implemented the genocide convention, the reasons given publicly, you will often find, are that the provisions with respect to homicide deal with the matter indirectly by making individual murder a crime and, therefore, the murder of many people is, logically, a similar crime ... a multiple crime. Consequently, it is argued that it is unnecessary. However, that is a

far cry from saying that the rules on homicide or the rules on counseling homicide or conspiracy or intent or attempt or inciting dealt with this kind of group destruction which may be advocated. The real question is: Ought there to be a place in Canada for advocating the destruction of an identifiable group of Canadians? And I say there is no place in Canada for that. (Canada 1968: 60)

Cohen acknowledged that if Canada had directly implemented legislation prohibiting genocide, its advocacy through conspiracy or incitement would also have been prohibited. However, to follow his logic, if genocide was equal to murder and this was already prohibited under the Criminal Code, would it not be the case that advocating genocide was also prohibited under similar and already existing provisions relating to the conspiracy to commit murder or other related charges? Not according to Cohen. There had to be something more to genocide than just murder "writ large." Why, then, insist on legislation limited to the advocacy of genocide rather than deal with its potential or actual committal, the responsibility Canada did acquire by signing the Genocide Convention, which addressed both the prevention of the crime and its punishment? Or, why "advocacy" rather than conspiracy, incitement, attempt to commit, or complicity in genocide, acts that do appear in Article III of the Convention? To focus on advocacy allows for genocidal policies or practices, in their outcome if not in the intent, to be imposed on "identifiable groups" like Aboriginal peoples as long as the stated purpose behind such policy is not vocalized as being to destroy the identifiable group "as such." However, as Jean-Paul Sartre asked following the Holocaust, can it reasonably be expected that a government would advocate publicly a policy of genocide (Moses 2000: 89–106)? Parliament proved reticent in dealing with even this limited aspect of the crime through legislation, and this third bill died following the dissolution of parliament on 23 April 1968.

Resurrected for a fourth time in the form of Bill S-21, nearly an exact copy of Bill S-49 and S-5, which retained a full definition of genocide in line with the Convention, this bill was referred to the Senate Committee on Legal and Constitutional Affairs on 22 January 1969.[21] The committee continued an extensive debate on the proposed amendments to the Criminal Code dealing with hate propaganda. Hesitancy was expressed in submissions by both the Canadian Jewish Congress (cjc) and the Canadian Civil Liberties Association (ccla) about whether criminalizing the incitement of hatred would impede free speech. Though the cjc took the position that this legislation would serve as an effective educational tool, the ccla commented that in a so-called democratic society, many useful utterances often bring up bitter feelings (Canadian Jewish Congress 1969; Canadian Civil Liberties Association 1969). They asked, "if an Indian were to heap blame for his poverty upon the white man, could he be said to be inciting 'hatred or contempt' for white peoples?" and concluded, "The deciding line between creative tension and destructive hate will often be very difficult to draw" (ccla 1969: 2).

Regarding the nature of genocide, the CCLA took the position that it should be defined much more narrowly than it was under international law. Completely disregarding internationally accepted legal understandings of the crime, but also indirectly acknowledging that the residential school policy in Canada was explicitly designed to destroy Aboriginal peoples and could be considered genocidal, they held that:

> Section 267 A (e) would make it an offence to advocate "forcibly transfer-ring children of the group to another group" with the intent of destroying the group. Could it be argued that the proposal to impose integrated education upon the children of Doukhobors or Indians, for example, might fall within this prohibition? The risk contained in this sub-section is that a court might be persuaded that the proposal to transfer children in such a way is intended to "destroy" a culture, i.e. a group. Clearly, whatever one thinks of compulsory integrated education, the advocacy of it in such circumstances should not constitute a criminal offence. In our view the concept of genocide should be limited to physical destruc-tion.[22] (CCLA 1969: 6)

In the face of such logic, it is only reasonable to wonder about the utility of laws crafted in such a manner as to explicitly exempt their authors from culpability for perpetuating policies that are formally prohibited as criminal under an international legal convention.

When re-called as a witness during these deliberations, Mr. Cohen, despite recommending in the Cohen Report that genocide encompass acts in sections (a), (c) and (d), now suggested that subsection (d), imposing measures intended to prevent births within the group, be left out completely. This exchange, which directly addresses the issue of sterilization, is quoted at length:

> Senator Prowse: Did I understand you to suggest, Dean Cohen, that subsection (d) should be left out?
> Dean Cohen: Yes, we should leave out subsection (d), which men-tions deliberately imposing measures intended to prevent births within the group.
> Senator Prowse: One of the types of things that come into this ques-tion of hate propaganda from time to time, so it seems to me, is the sugges-tion that you might solve a problem by sterilizing all of a particular group. I am wondering whether we go further than we should in taking that out.
> Dean Cohen: I think that is a very trenchant comment, Senator Prowse.
> Senator Prowse: This can upset people more than being killed.
> Dean Cohen: There is a fair amount of this dreadful literature in circulation at the present time advocating sterilization ...

Senator Prowse: We have in Alberta a sterilization act, I don't know if there is a better name for it, and because of this suggestion which I read about in the paper it seemed to me that the context of that recommenda-tion and the context of this legislation are sufficiently separate that there is no danger of the two forms of the act being confused. I do not think this legislation we are contemplating would in any way effect that enactment.
...

Senator Prowse: As I understood it the suggestion was made that people who have children and who have demonstrated an incapacity to take care of them as individuals should then be compulsory sterilized because they could not look after the children and there are the implica-tions, of course, that the children would not be much better.

Dean Cohen: Well, you have two defenses here. There is one that you mention that it will not be confused with therapeutic controls. The second is the way you define an identifiable group. That is a very specific consideration. It has nothing to do with a man or a woman looking after their children. (Canada 1969f: 357–58)

It was the opinion of Mr. Cohen that as long the sterilization of members of an identifiable group was not openly advocated, or as long as these sterilizations were performed for "therapeutic reasons," then there was no danger of the practice being construed as genocide under the proposed legislation. This possibility would be further assured by the outright removal of the clause relating to the imposition of measures to prevent births within a group from the list of enumerated acts that constituted genocide in Canada (Canada 1969f: 259).

Subsequent to this, it was officially recommended in the final report submit-ted by this committee to the Senate on 12 June 1969 that subsection (2) of the proposed new section 267A be struck out and substituted with a definition of genocide consisting only of (a) killing members of a group and (c) deliberately inflicting conditions of life calculated to bring about its physical destruction, acts limited solely to physical genocide (Canada 1969e). Professor Harry Arthurs from Osgoode Hall Law School at York University expressed reservations even to this latter item, arguing it might be employed to describe "benevolent measures" like those undertaken in relation to the resettlement of economically deprived com-munities or the integration of "Indians and Eskimos" into an urban society (Canada 1969e: 147). However, the Senate acted on these recommendations and the newly amended Bill S-21 passed third reading on 17 June 1969.[23] From there, it was sent to the House of Commons for consideration. Just two days later, on 19 June 1969, parliament prorogued yet again, causing the death of this piece of legislation.[24]

Finally, reintroduced as Bill C-3 and originating in the House of Commons, this bill was again subject to debate. Somewhat hypocritically, considering the rhetorical argument previously made by Pearson that Canada did not need to incorporate a full definition of genocide in line with the Convention because killing and its equivalents were covered under existing criminal law and there was no need for the same crime to be covered twice, Mr. Gerald William Baldwin, representative from Peace River, pointed out that it was already possible to lay a charge of defamatory libel under exactly the same facts and circumstances as set out in the first part of the proposed new section.[25] Despite the argument that legislation was unnecessary in one case, when attempting to avoid responsibility for crimes which fall under the definition of genocide in international law, the same argument appears not to have held in the other, when purportedly taking action against genocide in Canada.

The failure of these proposed amendments to hold the potential to adequately address the grievances of various groups in Canada that have been subject to conditions which could be argued to be genocidal was duly noted by Mr. Donald F. Mazankowski during these debates on 13 April 1970.[26] He pointed out the danger in allowing for the criminalization of dissent and was particularly aware of the situation of Aboriginal peoples. Speaking of men such as Harold Cardinal, who wrote of the injustices faced by Aboriginal peoples and the policy of assimilation outlined in the White Paper, he states:

> Men like Harold Cardinal are angry men. They feel injustice. They feel that their people have been deprived of the riches that many other Canadians enjoy. They feel that they are being disadvantaged, and they feel a sense of frustration and injustice. I ask you, Mr. Speaker is it right that we should take away their right to articulate their views simply because they are angry, simply because they may appear to be somewhat militant, simply because they feel the lethargy of our society forces them to be militant in their modes of expression?[27]

Baldwin argued the proposed amendment did nothing to address the concerns of Aboriginal peoples who cry genocide in the face of the situation created by Canadian policy and practice since colonization:

> I wonder what Bill C-3 proposes for dealing with the 97 per cent drop out rate of Indians from school, or what in fact it would propose to do about providing the equal opportunity that is necessary to enable these people to participate in the full riches of Canadian life. I wonder what this bill proposes to do about supplying them with an adequate water supply, or adequate housing, or about providing them with adequate jobs. And I wonder what it could do to remove the frustration that presently exists among the Indian population in Alberta with respect to medical treatment.[28]

Instead, government appeared more concerned in the passage of this bill as it stood with controlling and regulating the quantity and quality of dissent in this country than prohibiting acts of genocide.[29]

Notwithstanding these criticisms, on 14 April 1970 this bill was referred to the Senate. Despite nearly failing again due to a request that it first be referred to the Supreme Court of Canada for a judgment on whether its contents infringed on provisions included in the *Canadian Bill of Rights*, the bill was passed on 19 May 1970, and received Royal Assent on 11 June 1970.[30] *An Act to Amend the Criminal Code (Hate Propaganda)*, or Bill C-3, dealt with three separate offences: publicly advocating or promoting genocide; the breach of the peace resulting from the incitement of hatred against an identifiable group; and the willful promotion of hatred in other than private conversation (Kane 1970: 21–25). In response to the definition of genocide as it appeared in the bill, no objections were made and as Mr. Baldwin accurately stated, "I doubt very much if there will ever be any prosecutions launched in this country."[31]

The outcome of these voluminous discussions can be read as follows in the Criminal Code under the heading of "Hate Propaganda":

> Advocating genocide. — s. 267A
>
> 267A. (1) Every one who advocates or promotes genocide is guilty of an indictable offence and is liable to imprisonment for five years.
>
> "Genocide" defined. — s. 267A (2)
>
> (2) In this section "genocide" means any of the following acts committed with the intent to destroy in whole or in part any identifiable group, namely:
>> (a) killing members of the group, or
>> (b) deliberately inflicting on the group conditions of life calculated to bring about its physical destruction.
>
> Identifiable group defined. — s. 267A (4)
>
> (4) In this section "identifiable group" means any section of the public distinguished by colour, race, religion or ethnic origin.[32]

This is the first definition of genocide in Canadian law, limited to Article II (a) and (c) of the United Nations Genocide Convention, and referring solely to instances of its advocacy, not its actual committal. In other words, at this point, following Canada's purported attempt to meet international obligations through the enactment of implementing legislation, a person could still not be charged with genocide per se under Canadian law, only with its advocacy according to a narrow definition of the crime.

Despite government attempts to circumscribe the definition of genocide, the Convention has become part of the Common Law of Nations (Van der Vyver 1999: 287). In other words, and as is the case with laws pertaining to crimes against humanity, war crimes, piracy, slave-related practices and torture, genocide has been declared part of international customary law, or *jus cogens*. The Vienna Law of Treaties defines *jus cogens* as "norms accepted and recognized by the international community of States from which no derogation is permitted and which can be modified only by a subsequent norm of general international law having the same character."[33] The International Court of Justice, when considering the effect of reservations to the Convention, stated that "the prohibition of genocide is binding on states, even without any contractual obligation" (Van Schaak 1997: 2277). This could mean that the efforts by Canada to exempt itself from the Convention by reinterpretation are themselves contraventions of international law (Chrisjohn and Young 2006; Churchill 2002). Roland Chrisjohn points out, "A country cannot simply exempt itself from the Common Law of Nations (of which the Genocide Convention is a part), nor interpret the law to its own advantage" (Chrisjohn and Young 2006: 30). The fact that Canada, by refusing to acknowledge certain elements of the Convention, sought to excuse itself from international law does not change the fact that genocide accurately describes many of its policies concerning Aboriginal peoples. One should also consider that the primary defense advanced by the Nazi leadership at Nuremberg was that Germany had never accepted the international laws they were accused of violating. Instead, they argued the policies they carried out were legal under German law. The allied powers represented on the tribunal, including Canada, flatly rejected this argument (Wright 1972: 3–8, 30–43).[34] The wriggling of the Canadian government in this instance bears an uncomfortable resemblance to that of the Third Reich. By re-writing law in such a way as to narrowly define the crime of genocide, the Canadian government placed itself in a position of being able to argue that any actions taken against members living within its own borders and falling under the internationally accepted definition of genocide were in fact not considered crimes in Canada.

In the face of such attempts to limit potential accountability for acts which share such a great overlap with its treatment of Aboriginal peoples, we need to consider whether Canadian functionaries knew too well the dangers faced by a full and honest undertaking to prevent and punish genocide wherever it took place, including within Canadian borders. During the period between the ratification of the Convention and the definition of genocide appearing in the Criminal Code in 1970, another change was also made which rendered it increasingly difficult for a charge of genocide to arise with respect to the treatment of Aboriginal peoples in Canada. In 1956, the *Canadian Citizenship Act* was amended to include all First Nations, making them citizens of Canada (Paul 2000: 295; Statutes of Canada 1956). This Act was originally passed in 1947 to free the settler population of Canada from the British Crown and it conspicuously excluded Aboriginal peoples. The belated inclusion of the latter nine years later was made retroactive to 1947. Though purportedly a gesture of goodwill, this conveyance of citizenship has served to obscure the sovereign rights of Aboriginal Peoples vis-à-vis the Canadian state and has fostered the illusion that Indigenous polities have been more or less, for all practical purposes, fully assimilated into settler society. If Aboriginal peoples are fully assimilated, the argument is more easily made that they no longer constitute an identifiable group "as such." To declare Aboriginal peoples citizens could also be viewed as imposing a minority status, and this has implications in the avenues available to seek redress for grievances against the Canadian government. There is no individual or group complaint mechanism under the Genocide Convention and only states have access to international courts. This means Aboriginal peoples, as "minorities," were left no recourse in the international sphere to claim genocide in relation to their treatment at the hands of what becomes "their own government." It was left to another "Aboriginal-friendly state" to lodge a charge that Canada committed genocide against Indigenous peoples, a situation unlikely to occur (Tennant and Turpel 1990: 294). Moreover, given that no statute of limitations constrains prosecution on charges of genocide, by backdating Aboriginal citizenship to the year before the Convention was approved by the General Assembly, Canada positioned itself to argue that Aboriginal peoples were never covered by it.

Canada and the International Criminal Court

The discussion thus far has sought to highlight some of the ways that Canada, through its involvement in the formation of the *Convention on the Prevention and Punishment of Genocide* and in the manner in which it proceeded to enact enabling legislation, has limited our understanding of genocide and the avenues of redress available for crimes resulting from Indian policy in Canada. One of the most perverse consequences of its posture regarding genocide is that potential critics have been formally enjoined from using the term to characterize the treatment of Aboriginal peoples other than in such specific circumstances as to render reasonable usage virtually impossible. Assuming Canada does in fact lack a lawful basis upon which to derogate its international legal obligations by redefining genocide for its own purposes, the question remains whether there is now a recognized judicial venue wherein Indigenous peoples can bring charges of genocide against the Canadian government.

Article VI of the United Nations Genocide Convention states that persons charged with genocide should be tried by a competent tribunal either in the state or the territory in which the act was committed, or by an international penal tribunal whose jurisdiction is accepted by contracting parties. Despite the inclusion of this clause, no international penal tribunal was established to enforce the Convention for over forty years.[35] Not until 1998 were steps taken to create such a body for the purposes of presiding over the prosecution and punishment of genocidal acts. The *Rome Statute of the International Criminal Court* (icc) was adopted by diplomatic conference on 17 July 1998 and came into force on 1 July 2002.[36] Referred to as "an important milestone" (Kastrup 2000: 408) and "the first and crucial step toward erecting a standing international body capable of prosecuting future perpetrators of genocide" (Greenwalt 1999: 2262) this statute provides for a permanent court able to assert jurisdiction over cases involving genocide, crimes against humanity and war crimes.[37] While an in-depth analysis of the ICC is not undertaken here, a few key problems are highlighted, in keeping with this discussion, to establish that the attempt to evade accountability for genocidal practices against Aboriginal peoples in Canada is ongoing (Arsanjani 1999).

At the opening of the Rome Conference, Minister of Foreign Affairs Lloyd Axworthy urged states to create a "Court worth having," and to avoid creating "a regime that will allow States to gain the prestige of ratifying the court's statute without ever accepting the court's jurisdiction over a particular case."[38] Yet, if one considers its role in shaping the mandate and function of the court, and the implications of it becoming signatory to the Rome Statute, Canada has managed to do just this, at least with respect to its historical treatment of Aboriginal peoples. Canada played a pivotal role in advocating for the ICC and Canadian delegates were instrumental in shaping its development. On the website of the Department of Foreign Affairs and International Trade, the federal government boasts that through extensive lobbying, the funding of non-governmental organizations and by chairing a coalition of states that helped motivate the international community to adopt the Rome Statute, Canada was a leader in the promotion of the ICC. Canadian Philippe Kirsch, senior diplomat and former legal advisor of the Department of Foreign Affairs, served as Chair of the Whole at the Rome Conference from 15 June to 17 July 1998. He also played a lead role in outlining the statute of the court, its rules of procedure and evidence and elements of crimes, and he became the first president of the court, serving as a judge from 2003 to 2009. Political scientist Lana Wylie suggests that Canada has used this involvement to support its image as a model international citizen (Wylie 2006). However, with respect to Aboriginal peoples, its support and advocacy for this court is in keeping with past practice.

Specifically, Article XII of the Rome Statute establishes the international jurisdiction of the ICC, but this jurisdiction applies only if a state chooses to accept it. Article XI also constrains this jurisdiction only to crimes committed after the entry into force of the statute. There is now an international court capable of prosecuting acts of genocide as defined by the Genocide Convention, but prosecution can only be carried out if the state in which these acts took place agrees to be bound by the court, if it chooses not to undertake legal action of its own and then only if the acts in question transpired after the state became signatory to the statute. While purporting to be a great advance on the international stage with regard to the prevention and punishment of future genocidal acts, establishing this court leaves those who have been victimized by past genocidal acts without this legal recourse under international law, effectively resetting the clock regarding past atrocities or genocidal actions.

Canada was the first to incorporate the obligations of the Rome Statute into its national laws by adopting the *Crimes Against Humanity and War Crimes Act* (CAHWCA) on 24 June 2000 (Statutes of Canada 2000). The CAHWCA criminalized genocide, crimes against humanity and war crimes as outlined in the Rome Statute, and allowed Canada to ratify the Rome Statute on 9 July 2000 (Statutes of Canada 2000 c. 24, s. 4). However, because the ICC is not mandated to consider actions which took place prior to its enactment, by agreeing to be bound by the court, there is no possibility that a charge of genocide can be lodged in the ICC for actions carried out by any Canadian official, functionary, or citizen prior to the statute coming into effect. Interestingly, the CAHWCA incorporates a full definition of genocide as outlined in international law, meaning the definition of genocide in Canadian law now encompasses all enumerated acts as listed under Article II of the Genocide Convention (Arsanjani 1999: 30). Although it is difficult to view this act as anything but hypocrisy within the context of the present discussion and the consistent history — more than fifty years — of the Canadian government attempting to limit the definition of genocide in both international and domestic law, it is now possible for a charge of genocide to be lodged in Canadian courts.[39] Yet the CAHWCA is careful to specify that no proceeding can be commenced without the personal consent of the Attorney General or Deputy Attorney General of Canada, and that these proceedings must be conducted by the Attorney General or counsel acting on its behalf (Statutes of Canada 2000 c. 24, s. 9 (3)). However improbable it might be that this arm of government would agree to carry out an investigation on its own members or other functionaries acting on its direction, given there is no statute of limitations on the crime of genocide, it is technically possible (Schabas 2008: 51).

Genocide and Aboriginal Peoples Today

The current discussion makes obvious that Aboriginal peoples will experience many hurdles in attempting to prosecute Canadian officials or functionaries for genocidal policies and practices imposed on their peoples. The purpose here has not been to argue otherwise, but to demonstrate the ways the Canadian government has attempted to avoid responsibility for its actions by ensuring that however these are understood, they will not likely be subject to the scrutiny of the international community within a criminal court, nor will they be weighed according to the internationally accepted definition of genocide. The role Canada has played in shaping current understandings of genocide has limited the avenues for justice available to Indigenous peoples within national borders and abroad. As sociologist Leo Kuper writes, "One can see, in the controversies about the wording of the Convention, many of the forces which have rendered it so ineffective" (Kuper 1981: 24). Canada played a role in rendering the Genocide Convention ineffective through its involvement in its formation at the United Nations and on a national level by enacting domestic legislation that has attempted to confine genocide solely to instances of physical destruction.

There are few who accept the claim that genocide properly applies with respect to the past or current treatment of Aboriginal peoples in Canada. If genocide is equated solely with physical destruction, so the story goes, one need only refer to the fact that Indigenous populations are still here, and in many instances are increasing, to argue that this term is simply not appropriate. Or, because such few instances of one-sided mass killing have taken place within Canadian borders, Aboriginal peoples actually "fared so much better during the invasion than other Indigenous peoples in the Americas" (Chalk 1989: 159). Perhaps this is true in contrast to other areas, including the United States, where one-sided mass killings were undertaken in a more explicit and systematic way. However one is hard pressed to argue that the forced extinction of the Beothuk from Newfoundland, the practice of scalping by royal decree in the Maritime provinces or the many other policies that have resulted directly or indirectly in the physical destruction of Aboriginal peoples have been any less fatal (Palmater 2011b; Paul 2000; Upton 1977). Historian Norbert Finzsch clarifies that outright wars of extermination against Aboriginal peoples have most often proven too expensive and inefficient. A cheaper and more effective policy has been the territorialization of land and its sale to a large number of settlers (Finzsch 2008a). This, I argue, coupled with forceful assimilative policies which were also sometimes physically violent but in general did not involve such a disruptive affront to the rule of law that was "ideologically central to the cohesion of settler society" (Wolfe 2008: 120), was the preferred method pursued by Canadian officials in order to ensure access to territories and resources it did not own.

Simply because outright physical extermination was not the preferred course of action in a Canadian context does not negate the fact that the results of policy have proven genocidal for Aboriginal peoples in their outcomes, if not in their execution. Lemkin did not separate the larger process of colonialism from subsequent resulting deaths and he placed blame, even for unintentional deaths, squarely on the shoulders of the interlopers. On the genocidal effects of colonialism for Aboriginal Australians, he wrote:

> The blame for this destruction of a race lies on the cruelty and lack of understanding of human beings, on the cruelty of the selfish, grasping settlers and convicts who attacked and aroused the spirit of revenge of the originally peaceable natives, and on the lack of understanding of the men who in the end strove to protect them and make them conform to the standard of an alien civilization, and killed them with misguided kindness. (Barta 2008b: 117)

This "misguided kindness" is sometimes said to be the motivating factor behind Canadian Indian policy as well, that destructive policies of the past were carried out with the best intentions (Barman 2006; Miller 1996). The assumption here, of course, is that current policies and practices toward Aboriginal peoples are not destructive, or not intended, or both. When the question of intentions came up in the course of an independent inquiry into the forced transfer of Aboriginal children in Australia, debates clarified that an act or policy is still genocide even when it has a number of objectives, and policy does not need to be motivated by animosity or hatred (Barta 2008a: 207). An alternative version of this story is that if Aboriginal peoples died through the process of colonialism, these deaths were most often the result of disease and hence were either unintentional or the product of a certain biological inferiority. For instance, Alfred Crosby has written that the immune systems of Native populations "simply did not wear well" when they came into contact with European diseases (Crosby 1991: 124; Diamond 1997). More controversial still is the claim that genocide is a unique phenomenon that refers exclusively to the experience of Jewish people in the Holocaust (Katz 1994; Churchill 1997: 413–30).

A new trend among scholars which insists that because Aboriginal peoples actively resisted or negotiated with colonialism, often fighting back or "participating" in their own destruction by accepting relief, "cutting a deal" or sending their children to residential schools, this agency somehow negates the fact that imposed policies were destructive to their ways of life (Loo 1992; Tovias 2008). It is important to acknowledge that Indigenous peoples have indeed been more than simply victims, and their agency has been a force for policy makers and government officials to reckon with, but neither can we consider this agency apart from the larger structural factors informing it (Brownlie and Kelm 1994; Wolfe 2008). There is an increased willingness to refer to residential schools, the most well known Indian policy in Canada, as a form of "cultural genocide" or "ethnocide," but not as genocide proper (Chrisjohn and Young 2006; Tennant and Turpel 1990; Hudson and McKenzie 1981). Philosopher Claudia Card makes an important point in this respect, arguing that the very notion of "cultural genocide" is redundant and that cultural death is in fact present in all genocides (Card 2003). Genocide scholar Patrick Wolfe adds that implicit in the notion of a hyphenated genocide is the assumption that these cases are "not quite the real thing" (Wolfe 2008: 120). Robert Davis and Mark Zannis also remind us that:

> One should not speak lightly of "cultural genocide" as if it were a fanciful invention ... The cultural mode of extermination is genocide, a crime. Nor should "cultural genocide" be used in the game: "Which is more horrible, to kill and torture; or, to remove the reason and will to live?" Both are horrible. (Davis and Zannis 1973: 18)

In order to re-instill in these discussions this sense of moral and historical significance that Lemkin was trying to articulate when he coined the term, we must return to his work. This results in a reconfirmation that genocide does accurately describe the colonization and resultant destruction of many Indigenous communities. Lemkin considers acts perpetrated by the English and French in the Americas as equal instances of genocide, and in his unpublished and incomplete research he took note of some of these instances, which included:

> dispossessing Indigenous peoples of their land (with or without permission of central authorities), kidnapping, enslavement, removal, and deportation often involving forced marches, taking of children, disease through overcrowding on reservations with inadequate food and medicine, self-destruction brought on by introduction and sale of liquor, curtailing and deprivation of legal rights, cultural genocide (as in re-education of children in boarding schools, cutting off braids, forbidding native languages, prohibition on Indian culture and banning religious ceremonies, forcing children to become Christians), and mass death. (Docker 2004)

It is policies such as these, to which we could add the control of births in Indigenous communities through coercive sterilization, the indiscriminate prescription of birth control or abusive abortions, which can also be understood as genocide in a Canadian context.

Considering the range of disagreement over the applicability of the concept of genocide to the past and current treatment of Aboriginal peoples in Canada, it appears that the inclination to apply the term is driven by ideological preference or vested interests rather than an understanding of legal definitions or considerations of historical fact. If this is indeed the case, it is better to avoid getting bogged down in definitional quagmires. The fact remains that Aboriginal communities today face problems of epidemic proportions that are the direct or indirect result of the history of colonialism in Canada, a history which continues to include the mass theft of Aboriginal lands and resources and the undermining of Aboriginal peoples' abilities to exist on their own terms. Historian Tony Barta asks us to focus on what he terms "genocidal relations" rather than the specific acts or intentions of individuals in order to better understand how these underlying historical and material relations give rise to and provide meaning to actions. He quotes Marx:

> There are relationships, however, which determine the actions of private persons as well as those of individual authorities, and which are as independent as the movements in breathing. Taking this objective standpoint from the outset, one will not presuppose an exclusively good or bad will on either side. Rather, one will observe relationships in which only persons appear to act first. (Barta 1987: 239)

These relations are at their core relations of land and resource expropriation to the benefit of the current mode of production, and they are systemic and fundamental to Canadian society. It is these relations that give rise to and have consistently motivated the implementation of destructive policies and practices against Aboriginal peoples, and it is these relations for which the Canadian state has by and large been able to avoid responsibility. I use the term genocide in this respect, to call our attention to these relations in hopes of effecting their transformation.

Well known poet and educator Gabriela Mistral once wrote that genocide carries with it a moral judgment (Mistral 1956). A moral judgment is needed when it comes to the treatment of Indigenous peoples in Canada and beyond its border, and our failure to respect ways of life that do not conform or submit to the requirements of the capitalist system. Implicit in this is a moral judgment of the type of world in which we all live, which depends on the unlimited exploitation of the earth and its resources, and the consequent destruction of its peoples, to which Indigenous ways of life represent viable and living alternatives. If these are allowed to be destroyed, how long before we forget completely that alternative ways of life are not only possible, but necessary?

Notes

1. *Convention on the Prevention and Punishment of the Crime of Genocide,* Adopted by Resolution 260 (III) A of the United Nations General Assembly on 9 December 1948, hereafter referred to as *The Genocide Convention.*
2. The Russell Tribunal, held in 1967, investigated and evaluated American foreign policy and military intervention in Vietnam.
3. This point was highlighted to me by Ward Churchill.
4. As opposed to during times of war. The first legal reference to genocide appeared during the Nuremburg trials, referring to crimes committed during World War II. Article 6(c) of the Charter of the International Military Tribunal provided punishment of acts considered Crimes Against Humanity. German war criminals were charged with conducting "deliberate and systematic genocide, viz., the extermination of racial and national groups, against the civilian populations of certain occupied territories in order to destroy particular races and classes of people, and national, racial, or religious groups." XIX Trial of the Major War Criminals Before the International Military Tribunal (1950), 43–44 in Lippman (1985: 5).
5. The Economic and Social Council consists of eighteen members of the United Nations who serve for three-year terms. It conducts or initiates studies and reports on matters related to its mandate, and makes recommendations on such matters to the General Assembly for the purpose of promoting respect for the observance of human rights.
6. See the *Report of the Ad Hoc Committee on Genocide to the Economic and Social Council on the Meetings of the Committee Held at Lake Success, New York, from 5 April to 10 May 1948,* 7 U.N. ESCOR Supp. No. 6, U.N. Doc. E/794 (1948); U.N. ESCOR, Ad Hoc Comm. On Genocide, 6th Session, 1st- 28th mtgs., *Proceedings of the Ad Hoc Committee,* U.N. Doc. E/AC.25/SR.1 — E/AC.25/SR.28 (1948).
7. Two amendments suggested the adoption of an illustrative definition, but these were rejected by the Sixth Committee. UN Doc A/C.6/232/Rev.1 and UN Doc A/C.6/223 and Corr.1.
8. Javaid Rehman tells us that the *International Covenant on Civil and Political Rights* is unique among international law treaties for its inclusion of Article 27, which provides protection on the basis of the minority right characteristics of an individual. This article provides that a minority shall not be denied the right, in community with the other members of a group, to enjoy their own culture, to profess and practice their own religion or to use their own language. This provision was employed in the case *Sandra Lovelace v. Canada,* Communication No. 24/1977 (30 July 1981), in which Lovelace argued losing her Indian status as a result of her marriage to a non-Indian

man deprived her of right to return to her reserve lands, and was this was discriminatory and in breach of the ICCPR.

9. For example, the *International Covenant on Economic, Social and Cultural Rights*; the *International Covenant on Civil and Political Rights*; the *Convention for the Elimination of Racial Discrimination*.

10. Canada, *Commons Debates*, 21 May 1952, 2442.

11. During debates signing the Convention was spoken of as a means of cultivating the image of Canada as "upholder of humanitarian views and ... fearless champion of justice" whose "guidance and leadership" could be sought by less human and enlightened countries. Canada, *Commons Debates*, 21 May 1952, 2439.

12. Canada, *Commons Debates*, 21 May 1952, 2435.

13. Canada, *Commons Debates*, 21 May 1952, 2442.

14. Canada, *Commons Debates*, 21 May 1952, 2443.

15. The *Declaration on the Elimination of All Forms of Racial Discrimination* was adopted unanimously by the United Nations General Assembly on 21 November 1963.

16. The Committee met on 18 and 24 November 1964, 3 December 1964, 25 and 26 February 1965, and 12 and 24 March 1965.

17. The Committee was comprised of Dean Maxwell Cohen, Q.C., Chairman, Dean of the Faculty of Law, McGill University; Dr. J.A. Corry, Principal, Queens University; L'Abbé Gérard Dion, Faculty of Social Sciences, Laval University; Mr. Saul Hayes, Q.C., Executive Vice-President, Canadian Jewish Congress; Prof. Mark R. MacGuigan, Associate Professor or Law, University of Toronto; Mr. Shane MacKay, Executive Editor, Winnipeg Free Press; and Prof. Pierre Elliott Trudeau, Associate Professor of Law, University of Montreal.

18. Canada, *Senate Debates*, 9 November 1966, 1109–14.

19. Canada, *Senate Debates*, 9 May 1967, 14.

20. Canada, *Senate Debates*, 17 December 1968, 791.

21. This Bill was first introduced on 9 December 1968. Canada, *Senate Debates*, 9 December 1968, 710-711, 790; Canada, *Senate Debates*, 22 January 1969, 885–886.

22. The Doukhobor Sons of Freedom referred to the forceful seizure and institutionalization of their children by the state as an instance of genocide. In a telegram to the United Nations, they wrote that these abductions were an "international offence under the U.N. Genocide Convention," "a direct assault upon human rights" and "a final attempt to annihilate the identity of our group by assimilating our children into the common nationalistic pattern." Fraternal Council, Union of Christian Communities and Brotherhood of Reformed Doukhobors, Open letter to AA Gusskin, Sondalo, Italy, 1955, Simon Fraser University Doukhobor Collection. This complaint was not pursued by the United Nations (McLaren 2002, 278).

23. Canada, *Senate Debates*, 17 June 1969, 1620.

24. Canada, *Senate Debates*, 16 April 1970, 882.

25. "Every one who, by communicating statements in any public place, incites hatred against any identifiable group where such incitement is likely to lead to a breach of the peace." Canada, *Commons Debates*, 7 April 1970, 5579; *Martin's Criminal Code*, s. 267 B.

26. Canada, *Commons Debates*, 13 April 1970, 5785.

27. Canada, *Commons Debates*, 13 April 1970, 5785.

28. Canada, *Commons Debates*, 13 April 1970, 5785.

29.   Canada, *Commons Debates*, 13 April 1970, 5797.

30.   Canada, *Senate Debates*, 21 April 1970, 894-899.

31.   Canada, *Commons Debates*, 7 April 1970, 5579. The first person charged with promoting genocide in Canada was Salman Hossain, a twenty-five-year-old who, in 2010, faced five counts of promoting hatred and advocating or promoting genocide for posts made on his blog that called for a "violent regime change in Western nations in order to remove the presence of Jews" and for "the slaughter of Jews." Hossain subsequently left the country and a warrant is out for his arrest. <interpol.int/Wanted-Persons/%28wanted_id%29/2010-37029; AFP>; Google News, "Muslim Man Charged with Promoting Genocide of Canadian Jews," 9 July 2010, <google.com/hostednews/afp/article/ALeqM5ih3NR8BtGoVz9deLSdKl4klxxT4w>.

32.   *Martin's Criminal Code*. In 2010, this section begins in the *Criminal Code* at s. 318-320.

33.   The Vienna Convention Law of Treaties was drafted by the International Law Commission at the United Nations and was adopted on 22 May 1969. Canada acceded to it on 14 October 1970. The Convention came into force on 27 January 1980. *Vienna Convention on the Law of Treaties*, May 23, 1969, Art. 53, 1155 U.N.T.S. 331, 334.

34.   This connection was also brought to my attention by Ward Churchill.

35.   In May 1993, the United Nations established the International Criminal Tribunal for the former Yugoslavia to deal with the mass atrocities which took place in Croatia, and Bosnia and Herzegovina. The following year, in November 1994, the Security Council created the International Criminal Tribunal for Rwanda to prosecute persons responsible for genocide and other violations of international humanitarian law, committed in the territory of Rwanda between 1 January 1994 and 31 December 1994.

36.   *Rome Statute of the International Criminal Court*, U.N. Diplomatic Conference of Plenipotentiaries on the Establishment of an International Criminal Court, U.N. Doc. A/CONF.183/9, <un.org/icc/part1.htm> [*Rome Statute*].

37.   *Rome Statute* Art. 5(1), accessed online at <un.org/icc/part1.htm>.

38.   United Nations, Press Release, "Diplomatic Conference Begins Four Days of General Statements," 15 June 1998, <n.org/icc/pressrel/lrom7.htm>.

39.   The first charges under the CAHWCA were laid against Désiré Munganeza of Rwanda, a Canadian businessman, following a five-year investigation by the RCMP. He was arrested in 2005 and charged with two counts of genocide, two counts of crimes against humanity and three counts of war crimes for acts committed in Rwanda in 1994. Munganeza was sentenced on 29 October 2009 to life imprisonment with no chance of parole for twenty-five years. Ian Austen, "Canadian Judge Convicts Rwandan in Genocide," *New York Times*, 22 May 2009 <nytimes.com/2009/05/23/world/americas/23canada.html>.

Conclusion

The conquest of the Americas, that vast historical process that dispossesses undetermined numbers of Indigenous peoples to the advantage of European invaders, has not been completed. The liberal consciences of North America today acknowledge wrongdoings of the past, sometimes pausing to note that their own individual ancestors had not yet immigrated to this land (which is to say, they get a free pass on history), sometimes reflecting that past generations did not have the ethical luxury available in our own time, before moving on to other issues. One need not concern oneself so much with past generations and one's own ancestors. In the minutia of quotidian life, in the presuppositions of service providers, in the structures of State actions and inactions, in the continuing struggles over land use, in a whole trajectory of policies and plans, the work of conquest is being completed here and now. By our generation. It is our descendants, a hundred years from now, who will protest that they were not there when land claims were being negotiated, when Aboriginal rights were distorted beyond recognition, when the final acts of the great historical drama of conquest were performed. You who remain silent while this injustice continues, you are responsible. Here. And now.

But then again, so am I. (Kulchyski 2005: 3)

In the process of writing this work I relocated to Vancouver, British Columbia. Shortly after arriving, an Aboriginal woman was thrown from her Single Room Occupancy hotel room window in the Downtown Eastside and fell to her death on the sidewalk below.[1] Hers followed the death of another young woman who was also pushed out of a window of this very same hotel a year and a day prior. Dozens more Aboriginal women have been murdered or have gone missing from the Downtown Eastside in the past years and one need only walk down the streets of this part of town to see the most extreme outcomes of the current system at work. And yet Vancouver has been voted the "most livable city" in the world for nearly ten years in a row. No one appears to have asked Aboriginal women to vote in this poll.

This trend of denying the continued effects of colonialism, racism and sexism for Aboriginal peoples and hence, of treating the bodies of Aboriginal women as inherently violable and their lives as disposable, is certainly not unique to Vancouver (Simpson 2014). The Native Women's Association of Canada has documented that across the country over six hundred Aboriginal women are either missing or have been murdered in the past twenty years. Others, like Gladys Radek or Maryanne

Pearce, claim the number is much higher, currently at over twelve hundred (Pearce 2013). Couple this trend with the rampant social, economic and health problems experienced by many Aboriginal peoples and which lead some to resort to drugs, alcohol and prostitution to get by, or the increasingly high rates of incarceration of both Aboriginal men and women in prisons, and I am unsure how one cannot conclude these realities to be inherent problems of the system under which Indigenous peoples are forced to live.

Coercive sterilization is not unrelated to these other realities faced by Aboriginal women and their peoples. The central purpose of this work has been not only to begin the task of shedding light on how and why the practice of sterilization was imposed on Aboriginal women but to argue the connections between this practice and the larger historical material relations of Canadian society. Reproductive abuses like coercive sterilization must be understood as arising from and serving to perpetuate the very same system that has consistently sought to gain access to Indigenous lands and resources and to reduce consequent federal obligations, and hence that has consistently denied Aboriginal women and their peoples the right to exist on their own terms in the ways they so choose.

Aboriginal peoples in Canada know too well the realities their peoples have faced. As Canadians, we need to become aware not only of this past but also of the present choices our government is forcing on Aboriginal peoples, choices that inevitably require Indigenous peoples to give up the basic and inherent rights that not only define them as Indigenous peoples but also ensure their continued survival. More recent initiatives surrounding land claim negotiations, self-government agreements and economic development ventures in Aboriginal communities are often purported by federal bureaucrats to be positive advances for, and a change in official state policy towards, Aboriginal peoples. These initiatives are also said, sometimes by Aboriginal peoples as well, to be effective means of increasing economic opportunities; of providing much-needed funds to enable the development of schools, infrastructure and social programs on reserves; and as steps toward the long sought after independence from the Canadian state by ensuring a base upon which to rebuild nations. A few Aboriginal communities have managed opportunities presented to them and become economically successful in Indigenous-owned or -operated enterprises in mining and resource extraction, gaming on reserve or hospitality and tourism.

However, critics argue that the options being presented to Indigenous nations consistently fall short of what is needed to ensure the sovereignty of communities; that these often represent further steps toward assimilation by involving some Aboriginal peoples in the exploitation of their lands and resources, to the benefit of corporations and a select few individuals and in ways that are unsustainable from an ecological or human perspective. Scholar Taiaiake Alfred explains that without fundamentally questioning the approach to power taken by the Canadian state, the assumptions of colonialism continue to structure the relationship between

Indigenous and non-Indigenous peoples, and any progress made toward justice will be marginal. In fact, it will be tolerated only to the extent that it serves, or at least does not oppose, the interests of the state itself. Alfred writes:

> For example, the ongoing example of "aboriginal rights and title" by the Supreme Court since the 1980s is widely seen as progress. Yet, even with a legal recognition of collective rights to certain subsistence activities within certain territories, Indigenous peoples are still subject to state control in the exercise of their inherent freedoms and powers. They must meet state defined criteria for Aboriginal identity in order to gain access to these legal rights. Given Canada's shameful history, defining Aboriginal rights in terms of, for example, a right to fish for food and traditional purposes is better than nothing. But to what extent does the state regulated "right" to food-fish represent justice for people who have been fishing on their rivers and seas since time began? (Alfred 2009b: 81–82)

Expanding on this point, he continues:

> To argue on behalf of Indigenous nationhood within the dominant Western paradigm is self-defeating. To frame the struggle to achieve justice in terms of Indigenous "claims" against the state is implicitly to accept the fiction of state sovereignty. Indigenous peoples are by definition the original inhabitants of the land. They had complex societies and systems of government. And they never gave consent to European ownership of territory or the establishment of European sovereignty over them (treaties did not do this, according to both historic Native understandings and contemporary legal analysis). These are indisputable realities based on empirically verifiable facts. So why are Indigenous efforts to achieve legal recognition of these facts framed as claims? The mythology of the state is hegemonic, and the struggle for justice would be better served by undermining the myth of state sovereignty than by carving out a small and dependent space for Indigenous peoples within it. (Alfred 2009b: 148–49)

Others also criticize federal Indian policy as being a continuation of the same previously held goals: of separating Aboriginal peoples from their lands and resources and of reducing the number of those to whom the federal government has obligations. Scholar and activist Pamela Palmater argues the reliance of the federal government on the Indian Act and its attendant registration provisions is evidence of a continuing desire to undermine Indigenous ways of life and limit those considered Aboriginal. She writes:

> What is happening now is a legislated form of population reduction which is based on the government's previous goal of assimilation. The

ultimate effect of the legislation, despite changes in official policy with
regard to assimilation, is to reduce the number of people the government
must be accountable to in terms of protection, treaty obligations, land
rights, self-government, and other Aboriginal rights, including a whole
series of culturally specific programs and services that are provided today.
(Palmater 2011a: 47)

If followed to its natural progression, federal policy and practice as established
through the Indian Act, as set out in modern land claim negotiations or as laid
out most recently through the numerous pieces of legislation that impact nearly
every aspect of the lives of Aboriginal peoples, will slowly but surely eliminate the
number of those able to claim collective and inherent, constitutionally protected
and internationally recognized Aboriginal or Treaty rights to lands and resources
(Diabo 2012: Palmater 2011a: 43–54).[2] Canada will have managed to finally and
successfully deal with the "Indian problem" that has plagued it since its inception.

Although this final chapter has yet to be written, these criticisms tell us that
there are fundamental problems with the manner in which the federal government is
dealing with Indigenous grievances. The situation in many communities continues
to be extreme. Aboriginal peoples are often the first to experience the harmful health
and environmental effects of economic development initiatives on their lands, and
the course of action pursued by federal policies has created deep divides, sometimes between Aboriginal and non-Aboriginal peoples, and other times within or
between nations. Debate and differences are not to be shied away from. However,
the options and initiatives from which Aboriginal peoples are expected to choose
and the often dire circumstances in which they must make choices can hardly be
viewed as just. One must wonder what kind of choices Indigenous peoples would
make to ensure the survival of their nations if the choice was between more than
simply surviving and nothing at all.

Part of the problem with recent federal initiatives to address Aboriginal grievances has more to do with the fact that Canada refuses to view Aboriginal peoples
as nations in their own right. If it were to do so, it would need to recognize that
Aboriginal peoples are entitled to all that other peoples are entitled to, without
stipulations, including: the land and resource base upon which to subsist, and the
right to make use of these on their own terms; the right to develop and implement
their own institutions based on their own values, ideologies and histories, and to
have these respected as such; and the right to make their own decisions about who
belongs to their nations, and to teach their children in ways that are in keeping with
their own ways of life. These rights have been most recently affirmed and recognized
in the *United Nations Declaration on the Rights of Indigenous Peoples* adopted by the
General Assembly in 2007, and which Canada eventually committed to uphold-
ing in 2010.[3] Once the sovereign rights of Aboriginal peoples are respected, there
exists the possibility that they might continue along the path already set out, and

this choice is for Aboriginal peoples to make. However, with this freedom also comes the possibility that Indigenous peoples might choose to make decisions that are contrary to the needs of the political economy, to the desires of the Canadian government and to the wants of private corporations, and this is what is feared most by those in power.

Indigenous ways of life have consistently stood in opposition to the ideologies, values and ways of relating to each other and the natural world that are inherent to the capitalist mode of production of Canadian society and by and large they continue to stand in opposition to these today, as evidenced by the many instances of Indigenous peoples as the first line of defense against environmentally destructive resources-extraction projects. It is exactly these ways of life which need to be respected in order to properly address grievances against Aboriginal peoples. Patricia Monture tells us:

> Whatever the issue, be it child welfare, criminal justice, family violence, alcohol and drugs, or lack of education or employment, the same path can be traced to a conflict in the basic values of the two societies — force and coercion versus consensus and cooperation. This realization, then, can take us to only one conclusion: First Nations demands for self-determination (sovereignty) must be realized ... Failure to meet this challenge will continue to result in further piecemeal legislative reforms. The inevitable consequence will be the genocide of First Nations people. (Monture 1991: 195)

However troublesome a proposal this might be to those who benefit from the current order of things, the possibilities that come from Aboriginal peoples exerting their inherent rights to live according to their own ways should represent exciting alternatives for Canadian citizens. Whether or not Canadians are aware of their own exploitation that results from the current political and economic system, and whether or not they are prepared to advocate for revolutionary changes to the relations that exist between them, their government and the corporations that assert increasing control over all aspects of their lives, growing numbers do agree that something is simply not working with respect to the current system; that it is indeed having grave negative impacts on their own health and wellbeing and that of their families, and that it is destroying the environment. To stand up and speak out against the longstanding policies and practices imposed on Aboriginal peoples by the Canadian state is not only necessary and just, and part of the responsibility Canadians have acquired as treaty partners and settlers on these lands, but it also holds the possibility of creating a better world for all of us to enjoy. Monture continues:

> I think it is now time that the tables were turned and we question the motivations of those who staunchly refuse to agree to the positive changes

> Aboriginal peoples seek. Non-Aboriginal people could be of great as-
> sistance if they assisted us in turning the conversation around so that
> Canada is required to be accountable for the wrongs it has perpetuated.
> (Monture 1991: 253)

Canadians have a role to play in ensuring the survival of Aboriginal peoples as distinct and independent peoples. We also need to understand that the choices we make in this respect will determine our survival as well.

Over thirty years ago, longtime activist and scholar George Manuel wrote that the failure of Canadians to heed the plea for a new approach to Indigenous–settler relations is a failure of the imagination (Manuel and Posluns 1974: 224). Canadians need to exercise their imagination while coming to terms with the past in order to create new ways of interrelating with each other, ways that are not destructive to us, others or the natural world on which we all depend. Paulette Regan stresses that neither can we leave the critical task of social change up to governments and courts. We, as people, must lead the way. She implores us to shake ourselves from the complacency that comes with being the dominant culture; to think about who we have been and to face this history honestly and with courage; and to challenge the assumptions and myths of our history so that we can engage in a deeper dia-logue with Indigenous peoples about what really constitutes a just reconciliation and peace (Regan 2005). In the spirit of these goals, this work seeks to contrib-ute to existing scholarship by buttressing longstanding claims that the coercive sterilization of Aboriginal women did indeed take place. It begins the process of documenting instances of abuse while also providing a context in which to make sense of these crimes. By highlighting the role of the federal government in allow-ing coercive sterilization to take place it poses pressing questions about federal actions and inactions for which Aboriginal peoples and the general public deserve answers. Moreover, this work links past practices to present policies by providing a larger historical and material context in which to understand many of the reali-ties faced by Aboriginal women and their peoples, and by encouraging us to take a broader view of the attack on the reproductive lives of Indigenous women, one which connects this to the longstanding struggles of Indigenous peoples for basic human rights and services, for control over lands and resources and ultimately, for self-determination. As was indicated by Martin Lukacs in his piece on the Commission of Inquiry into the large number of missing and murdered women in Vancouver, an inquiry that lost credibility before it even began in the eyes of those who live and struggle daily with the realities of marginalization and exploitation:

> It is not sexism or racism alone that is to blame. It is an entire system of
> inhumane relations with Aboriginal peoples, upheld by a society that
> has swallowed the country's forests, rivers, minerals and their original
> owners and spit them out as strangers in their own land. Dispossessed
> and subjected to wrenching poverty, culturally demeaned and lacking

access to services and housing, Aboriginal women are left exposed and vulnerable to all-too-ordinary predators. Predators who act assuming their victims will not be missed. Predators who believe they will escape with impunity. (Lukacs 2011)

The Canadian state and private interests have been the biggest predators of all when one considers the historical and present-day mistreatment of Indigenous women and their peoples. And they too have, up to this point, been allowed to escape with relative impunity. It is up to all of us to decide how long these injustices are allowed to continue.

Notes

1. A Single Room Occupancy, or SRO, is a multiple-tenant building that houses people in individual rooms, often with the shared use of a bathroom and/or kitchen. Many SROs in the Downtown Eastside are considered unsafe and inadequate housing, often in dilapidated conditions, infested with pests and lacking security.

2. Some examples of these bills include: Bill C-27: *First Nations Financial Transparency Act*; Bill C-45: *Jobs and Growth Act, 2012*; Bill S-2: *Family Homes on Reserves and Matrimonial Interests or Rights Act*; Bill S-6: *First Nations Elections Act*; Bill S-8: *Safe Drinking Water for First Nations*; Bill C-428: *Indian Act Amendment and Replacement Act*; Bill S-207: *An Act to Amend the Interpretation Act (non derogation of Aboriginal and treaty rights)*; Bill S-212: *First Nations Self-Government Recognition*; Bill C-10: *Safe Streets and Communities Act*.

3. The *United Nations Declaration on the Rights of Indigenous Peoples*, Resolution adopted by the General Assembly, 13 September 2007, <un.org/esa/socdev/unpfii/documents/DRIPS_en.pdf>. Despite the Declaration not being legally binding, Canada initially refused to endorse it, citing concerns with its provisions including: ownership over lands, territories and resources; free, prior and informed consent when used as a veto; self-government without recognition of the importance of negotiations; intellectual property; military issues; and the need to achieve an appropriate balance between the rights and obligations of Indigenous peoples, the state and third parties. Canada eventually signed the Declaration on 12 November 2010. It has yet to take any formal steps to implement legislation to enforce it, and it continues to make decisions on issues affecting Aboriginal peoples and their lands, territories and lives without obtaining their free, prior and informed consent.

References

Archival Sources

British Columbia Archives and Record Services, GR 496, "Some Aspects of Eugenical Sterilization in British Columbia with Special Reference to Patients Sterilized from Essondale Provincial Mental Hospital Since 1935," Box 38, file 3, Provincial Secretary Correspondence, M. Stewart, 17 August 1945.

Library and Archives Canada, MG 28 I 233, "Prevention of Blindness — Sterilization Project," Volume 21, File 8, 1936-1939, Correspondence from A.R. Kaufman to CNIB, Toronto Chapter, 2 December 1938.

____. RG 58-C-1, Attest Audit Files, "Historical Files From 1974 and Prior Department of Health and Welfare Coqualeetza Indian Hospital — Audit (1964)." Volume 256, File Part 1, 1964, Report by G.P. Anderson, Audit of Coqualeetza Indian Hospital Report, Submitted to Mr. Douglas, 28 September 1964.

____. RG 85, "Sterilization of Imbeciles," Volume 901, File 10109, Correspondence from Gibson to Daly, 30 December 1938.

____. RG 85, "Sterilization of Imbeciles," Volume 901, File 10109, Correspondence from Daly to Gibson, 4 January 1939.

____. RG 85, "Sterilization of Imbeciles," Volume 901, File 10109, Précis, Northwest Territories Council, pp.1-2, 14 January 1939.

____. RG 85, "Sterilization of Imbeciles," Volume 901, File 10109, Memorandum from Deputy Commissioner Gibson to Major McKeand, member of the Northwest Territories Council, 17 January 1939.

____. RG 85, "Sterilization of Imbeciles," Volume 901, File 10109, Correspondence from J.A. Bildfell, M.D. to the Director, Northwest Territories Division of the Department of Mines and Resources, 17 September 1941.

____. RG 85, "Sterilization of Imbeciles," Volume 901, File 10109, Correspondence, letter returned to D.L. McKeand, from Deputy Commissioner Gibson, 14 November 1941.

____. RG 85, "Sterilization of Imbeciles," Volume 901, File 10109, Extract from the Minutes of the One Hundred and Thirty-fourth Session of the Northwest Territories Council held on 21 November 1941.

____. RG 85, "Sterilization of Imbeciles," Volume 901, File 10109, Correspondence from J.J. Heagerty, M. D. to R.A. Gibson, 25 November 1941.

____. RG 29, "Mental Diseases," Volume 2971, File 851-4-300 pt. 1A, Correspondence from P.E. Moore, Director, Indian Health Services to Deputy Minister of National Health, 3 November 1953.

____. RG 29, "Mental Diseases," Volume 2971, File 851-4-300 pt. 1A, Correspondence from C.A. Roberts, M.D., Chief, Mental Health Division, to Director, Health Insurance Studies, 10 November 1953.

____. RG 29, "Mental Diseases," Volume 2971, File 851-4-300 pt. 1A, Correspondence from Gordon E. Wride, M.D., Assistant Director, Health Insurance Studies, to G.D.W.

Cameron, M.D., Deputy Minister of National Health, 14 November 1953.

____. RG 29, "Mental Diseases," Volume 2971, File 851-4-300 pt. 1A, Correspondence from W. S. Barclay, Regional Superintendent, Pacific Region, Indian Health Services, to A. L. Henderson, Research Analyst, Hospital for Mental Diseases, Brandon Manitoba, 23 February 1956.

____. RG 29, "Mental Diseases," Volume 2971, File 851-4-300, pt. 1A, Correspondence from C.A. Roberts, M.D., Principal Medical Officer, Mental Health, to Director, Indian Health Services, 28 September 1956.

____. RG 29, "Mental Diseases," Volume 2971, File 851-4-300, pt. 1A, Correspondence from the Department of Indian Affairs to P.E. Moore, Director, Indian and Northern Health Services, Department of National Health and Welfare, 10 January 1957.

____. RG 29, "Birth Control," Volume 2869, File 851-1-5 pt. 1 A, Correspondence from P. E. Moore to Regional Superintendent, Saskatchewan, 20 August 1957.

____. RG 29, "Birth Control," Volume 2869, File 851-1-5, pt. 1A, Correspondence from S. Mallick, Sioux Lookout Zone Superintendent, to H. A. Proctor, Director General, Medical Services, 15 December 1964.

____. RG 29, "Birth Control," Volume 2869, File 851-1-5, pt. 1A, Directives issued by the Department of National Health and Welfare, Medical Services, to Zone Superintendents, 5 April 1965.

____. RG 29, "Birth Control," Volume 2869, File 8851-1-5 pt.1A, Correspondence from H.A. Proctor to Zone Superintendents, 27 August 1965.

____. RG 29, "Birth Control," Volume 2869, File 851-1-5, pt.1A, Correspondence from C.S. Gamble, Superintendent, Nanaimo Region, to Pacific Region Superintendent, 2 September 1965.

____. RG 29, "Birth Control," Volume 2869, File 851-1-5, pt. 1A, Correspondence from Regional Superintendent, Saskatchewan Region to H.A. Proctor, Director General, Medical Services, 3 September 1965.

____. RG 29, "Birth Control," Volume 2869, File 851-1-5, pt. 1A, Correspondence from Inuvik Zone Superintendent to Foothills Superintendent, 8 September, 1965.

____. RG 29, "Birth Control," Volume 2869, File 851-1-5, pt. 1A, Correspondence from J.D. Galbraith, Coqualeetza Hospital, Zone Superintendent, Sardis, to Regional Superintendent, Pacific Region, 8 September 1965.

____. RG 29, "Birth Control," Volume 2869, File 851-1-5, pt. 1A, Correspondence from R.D. Thompson, Superintendent, Pacific Region, to H.A. Proctor, Director General, Medical Services, Department of National Health and Welfare, 13 September 1965.

____. RG 29, "Birth Control," Volume 2869, File 851-1-5, pt. 1A, Correspondence from L.R. Hurtle, Superintendent, Atlantic Zone, 20 September 1965.

____. RG 29, "Birth Control," Volume 2869, File 851-1-5, pt. 1A, Correspondence from M. Savoie, Superintendent, Quebec Zone, to Eastern Region Superintendent, 21 September 1965.

____. RG 29, "Birth Control," Volume 2869, File 851-1-5, pt. 1A, Correspondence from M.E. Gordon, Zone Superintendent, Prince Rupert, to R. D. Thompson, Regional Superintendent, Pacific Region, and forwarded to H. A. Proctor, 24 September 1965.

____. RG 29, "Birth Control," Volume 2869, File 851-1-5, pt. 1A, Correspondence from H.A. Proctor, to Commander J. Coulter, Special Planning Secretariat, 1 October 1965.

____. RG 29, "Birth Control," Volume 2869, File 851-1-5, pt. 1A, Internal handwritten memo written by Proctor, n.d.

____. RG 29, "Birth Control," Volume 2869, File 851-1-5, pt. 1A, Correspondence from Kahn Tineta Horn, to R. F. Battle, Director, Indian Affairs Branch, Indian and Northern Affairs, 28 January 1966.

____. RG 29, "Birth Control," Volume 2869, File 851-1-5, pt. 1A, Correspondence from H.A. Proctor to Chief Delisle, 17 February 1966.

____. RG 29, "Birth Control," Volume 2869, File 851-1-5, pt. 1A, Correspondence from T. J. Orford, Regional Director, Saskatchewan, to H. A. Proctor, Director General, Medical Services, 16 March 1966.

____. RG 29, "Birth Control," Volume 2869, File 851-1-5, pt. 1A, Correspondence from H. A. Proctor, Director General, Medical Services, 6 April 1966.

____. RG 29, "Birth Control," Volume 2869, File 851-1-5, pt. 1A, Memorandum from Minister of Health to Dr. J. N. Crawford, Deputy Minister of Health, 12 February 1969.

____. RG 29, "Birth Control," Volume 2869, File 851-1-5, pt. 1B, Correspondence from J.H. Wiebe, M.D., Director, Medical Services, 2 October 1970.

____. RG 29, "Birth Control," Volume 2869, File 851-1-5, pt. 1B, Correspondence from J.H. Wiebe, M.D., Director, Medical Services, to Maurice Leclair, M.D., Deputy Minister of National Health, 27 October 1970.

____. RG 29, "Birth Control," Volume 2869, File 851-1-5, pt. 2, Newspaper clipping, "Eskimo Sterilization Inhumane — Lewis," n.d.

____. RG 29, "Birth Control," Volume 2869, File 851-1-5, pt. 2, Correspondence from A.P. Abbott, to J. MacDonald, 28 July 1971.

____. RG 29, "Birth Control," Volume 2869, File 851-1-5, pt. 2, Correspondence from J. H. Wiebe, M. D., Director, Medical Services, to Regional Directors, 8 October 1971.

____. RG 29, "Birth Control," Volume 2869, File 851-1-5, pt. 2, Memorandum from J.H. Wiebe, M.D., Director, Medical Services, to Dr. Maurice Leclair, Deputy Minister of Health, 19 October 1971.

____. RG 29, "Birth Control," Volume 2870, File 851-1-5, pt. 3A, Guidelines for Tubal Ligation issued to Regional Director, Northern Region from O. J. Rath, Regional Director, Alberta Region, 1 April 1970.

____. RG 29, "Birth Control," Volume 2870, File 851-1-5, pt. 3A, Correspondence from Regional Director, Medical Services, Northern Region, Guidelines for Approval of Sterilization Procedures, 10 November 1970.

____. RG 29, "Birth Control," Volume 2870, File 851-1-5, pt. 3A, Memorandum from R. P. Beck, M. D. Professor and Chairman of the Department of Obstetrics and Gynaecology from the University of Alberta, to Attending staff and nurses, 20 September 1971.

____. RG 29, "Birth Control," Volume 2870, File 851-1-5, pt.3A, Correspondence from R.R.M. Croome, M. D. Executive Director, Charles Camsell Hospital, to Dr. O. J. Rath, Regional Director, Alberta Region, 24 February 1972.

____. RG 29, "Birth Control," Volume 2870, File 851-1-5, pt. 3A, Correspondence from M.L. Webb, Assistant Deputy Minister, Medical Services, to Dr. O. J. Rath, Regional Director, Alberta Region, 12 April 1972.

____. RG 29, "Birth Control," Volume 2870, File 851-1-5, pt. 3A, Correspondence from M. L. Webb, Assistant Deputy Minister, Medical Services, to Dr. Maurice Leclair, Deputy Minister of National Health, 5 April 1973.

____. RG 29, "Birth Control," Volume 2870, File 851-1-5, pt. 3A, Transcript of interview conducted by Jim Eayrs with Brian Gunn, Canadian Broadcasting Corporation program, Weekend, 8 April 1973, 8.

____. RG 29, "Birth Control," Volume 2870, File 851-1-5, pt.3A, Correspondence from M. L. Webb, Assistant Deputy Minister, Medical Services, to Dr. Maurice Leclair, Deputy Minister of National Health, 13 April 1973.

____. RG 29, "Birth Control," Volume 2870, File 851-1-5, pt. 3A, Correspondence from Marc Lalonde to Laurent Picard, President, Canadian Broadcasting Corporation, 6 April 1973. Also reprinted in The MacKenzie Pilot, May 3, 1973, pp. 29–30.

____. RG 29, "Birth Control," Volume 2870, File 851-1-5, pt. 3B, Correspondence from V.L. Urbanoski, Zone Director to F.J. Covill, Regional Director, Medical Services, Northwest Territories Region, n.d.

____. RG 29, "Birth Control," Volume 2870, File 851-1-5, pt. 3B, Correspondence, "Sterilizations — Minister's Briefing Book," from N.L. Fraser, Zone Director, Ontario, to Director General, Medical Services, n.d.

____. RG 29, "Birth Control," Volume 2870, File 851-1-5, pt. 3B, Correspondence from M.L. Webb, M.D., Assistant Deputy Minister, Medical Services, to the Regional Director, Northern Region, Therapeutic Abortions at the Frobisher Bay General Hospital, 7 April 1972.

____. RG 29, "Birth Control," Volume 2870, File 851-1-5, pt. 3B, C.M.L. Webb, Assistant Deputy Minister, Medical Services, to A.D. Hunt, Assistant Deputy Minister, Northern Affairs Program, 1 May 1973.

____. RG 29, "Birth Control," Volume 2870, File 851-1-5, pt. 3B, A.D. Hunt, Assistant Deputy Minister, Northern Affairs Program, 1 June 1973.

____. RG 29, "Birth Control," Volume 2870, File 851-1-5, pt. 3B, Correspondence, "Sterilizations — Minister's Briefing Book," from Hospital Administrator, Frobisher Bay Hospital, N.W.T. to Director General, Medical Services Branch, 31 January 1974.

____. RG 29, "Birth Control," Volume 2870, File 851-1-5, pt. 3B, Correspondence, "Sterilizations — Minister's Briefing Book," from A. Schwartz, Regional Director, Manitoba Region, to Dr. L.B., Director General, Medical Services Branch, 5 February 1974.

____. RG 29, "Birth Control," Volume 2870, File 851-1-5, pt. 3B, Correspondence, "Sterilizations — Minister's Briefing Book," from W.G. Goldthorpe, Zone Director, Sioux Lookout, to Director General, Medical Services Branch, 6 February 1974.

____. RG 29, "Birth Control," Volume 2870, File 851-1-5, pt. 3B, Correspondence, "Sterilizations — Minister's Briefing Book," from M.P.D. Waldron, Acting Regional Director, Alberta Region, to Director General, Medical Services Branch, 12 February 1974.

____. RG 29, "Birth Control," Volume 2870, File 851-1-5, pt. 3B, Correspondence, "Sterilizations — Minister's Briefing Book," from Zone Director, Inuvik Zone, to Director General, Medical Services Branch, 28 February 1974.

____. RG 29, "Birth Control," Volume 2870, File 851-1-5, pt. 3B, Correspondence from Maurice Leclair to B.D. Dewar, Assistant Deputy Minister of Medical Services on 24 May 1974.

____. RG 29, "Birth Control," Volume 2870, File 851-1-5, pt. 3B, Correspondence from F.J. Covill, Regional Director, Medical Services, Northwest Territories Region, to Director General, Program Management, Medical Services Branch, 11 June 1974.

____. RG 29, "Birth Control," Volume 2870, File 851-1-5, pt. 3B, Correspondence from Mr. Bell to Minister Lalonde, 19 December 1974.

____. RG 29, "Birth Control," Volume 2870, File 851-1-5, pt. 3C, Abortions and

Sterilizations, 1974, at Medical Services Branch Hospitals, n.d.

____. RG 29, Volume 2870, File 851-1-5, pt. 3C, Robert Lechat, "Sterilization of Inuit is Exposed as National Scandal," Sunday Express, 4 pps., n.d.

____. RG 29, "Birth Control," Volume 2870, File 851-1-5, pt. 4, Correspondence from Parliamentary Returns Division, to Mr. Charles Caron, Assistant Deputy Minister, Medical Services, regarding question No. 765, 25 October 1976.

____. RG 29, "Birth Control," Volume 2870, File 851-1-5, pt. 4, Information Release, Parliamentary Returns Officer, 1 December 1976.

Provincial Archives of Ontario, RG 8-5, Correspondence of the Provincial Secretary, "Sterilization [between 1934 and 1943]," Box 115, Correspondence from J.L. Dixon to Honourable H.C. Nixon, Provincial Secretary, 20 March 1942.

____. RG 10-1, "Correspondence of Dennis R. Timbrell, Minister of Health, 1979-1981," RG 10-1-3.

____. RG 10-107, Container 80: "Indian Patients 1926-1949," Files Reference Code RG 10-107-0-516, Correspondence, H.M. Robbins, Deputy Provincial Secretary, to Bursar, Ontario Hospital, Hamilton Ontario, 18 August 1926.

____. RG 10-107, Container 147: "Dept. of Indian Affairs 1950," File Reference Code RG 10-107-0-942, Correspondence, T.M. Gourlay, Executive Officer, Ontario Department of Health, to all Superintendents, 25 August 1953.

____. RG 10-6, Correspondence of the Deputy Minister of Health, "Legislation — Sexual Sterilization Act. 1948-1960," File Reference Code RG 10-6-0-1072.

____. RG 10-6, Correspondence of the Deputy Minister of Health, "Legislation — Sexual Sterilization Act. 1948-1960," File Reference Code RG 10-6-0-1072, Correspondence from B.T. McGhie, M.D. to Dr. S.J.W. Horne, 11 September 1933.

____. RG 10-6 Correspondence of the Deputy Minister of Health, "Legislation — Sexual Sterilization Act. 1948-1960," File Reference Code RG 10-6-0-1072, Correspondence from R.C. Montgomery, M.D. to Dr. S.J.W. Horne, 17 February 1938.

Court Cases

A.W. and D.W. By Litigation Guardian, the Public Guardian and Trustee of B.C. v. British Columbia, 2002 BCSC 976.

A.W. and D.W. v. British Columbia; Richard v. British Columbia, 2003 BCCA 589, 31 October 2003.

Arishenkoff v. British Columbia, 2002 BCSC 951, 22 July 2002.

Arishenkoff v. British Columbia, 2005 BCCA 481, 6 October 2005.

Base v. Hadley et al., 2006 NWTSC 04, 1 January 2006.

Beadle v. British Columbia, 1996 BCSC 8661, 11 October 1996.

D.E. (Guardian ad litem) v. British Columbia, 2003 BCSC 1013, 23 June 2003.

D.E. (Guardian ad litem) v. British Columbia, 2005, 252 DLR BCLR (4th) 713.

D.L.W. v. Alberta (Minister of Social Services), 1992 A.J. 530, 5 June 1992.

J.H. v. British Columbia, 1998 BCJ, 2926, 8 December 1998.

K.L.B. v. British Columbia, 1996 BCJ, 3036, 11 October 1996.

Lytton v. Alberta; Barrett v. Alberta; Busch v. Alberta, Alberta Court of Queen's Bench, 1996 ABQB 895, 18 October 1996.

Lytton v. Alberta, 1999 ABQB 421, 10 May 1999.

L.R. v. British Columbia, 1999 BCCA 698, 26 November 1999.

M.S.Z. v. M., 2008 YKSC 73, 1 October 2008.

Murray v. McMurchy, 1949 BCSC 989.

People v. Johnson, California Supreme Court, No. 29390, 2 January 1991.

Re Eskimos, 1939 SCR 10.

Reibl v. Hughes, 1980 SCC 880.

Richard v. British Columbia, 2003 BCJ 1466.

Richard v. British Columbia; A.W. and D.W. (Litigation Guardian of) v. British Columbia, 2004 BCCA 337, 15 June 2004.

Richard v. British Columbia; A.W. and D.W. By Litigation Guardian, the Public Guardian and Trustee of B. C. v. British Columbia, 2003 BCSC 976, 20 June 2003.

Richard v. British Columbia; A.W. and D.W. (Litigation Guardian of) v. British Columbia, 2004 BCCA 337, 15 June 2004.

Richard v. British Columbia, 2007 BCSC 1107, 7 and 8 June 2007.

Richard v. British Columbia, 2007 BCSC 1107, 23 July 2007.

Richard v. British Columbia, 2007 BCCA 570, 9 November 2007.

Richard v. British Columbia, 2008 BCCA 53, 1 February 2008.

Richard v. British Columbia, 2008 BCSC 1274, 22 September 2008.

Richard v. British Columbia, 2008 BCCA 549, 1 December 2008.

Richard v. British Columbia, 2009 BCCA 77, 13 February 2009.

Richard v. British Columbia, 2009 BCCA 185, 30 April 2009.

Richard v. British Columbia, 2010 BCJ 1363, 7 July 2010.

Rumley v. British Columbia, 2002 BCSC 1300, 6 September 2002.

Muir v. Alberta, [1996] 132 DLR (4th) 695.

Winnipeg Child and Family Services (Northwest Area) v. G. (D.F.), 1997 SCR 925, 31 October 1997.

Statutes

Statutes of Canada. 2000. *Crimes Against Humanity and War Crimes Act*, SC 2000, c. 24.

____. 1985. *Canadian Criminal Code*, RS, c. C-34, s. 45.

____. 1982. *Charter of Rights and Freedoms*, Part I of the *Constitution Act*, 1982 being Schedule B to the *Canada Act* 1982 (U.K.), 1982, c. 11.

____. 1969. *Omnibus Bill C-150, The Criminal Law Amendment Act*, 1968-69, c. 38.

____. 1960. *Canadian Bill of Rights: An Act for the Recognition and Protection of Human Rights and Fundamental Freedoms*, SC 1960, c. 44.

____. 1956. *An Act to Amend the Canadian Citizenship Act*, RSC 1956, c. 6, s. 9.

____. 1952. Indian Health Regulations, s. 72(1)(f) of the *Indian Act* of 1952, RSC c. 149.

____. 1951. *An Act to Amend the Indian Act*, RSC 1951, c. I-5.

____. 1946. *Canadian Citizenship Act*, SC 1946, c. 15.

____. 1927. *The Indian Act*, SC 1927, c. 98.

____. 1914. *An Act to Amend the Indian Act*, SC 1914, c. 35.

____. 1898. *An Act to Amend the Indian Act*, RSC 1898, c. 34.

____. 1886. *The Indian Act*, SC 1886, c. 28, s.5.

____. 1884. *An Act to Further Amend the Indian Act*, 1880, SC 1884, c. 27, s. 5.

____. 1880. *An Act to Amend the Indian Act*, SC 1880, 43 c. 28.

____. 1879. *The Indian Act*, SC 1879, 42, c. 34.

____. 1872. *An Act Respecting the Public Lands of the Dominion* (April 14).

Statutes of Alberta. 2008. *Alberta Evidence Amendment Act*, RSA 2008, Amending RSA 2000 c. A-18.

____. 1980. *Limitation of Actions Act*, RSA 1980, c. L-5, s. 53.

____. 1972a. *Individual Rights Protection Act*, SA 1972, c. 2

____. 1972b. *Sexual Sterilization Repeal Act* 1972 c. 87, s. 1.

____. 1966. *Alberta Human Rights Act*, RSA 1966, c. 39.

____. 1942. *Sexual Sterilization Act*, RSA 1942, c. 194.

____. 1937. *Sexual Sterilization Act*, RSA 1937, c. 47.

____. 1928. *Sexual Sterilization Act*, SA 1928, c. 37.

Statutes of British Columbia. 2006. *Apology Act*, SBC 2006, c. 19.

____. 1996. *Limitation Act*, RSBC 1996, c. 266.

____. 1974. *Crown Proceedings Act*, SBC 1974, c. 24.

____. 1973a. *Human Rights Code of British Columbia Act*, SBC 1973, c. 119.

____. 1973b. *Sexual Sterilization Act Repeal Act*, SBC 1973.

____. 1933. *Sexual Sterilization Act*, SBC 1933, c. 59.

United Nations General Assembly. 1948a. *Universal Declaration of Human Rights*, December 10. 217A (III). <unhcr.org/refworld/docid/3ae6b3712c.html>.

____. 1948b. *Convention on the Prevention and Punishment of the Crime of Genocide*, December 9. A/RES/260. <unhcr.org/refworld/docid/c3b00f0873.html>.

Government Publications

Alberta. *Hansard*, 11 March 1998.

____. *Hansard*, 10 March 1998.

____. *Hansard*, 9 March 1998.

____. *Hansard*, 7 November 1994.

____. *Hansard*, 31 May 1972.

____. *Hansard*, 14 April 1972.

British Columbia, *Hansard*, 6 March 2008.

____. *Hansard*, 25 April, 2006.

____. *Hansard*, 6 April, 2006.

____. *Hansard*, 29 March, 2006.

____. *Hansard*, 24 November 2005.

____. *Hansard*, 1 March 2005.

____. *Hansard*, 5 April 1973.

Canada, *House of Commons Debate*, 17 March 1977.

____. *House of Commons Debate*, 25 February 1977.

____. *House of Commons Debate*, 25 October 1976.

____. *House of Commons Debate*, 10 October 1974.

____. *House of Commons Debate*, 11 January 1974.

____. *House of Commons Debate*, 2 April 1973.

____. *House of Commons Debate*, 1 November 1971.

____. *House of Commons Debate*, 14 October, 1970.

____. *House of Commons Debate*, 9 October, 1970.

____. *House of Commons Debate*, 13 April 1970.

____. *House of Commons Debate*, 7 April 1970

____. *House of Commons Debate*, 21 May 1952.

____. *House of Commons Debates* 22 May 1883.

____. *Senate Debates*, 21 April 1970.

____. *Senate Debates*, 16 April 1970.

____. *Senate Debates*, 22 January 1969.

____. *Senate Debates*, 17 June 1969.

____. *Senate Debates*, 17 December 1968.

____. *Senate Debates*, 9 December 1968.

____. *Senate Debates*, 9 May 1967.

____. *Senate Debates*, 9 November 1966.

____. *Sessional Papers*, Volume 11, Number 27, 1904.

Northwest Territories, *Hansard*, 4 June 1998.

Badgley, R.F. 1977. *Report of the Committee on the Operation of the Abortion Law*. Ottawa: Supply and Services.

Blair, W.R.N. 1969. *Mental Health in Alberta: A Report on the Alberta Mental Health Study, 1968*. Edmonton: Government of Alberta.

British Columbia. 2003. Executive Council. "Woodlands Apology." *Transcript of Open Cabinet Meeting*, May 30. <corporate.gov.bc.ca/open_cabinet/down/tran/open_cabinet_meeting_may_30_2003.htm>.

British Columbia Task Force on Access to Contraception and Abortion Services. 1994. *Realizing Choices: The Report of the British Columbia Task Force on Access to Contraception and Abortion Services*. Victoria: Province of British Columbia.

Bryce, Peter H. 1907. *Report on the Indian Schools of Manitoba and the North-West Territories*. Ottawa: Government Printing Bureau.

Canada. 2002. Commission on the Future of Health Care in Canada. *Building on Values: The Future of Health Care in Canada — Final Report*. Ottawa: Canadian Government Publishing, 2002. <hcsc.gc.ca/english/care/romanow/hcc0086.html>.

____. 1996. *The Report of the Royal Commission on Aboriginal Peoples*. Ottawa: Minister of Supply and Services.

____. 1995. *Report of an Interdepartmental Working Group to the Committee of Deputy Ministers on Justice and Legal Affairs, Fiduciary Relationship of the Crown with Aboriginal Peoples: Implementation and Management Issues — A Guide for Managers*. Ottawa: n.p.

____. 1971. *Annual Report of the Department of National Health and Welfare, 1971*. Ottawa: Queen's Printer.

____. 1969a. *Minutes of the Standing Committee on Indian Affairs and Northern Development*. December 16. Ottawa: Queen's Printer.

____. 1969b. Indian Affairs and Northern Development. *Statement of the Government of Canada on Indian Policy* (The White Paper, 1969). Ottawa: Queen's Printer. <aadnc-aandc.gc.ca/eng/1100100010189/1100100010191>.

____. 1969c. Senate of Canada. *Proceedings of the Senate Committee on Legal and Constitutional Affair*. First Session, Twenty Eighth Parliament, 1968-1969. Ottawa: The Queen's Printer.

____. 1969d. Senate of Canada. *Proceedings of the Senate Committee on Legal and Constitutional Affair*. Second Session, Twenty Eighth Parliament, 1969-1970. Ottawa: The Queen's Printer.

____. 1969e. Standing Committee on Legal and Constitutional Affairs. *Report of the Committee: Evidence*. June 11. Ottawa: The Queen's Printer.

____. 1969f. Standing Committee on Legal and Constitutional Affairs. *Minutes of Proceedings: Evidence*. May 1. Ottawa: The Queen's Printer.

____. 1968. Senate of Canada. *Proceedings of the Special Committee on the Criminal Code (Hate Propaganda)*. Second Session, Twenty Seventh Parliament, 1967-1968. Ottawa:

The Queen's Printer.

____. 1965a. *Annual Report of the Department of National Health and Welfare, 1964*. Ottawa: Queen's Printer.

____. 1965b. House of Commons. Standing Committee on External Affairs. *Minutes of Proceedings and Evidence*, No. 38. March 12. Ottawa: The Queen's Printer.

____. 1964. House of Commons. Standing Committee on External Affairs. *Minutes of Proceedings and Evidence*. October 23. Ottawa: The Queen's Printer.

____. 1948a. Department of External Affairs. *Canada and the United Nations*. Ottawa: Department of External Affairs.

____. 1948b. Special Joint Committee of the Senate and the House of Commons on Human Rights and Fundamental Freedoms. *Minutes of Proceedings and Evidence*. Ottawa: King's Printer, 1948.

____. 1885–1900. *Department of Indian Affairs Annual Report, 1885-1900*. Ottawa: Queen's Printer.

Canadian Civil Liberties Association. 1969. *Submission Standing Committee on Legal and Constitutional Affairs: Legislation on Hate Propaganda*, April 22. Ottawa: Queen's Printer.

Canadian Jewish Congress. 1969. Brief of the Canadian Jewish Congress on Bill S-21 (Hate Propaganda) to the Senate Standing Committee on Constitutional and Legal Affairs, February 25. Ottawa: Queen's Printer.

Cohen, Maxwell. 1966. *Report of the Special Committee on Hate Propaganda in Canada*. Ottawa: Queen's Printer.

Government of Alberta, *Expression of Regret* (November 2, 1999). <gov.ab.ca/acn/199911/8353.html>.

Hawthorn, Harry, ed. 1966-67. *A Survey of the Contemporary Indians of Canada: Economic, Political, Educational Needs and Policies*. 2 vols. Ottawa: Queen's Printer Press. <ainc-inac.gc.ca/ai/arp/ls/phi-eng.asp>.

Hodgins, Frank Egerton. 1919. *Report on the Care and Control of the Mentally Defective and Feebleminded in Ontario*. Toronto: A.T. Wilgress.

Institute of Law Research and Reform. 1988. *Sterilization Decisions: Minors and Mentally Incompetent Adults. Report for Discussion No. 6*. Edmonton, Alberta.

Law Reform Commission of Canada. 1979. *Sterilization: Implications for Mentally Retarded and Mentally Ill Persons, Working Paper*. Ottawa: Ministry of Supply and Services.

McCallum, Dulcie. 2001. *The Need to Know: Woodlands School Report, An Administrative Review*. British Columbia: Ministry of Children and Family Development.

Munro, John. 1970. "Federal Government Initiates Family Planning Program." *News Release* (September 18).

Northwest Territories. 1993. Department of Health. *Status Report: Implementation Plan for Recommendations of the Abortion Services Review Committee*. Department of Health: Government of the Northwest Territories.

____. 1992. Department of Health. *Report of the Abortion Services Review Committee*. Department of Health: Government of the Northwest Territories.

Ontario. 1979a. Inter-ministerial Committee on Medical Consent. *Options on Medical Consent* Ontario: Ministry of Health (September).

____. 1979b. Inter-ministerial Committee on Medical Consent. *Options on Medical Consent — Part 2: Recommendations and Draft Legislation*. Ontario: Ministry of Health (December).

Secondary Sources

Adams, Mary Louise. 1994. "In Sickness and in Health: State Formation, Moral Regulation and Early VD Initiatives in Ontario." *Journal of Canadian Studies* 28, 4.

Akwesasne Notes. 1977. "Killing Our Future: Sterilization and Experiments." 9.

Alfred, Taiaiake. 2009a. "Restitution is Real Pathway to Justice for Indigenous Peoples." In *Response, Responsibility, and Renewal: Canada's Truth and Reconciliation Journey.* Ottawa: Aboriginal Healing Foundation.

____. 2009b. *Peace, Power, Righteousness: An Indigenous Manifesto,* 2nd Edition. Canada: Oxford University Press, 2009,

Allen, Robert S. 1993. *His Majesty's Allies: British Indian Policy in the Defence of Canada, 1774-1815.* Toronto: Dundurn Press.

Alonzo-Maizlish, David. 2002. "In Whole or In Part: Group Rights, the Intent Element of Genocide, and the 'Quantitative Criterion.'" *New York University Law Review* 77, 5.

Anaya, S. James. 2004. *Indigenous Peoples in International Law,* 2nd Ed. New York: Oxford University Press.

Anderson, Karen. 1991. *Chain Her by One Foot: The Subjugation of Native Women in Seventeenth Century New France.* London: Routledge Press.

____. 1988. "As Gentle as Little Lambs: Images of Huron and Montagnais-Naskapi Women in the Writings of the 17th Century Jesuits." *Canadian Review of Sociology and Anthropology* 25, 4.

Anderson, Kim. 2011. *Life Stages and Native Women: Memory, Teachings, and Story Medicine.* Winnipeg: University of Manitoba Press.

____. 2000. *A Recognition of Being: Reconstructing Native Womanhood.* Toronto: Second Story Press.

Arens, Richard (ed.). 1976. *Genocide in Paraguay.* Philadelphia: Temple University Press.

Arsanjani, Mahnoush H. 1999. "The Rome Statute of the International Criminal Court." *American Journal of International Law* 93, 1.

Austen, Ian. 2009. "Canadian Judge Convicts Rwandan in Genocide." *New York Times,* May 22. <nytimes.com/2009/05/23/world/americas/23canada.html>.

Bacchi, Carol. 1978. "Race Regeneration and Social Purity: A Study of the Social Attitudes of Canada's English Speaking Suffragists." *Histoire Sociale/ Social History* 11.

____. 1983. *Liberation Deferred? The Ideas of the English-Canadian Suffragists, 1877–1918.* Toronto: University of Toronto Press.

Backhouse, Constance. 1985. "Nineteenth-Century Canadian Prostitution Law: Reflection of a Discriminatory Society." *Social History* 18, 36.

Barman, Jean. 2006. *Good Intentions Gone Awry: Emma Cosby and the Methodist Mission on the Northwest Coast.* Vancouver: UBC Press.

Barron, F. Laurie, and James B. Waldram (eds.). 1986. *1885 and After: Native Society in Transition.* Regina: University of Regina Canadian Plains Research Centre.

Barta, Tony. 2008a. "Sorry, and Not Sorry, in Australia: How the Apology to the Stolen Generations Buried a History of Genocide." *Journal of Genocide Research* 10, 2.

____. 2008b. "With Intent to Deny: On Colonial Intentions and Genocide Denial." *Journal of Genocide Research* 10, 1.

____. 1987. "Relations of Genocide: Land and Lives in the Colonization of Australia." In Isidor Walliman and Michael N. Dobkowski (eds.), *Genocide and the Modern Age: Etiology and Case Studies of Mass Death.* New York: Greenwood Press.

Battiste, Marie, and James Y. Henderson. 2000. *Protecting Indigenous Knowledge and Heritage:*

A Global Challenge. Saskatoon: Purich Publishing.

Bear Nicholas, Andrea. 2001. "Canada's Colonial Mission: The Great White Bird." In K.P. Binda, and Sharilyn Calliou (eds.), *Aboriginal Education in Canada: A Study in Decolonization.* Mississauga, ON: Canadian Educators' Press.

____. 1994. "Colonialism and the Struggle for Liberation: The Experience of Maliseet Women." *University of New Brunswick Law Journal* 43.

Bebel, August. 1971. *Woman and Socialism.* New York: Schocken Books.

Bender Zelmanovits, Judith. 2003. "'Midwife Preferred': Maternity Care in Outpost Nursing Stations in Northern Canada, 1945–1988." In G.D. Feldberg (ed.), *Women, Health and Nation: Canada and the United States Since 1945.* Montreal: McGill-Queen's University Press.

Bennett, Marlyn, Cindy Blackstock, and Richard De La Ronde. 2005. *A Literature Review and Annotated Bibliography on Aspects of Aboriginal Child Welfare in Canada,* 2nd ed. The First Nations Site of the Centre of Excellence for Child Welfare and the First Nations Child and Family Caregiving Society of Canada.

Benoit, Cecilia, and Dena Carroll. 2001. *Marginalized Voices from Vancouver's Downtown Eastside: Aboriginal Women Speak About their Health Care Experiences.* Ottawa: Research Bulletin.

Biard, Father Pierre. 1612. *Jesuit Relations II.*

Black, Edwin. 2003. *War Against the Weak: Eugenics and America's Campaign to Create a Master Race.* New York: Four Walls Eight Windows.

Blackstock, Cindy, Nico Trome and Marlyn Bennett. 2004. "Child Maltreatment Investigations among Aboriginal and Non-Aboriginal Families in Canada." *Violence Against Women* 10, 8.

Blaney, Fay. 1995. "Backlash Against First Nations: Never Ending Robbery." *Kinesis* (July/August).

Bock, Gisela. 1983. "Racism and Sexism in Nazi Germany: Motherhood, Compulsory Sterilization, and the State." *Signs* 8, 3.

Boldt, E.D., L.W. Roberts and A.H. Latif. 1982. "The Provision of Birth Control Services to Unwed Minors: A National Survey of Physician Attitudes and Practices." *Canadian Journal of Public Health* 73, 6.

Boldt, Menno. 1993. *Surviving as Indians: The Challenge of Self Government.* Toronto: University of Toronto Press.

Borrows, John. 1997. "Wampum at Niagara: The Royal Proclamation, Canadian Legal History, and Self-Government." In Michael Asch (ed.), *Aboriginal and Treaty Rights in Canada: Essays on Law, Equality, and Respect for Difference.* Vancouver: University of British Columbia Press.

Bourgeault, Ron. 1983. "The Indian, the Métis and the Fur Trade: Class, Sexism and Racism in the Transition from 'Communism' to Capitalism." *Studies in Political Economy* 12.

Bowker, W.F. 1980. "Minors and Mental Incompetents: Consent to Experimentation, Gifts of Tissue and Sterilization." *McGill Law Journal* 26.

Bradford, William C. 2006. "Acknowledging and Rectifying the Genocide of American Indians: 'Why Is it that They Carry Their Lives on Their Fingernails?'" *Metaphilosophy* 37.

____. 2002. "'With Very Great Blame on Our Hearts': Reparations, Reconciliation, and an American Indian Plea for Peace with Justice." *American Indian Law Review* 27.

Brewin, Andrew. 1967. "The Report of the Special Committee on Hate Propaganda."

University of Toronto Law Journal 17, 1.

British Columbian Coalition of People with Disabilities. n.d. "Woodlands Backgrounder." <bccpd.bc.ca/campaigns/woodlands/default.htm>.

Brodie, Janine. 1992. "Choice and No Choice in the House." In Janine Brodie, Shelley Gavigan and Jane Jensen (eds.), *The Politics of Abortion*. Toronto: Oxford University Press.

Brown, Jennifer S.H. 1980. *Strangers in Blood: Fur Trade Company Families in Indian Country*. Vancouver: University of British Columbia Press.

Brownlie, Robin, and Mary-Ellen Kelm. 1994. "Desperately Seeking Absolution: Native Agency as Colonist Alibi?" *Canadian Historical Review* 75, 4.

Bryce, Peter H. 1907. *Report on the Indian Schools of Manitoba and the North-West Territories*. Ottawa: Government Printing Bureau.

Broberg, Gunnar, and Nils Roll-Hansen. 1996. *Eugenics and the Welfare State: Sterilization Policy in Norway, Sweden, Denmark and Finland*. East Lansing: Michigan State University Press.

Buffalohead, Priscilla K. 1983. "Farmers, Warriors, Traders: A Fresh Look at Ojibway Women." *Minnesota History* (Summer).

Burdett, Carolyn. 1998. "The Hidden Romance of Sexual Science: Eugenics, the Nation and the Making of Modern Feminism." In Lucy Bland and Laura Doan (eds.), *Sexology in Culture: Labeling Bodies and Desires*. Chicago: University of Chicago Press.

Burnett, Kristin. 2011. "Obscured Obstetrics: Indigenous Midwives in Western Canada." In Sarah Carter and Patricia McCormack (eds.), *Recollections: Lives of Aboriginal Women of the Canadian Northwest and Borderlands*. Edmonton: Athabasca University Press.

____. 2010. *Taking Medicine: Women's Healing Work and Colonial Contact in Southern Alberta, 1880-1930*. Vancouver: UBC Press.

Butler, Don. 2012. "The Dark Side of Honoring Dr. Helen MacMurchy." *Ottawa Citizen* (October 5). <ottawacitizen.com/health/dark+side+honouring+Helen+MacMurc hy /7346152/story.html.>

Canadian Medical Association Journal. 1970. "Sexual Sterilization for non-Medical Reasons." 102.

Canadian Medical Protective Association. 1971. "Control of Fertility by Sterilization." *Canadian Medical Association Journal* 104.

____. 1970. "Sexual Sterilization for Non-Medical Reasons." *Canadian Medical Association Journal* 102.

Card, Claudia. 2003. "Genocide and Social Death." *Hypatia* 18, 1.

Cardinal, Harold. 1969. *The Unjust Society: The Tragedy of Canada's Indians*. Vancouver: Douglas & McIntyre.

Carew, Jan. 1988a. *Fulcrums of Change*. New Jersey: Africa World Press.

____. 1988b. "Columbus and the Origins of Racism in the Americas: Part One." *Race and Class* 29, 1.

Carpio, Myla. 2004. "The Lost Generation: American Indian Women and Sterilization Abuse." *Social Justice* 31, 4.

Carter, Sarah. 1997. *Capturing Women: The Manipulation of Cultural Imagery in Canada's Prairie West*. Montreal: McGill-Queen's University Press.

____. 1996. "First Nation Women of Prairie Canada in the Early Reserve Years, the 1870's to the 1920's: A Preliminary Inquiry." In C. Miller and P. Churchryk (eds.), *Women of the First Nations: Power, Wisdom and Strength*. Manitoba: University of Manitoba Press.

____. 1990. *Lost Harvest: Prairie Indian Reserve Farmers and Government Policy*. Montreal and Kingston: McGill-Queen's University Press.

Caufield, Timothy, and G. Robertson. 1996. "Eugenic Policies in Alberta: From the Systematic to the Systemic?" *Alberta Law Review* 35, 1.

CBC *News Online*. February 20, 2006. "Sterilized Woman Took too Long to Sue, Court Rules." <cbc.ca/north/story/sterilization-nwt-13022006.html>.

____. December 22, 2005. "Cash Settlement for Sterilized Women." <cbc.ca/bc/story/bc_sterilized-women20051222.html>.

____. April 23, 2005. "Cost of Administering Residential School Program 'Staggering.'" <cbc.ca/news/canada/story/2005/04/22/residentialschool050422.html>.

____. February 8, 2004. "Sterilized Woman Sues Hospital." <cbc.ca/north/story/aug02stantonsuit02082004.html>.

____. February 7, 2003. "B.C. Faces Forced Sterilization Lawsuit." <cbc.ca/canada/story/2003/02/07/bc_sterilesuit030207.html>.

____. January 23, 2001. "New Questions about Sterilization Claims." <cbc.ca/news/story/2001/01/23/claim230101.html.>

____. September 22, 2000. "Sterilization Victims Offered Help With Lawyers' Bills." <cbc.ca/news/story/2000/09/22/strlcmp000922.html>.

____. November 2, 1999. "Alberta Apologizes for Forced Sterilization." <cbc.ca/canada/story/1999/11/02/sterilize991102.html>.

____. October 31, 1999. "Sterilization Compensation to be Announced This Week." <cbc.ca/news/story/1999/10/31/sterile991031.html>.

____. April 8, 1999. "Alberta Sterilization Settlement Challenged." <cbc.ca/canada/story/1999/04/08/ab_sterile990408.html>.

____. June 5, 1998. "Alberta Compensates Sterilization Victims." <cbc.ca/news/story/1998/06/05/altacomp980605ba.html>.

____. March 10, 1998. "Alberta Imposes Compensation Package." <cbc.ca/news/story/1998/03/10/alberta980310b.html>.

Chalk, Frank. 1989. "'Genocide in the 20th Century' Definitions of Genocide and Their Implications for Prediction and Prevention." *Holocaust and Genocide Studies* 4, 2.

Chalk, Frank, and Kurt Jonassohn. 1990. *The History and Sociology of Genocide: Analyses and Case Studies*. New Haven: Yale University Press.

Charny, Israel. 1994. "Toward a Generic Definition of Genocide." In George Andreopoulos (ed.), *Genocide: Conceptual and Historical Dimensions*. Philadelphia: University of Pennsylvania Press.

Chase, Allan. 1977. *The Legacy of Malthus: The Social Costs of the New Scientific Racism*. New York: Alfred A. Knopf, Inc.

Chrisjohn, Roland. 1999. "'You Have to be Carefully Taught: Special Needs and First Nations Education:' A Report to the National Indian Education Council, The Assembly of First Nations, and the Chiefs Council on Education." <natpsycdn.brandonu.ca/News%209911.htm>.

Chrisjohn, Roland, and Tanya Wasacase. 2009. "Half Truths and Whole Lies: Rhetoric in the 'Apology' and the Truth and Reconciliation Commission." In *Response, Responsibility, and Renewal: Canada's Truth and Reconciliation Journey*. Ottawa: Aboriginal Healing Foundation.

Chrisjohn, Roland, and Sherri Young with Michael Maraun. 2006. *The Circle Game: Shadows and Substance in the Indian Residential School Experience in Canada*. Vancouver: Theytus

Press.

Chrisjohn, Roland et al. 2002. "Genocide and Indian Residential Schools: The Past is Present." In R.D. Wiggers and A.L. Griffiths (eds.), *Canada and International Humanitarian Law: Peacekeeping and War Crimes in the Modern Era.* Halifax: Dalhousie University Press.

Christian, Timothy. 1974. "The Mentally Ill and Human Rights in Alberta: A Study of the Alberta Sexual Sterilization Act." Edmonton: University of Alberta, Faculty of Law.

Churchill, Ward. 2002. *Perversions of Justice: Indigenous Peoples and Anglo-American Law.* San Francisco, CA: City Lights Books.

____. 2000. "Forbidding the 'G Word': Holocaust Denial and Judicial Doctrine in Canada." *Other Voices* 2, 1. <othervoices.org/2.1/churchill/denial.php>.

____. 1997. *A Little Matter of Genocide: Holocaust and Denial in the Americas 1492 to the Present.* San Francisco: City Lights Publishing.

____. 1995. *Since Predator Came: Notes from the Struggle for American Indian Liberation.* Colorado: Aigis Publications.

____. 1994. *Indians Are Us? Culture and Genocide in Native North America.* Toronto: Between the Lines Press.

Cohen, Jamie, and T.F. Baskett. 1978. "Sterilization Patterns in a Northern Canadian Population." *Canadian Journal of Public Health* 69.

Colbourne, Jeff. 1998. "Sterilized Victims Quiet." *Northern News Services,* June 29. <nnsl.com/frames/newspapers/199806/jun29_98ster.html>.

Cole, Madeline. 2001. "The Shot Is Where It's At." *Nunatsiaq News,* November 23. <nunatsiaqonline.ca/archives/nunavut011130/news/editorial/columns.html#sexed_november23>.

Cole, Yolande. 2001. "Two Other Groups Withdraw From B.C. Missing Women Inquiry." *The Straight,* August 9. <straight.com/article-419657/vancouver/two-other-groups-withdraw-bc-missing-women-inquiry>.

Colodny, Nikki. 1989. "The Politics of Birth Control in a Reproductive Rights Context." In Christine Overall (ed.), *The Future of Human Reproduction.* Toronto: The Women's Press.

Cooper, John. 2008. *Rapheal Lemkin and the Struggle for the Genocide Convention.* New York: Palgrave Macmillan.

Corntassel, Jeff, and Cindy Holder. 2008. "Who's Sorry Now? Government Apologies, Truth Commissions, and Indigenous Self-Determination in Australia, Canada, Guatemala, and Peru." *Human Rights Review* 9.

Crichlow, Wesley. 2002. "Western Colonization as Disease: Native Adoption and Cultural Genocide." *Critical Social Work* 3, 2. <uwindsor.ca/criticalsocialwork/western-colonization-as-disease-native-adoption-cultural-genocide>.

Crosby, Alfred W. 1991. "Infectious Disease and the Demography of the Atlantic Peoples." *Journal of World History* 2, 2.

CTV News Online. December 16, 2009. "Government Must Agree to Justice For All Woodlands Survivors, Says NDP." <bcndp.ca/newsroom/gov%E2%80%99t-must-agree-justice-all-woodlands-survivors-says-ndp>.

Cull, Randi. 2006. "Aboriginal Mothering Under the State's Gaze." In D. Memee Lavell-Harvard and Jeannette Corbiere Lavell (eds.), *"Until our Hearts Are On the Ground," Aboriginal Mothering, Oppression, Resistance and Rebirth.* Toronto: Demeter Press.

Cumming, Peter A., and Neil Mickenberg. 1972. *Native Rights in Canada.* Ottawa: Indian-

Eskimo Association.

Daisley, Brad. 1996. "Government's Actions 'Warped' Plaintiff's Life: Alta. Judge — Alta. Must Pay for Wrongful Sterilization." *The Lawyers Weekly* 15, 39.

Darwin, Charles. 2001. *Origin of the Species by Means of Natural Selection: or, The Preservation of Favored Races in the Struggle for Life.* London: Electric Book Co.

___. 1871. *The Descent of Man, and Selection in Relation to Sex.* London, John Murray.

Davis, Robert, and Mark Zannis. 1973. *The Genocide Machine in Canada: The Pacification of the North.* Montréal: Black Rose Books.

Degler, Carl N. 1991. *In Search of Human Nature: The Decline and Revival of Darwinism in American Social Thought.* London: Oxford University Press.

Denys, Nicolas. 1908. *The Description & Natural History of the Coasts of North America.* Toronto: Champlain Society.

Devereux, Cecily. 2005. *Growing a Race: Nellie L. McClung and the Fiction of Eugenic Feminism.* Montreal & Kingston: McGill-Queen's University Press.

Diabo, Russell. 2012. "Harper Launches Major First Nations Termination Plan: As Negotiating Tables Legitimize Canada's Colonialism." *First Nations Strategic Bulletin, First Nations Strategic Policy Counsel* 10 (June–October).

Diamond, Jared. 1997. *Guns, Germs, and Steel: The Fates of Human Societies.* New York: W.W. Norton.

Dickens, Bernard M. 1985. "Reproduction Law and Medical Consent." *The University of Toronto Law Journal* 35, 3.

Dickin McGinnis, Janice. 1980. "From Health to Welfare: Federal Government Policies Regarding Standards of Public Health for Canadians, 1919–1945." PhD diss., University of Alberta.

Docker, John. 2004. " Raphael Lemkin's History of Genocide and Colonialism." Paper presented at the United States Holocaust Memorial Museum, Centre for Advanced Holocaust Studies, Washington DC, February 26.

Dodd, Dianne. 1991. "Advice to Parents: The Blue Books, Helen MacMurchy, MD, and the Federal Department of Health, 1920–1934." *Canadian Bulletin of Medical History* 8.

___. 1985. "The Canadian Birth Control Movement: Two Approaches to the Dissemination of Contraceptive Technology." *Scientia Canadensis: Canadian Journal of the History of Science, Technology and Medicine* 9, 1.

Donovan, Allan. 2006. "Commentary: Residential Schools Package Fails to Provide a Foundation for Fair Resolution." *Lawyers Weekly*, April 21. <lawyersweekly.ca/index. php?section=article&articleid=269>.

Doran, Beverly. 2010. "500 Woodlands School Survivors Denied Justice by B.C. Government." *The Georgia Straight*, February 25. <straight.com/article-293909/ vancouver/beverley-doran-500-woodlands-school-survivors-denied-justice-bc- government>.

Dowbiggin, Ian. R. 2008. *The Sterilization Movement and Global Fertility in the Twentieth Century.* New York: Oxford University Press.

___. 1997. *Keeping America Sane: Psychiatry and Eugenics in the United States and Canada, 1880–1940.* New York: Cornell University Press.

Downey, Michael. 1999. "Canada's Genocide." *Maclean's Magazine*, April 26.

Dyck, Eryka. 2013. *Facing Eugenics: Reproduction, Sterilization, and the Politics of Choice.* Toronto: University of Toronto Press.

Economist. 1996. "Sterilized in Alberta." September 11.

Ellis, David, Bluma Tischler, and David Lirenman. 1970. "Supra Pubic Aspiration of Urine in the Mentally Retarded Child." *The American Journal of Diseases of Children* 120, 3.

Ellis, Havelock. 1914. *The Task of Social Hygiene*. Boston: Houghton Mifflin.

Engels, Frederick. 2004. *The Origin of the Family, Private Property and the State*. Australia: Resistance Books.

____. 1976. "The Origin of the Family, Private Property and the State." In *Collected Works*, vol. v. Karl Marx and Friedrich Engels (eds.). Moscow: Progress Publishers.

____. 1884. *Outline of a Critique of Political Economy*. Deutsche-Franzosische Jarhrbucher.

Etienne, Mona, and Eleanor Leacock (eds.). 1980. *Women and Colonization*. New York: Praeger Publishers.

Evans, Kenneth G. 1980. "Sterilization of the Mentally Retarded — A Review." *Canadian Medical Association Journal* 123.

Federici, Silvia. 2004. *Caliban and the Witch*. Brooklyn, NY: Autonomedia.

Fiamengo, Janice. 2006. "Rediscovering our Foremothers Again: Racial Ideas of Canada's Early Feminists, 1885--1945." In M. Gleason and A. Perry (eds.), *Rethinking Canada: The Promise of Women's History*, 5th ed. Toronto: Oxford University Press.

Finzsch, Norbert. 2008a. "'The Aborigines ... Were Never Annihilated, and Still They Are Becoming Extinct': Settler Imperialism and Genocide in Nineteenth-century America and Australia." In A. Dirk Moses (ed.), *Empire, Colony, Genocide: Conquest, Occupation, and Subaltern Resistance in World History*. New York: Berghahn Books.

____. 2008b. "'[...] Extirpate or Remove that Vermine': Genocide, Biological Warfare, and Settler Imperialism in the Eighteenth and Early Nineteenth Century." *Journal of Genocide Research* 10, 2.

____. 2005. "'It Is Scarcely Possible to Conceive that Human Beings Could Be so Loathsome': Discourses of Genocide in Eighteenth- and Nineteenth-Century America and Australia." *Patterns of Prejudice* 39, 2.

Fiske, Jo-Anne, 1995. "Political Status of Native Indian Women: Contradictory Implications of Canadian State Policy." *American Indian Journal of Culture and Research* 19, 2.

Foulkes, R.G. 1962. "Medics in the North: A History of the Contributions of the Royal Canadian Air Force to the Medical Care of Civilians in the Fort Nelson Area of British Columbia, Part II." *Medical Services Journal, Canada* 18 (September).

Fournier, Suzanne. 2011. "Missing Women Inquiry Head Wally Oppal Says Boycott Won't Impact Probe." *The Province*, May 26. <theprovince.com/news/Marginalized+gro ups+withdraw+from+Missing+Women+Inquiry+over+lack+funding/4839805/ story.htm>.

Franks, Angela. 2005. *Margaret Sanger's Eugenic Legacy: The Control of Female Fertility*. London: McFarland & Company.

Gibbons, Sheila. 2014. "'Our Power to Remodel Civilization': The Development of Eugenic Feminism in Alberta, 1909–1921." *Canadian Bulletin of Medical History* 31, 1.

Gibson, David. 1974. "Involuntary Sterilization of the Mentally Retarded: A Western Canadian Phenomenon." *Canadian Psychiatric Association Journal* 19.

Gimenez, Martha E. 2005. "Capitalism and the Oppression of Women: Marx Revisited." *Science and Society* 1, 1.

Glauner, Lindsay. 2002. "The Need for Accountability and Reparation: 1830–1976; The United States Government's Role in the Promotion, Implementation, and Execution of the Crime of Genocide Against Native Americans." *DePaul Law Review* 51.

Globe and Mail. 1976. "Many Inuit Sterilized, RC Says." October 9.

____. 1974. "Staff Squabbling Hurt Patient Care, Stony Plains Doctor Tells Inquiry." November 16.

Gordon, Linda. 2002. *The Moral Property of Women: A History of Birth Control Politics in America*. University of Illinois Press.

Gould, Stephen J. 2002. *The Structure of Evolutionary Theory*. Cambridge, MA: Belknap Press.

____. 1981. *The Mismeasure of Man*. New York: W.W. Norton Press.

Gray, John. 1974. "The Oddity of Canada's Abortion Law." *The Ottawa Citizen*, October 24.

Green, Joyce. 1985. "Sexual Equality and Indian Government: An Analysis of Bill C-31 Amendments to the Indian Act." *Native Studies Review* 1, 2.

Greenwalt, Alexander K.A. 1999. "Note, Rethinking Genocidal Intent: The Case for a Knowledge-Based Interpretation." *Columbia Law Review* 99.

Gregory, Roxanne. 2009. "Woodlands Survivors See Legal Opening." *The Georgia Straight*, April 9. <straight.com/article-213248/woodlands-survivors-see-legal-opening>.

____. 2007a. "Woodlands Justice on Hold." *The Georgia Straight*, April 5. <straight.com/article-82907/woodlands-justice-on-hold>.

____. 2007b. "Woodlands Survivors Face More Delays." *The Georgia Straight*, November 29. <straight.com/article-120341/woodlands-survivors-face-more-delays>.

____. 2006. "Woodlands Justice in Doubt." *The Georgia Straight*, March 23. <straight.com/article/woodlands-justice-in-doubt>.

Grekul, Jana. 2008. "Sterilization in Alberta, 1928 to 1972: Gender Matters." *The Canadian Review of Sociology* 45, 3.

____. 2002. "The Social Construction of the Feebleminded Threat: Implementation of the Sexual Sterilization Act in Alberta, 1929–1972." PhD diss., University of Alberta.

Grekul, Jana, Harvey Krahn and Dave Odynak. 2004. "Sterilizing the 'Feeble-Minded': Eugenics in Alberta, Canada, 1929–1972." *Journal of Historical Sociology* 17, 4.

Hagen, Greg. 2005. "Commentary: On ADR for Residential School Claims." *The Lawyers Weekly*, April 1. <lawyersweekly.ca/index.php?section=article&articleid=62>.

Haller, Mark H. 1963. *Eugenics: Hereditarian Attitudes in American Thought*. New Brunswick: Rutgers University Press.

Hamlin, Kimberly Ann. 2007. "Beyond Adam's Rib: How Darwinian Evolutionary Theory Redefined Gender and Influenced American Feminist Thought, 1970–1920." PhD diss., University of Texas at Austin.

Hartley, Jackie, Paul Joffe and Jennifer Preston (eds.). 2010. *Realizing the UN Declaration on the Rights of Indigenous Peoples: Triumph, Hope, and Action*. Saskatoon, Purich Publishing.

Hawaleshka, Danylo. 2005. "A Shot in the Dark?" *Maclean's Magazine*, November 28.

Henderson, Jennifer. 2003. *Settler Feminism and Race Making in Canada*. Toronto: University of Toronto Press.

Hernstein, Richard J., and Charles Murray. 1994. *The Bell Curve*. New York: The Free Press.

Hillel, Marc, and Clarissa Henry. 1976. *Of Pure Blood*. New York: McGraw-Hill.

Hodson, Cora B.S. 1934. *Human Sterilization Today: A Survey of the Present Position*. London: Watts & Co.

Hogg, Peter W. *Constitutional Law of Canada, Vol. 1*. Toronto: Carswell, 1999.

Horowitz, Irving L. 1976. *Taking Lives: Genocide and State Power*. New Jersey: Transaction Books.

Hudson, Pete, and Brad McKenzie. 1981. "Child Welfare and Native People: The Extension of Colonialism." *The Social Worker* 49, 2.

Indian Chiefs of Alberta. 2011. "Citizens Plus (Red Paper)" reprinted in *aboriginal policy studies* 1, 2.

Jamieson, Elmer, and Peter Sandiford. 1928. "The Mental Capacity of Southern Ontario Indians." *Journal of Educational Psychology* 19.

Jamieson, Kathleen. 1989. "Sex Discrimination and the Indian Act." In R. Ponting (ed.), *An Arduous Journey: Canadian Indians and Decolonization*. Toronto: McClelland & Stewart.

____. 1978. *Indian Women and Law in Canada: Citizens Minus*. Canada: Advisory Council on the Status of Women.

Jasen, Patricia. 1997. "Race, Culture, and the Colonization of Childbirth in Northern Canada." *Social History of Medicine* 10, 3.

Jensen, Arthur R. 1980. *Bias in Mental Testing*. New York: The Free Press.

Jensen, Jane. 1992. "Getting to Morgentaler: From One Representation to Another." In Janine Brodie, Shelley Gavigan and Jane Jensen (eds.), *The Politics of Abortion*. Toronto: Oxford University Press.

Johansen, Bruce E. 1998. "Reprise/Forced Sterilizations." *Native Americas: Akwe:kon's Journal of Indigenous Studies* (Winter).

Johansen, David, and Philip Rosen. 2008. *The Notwithstanding Clause of the Charter*. Library of Parliament: Parliamentary Information and Research Service.

Johnston, Patrick. 1983. *Native Children and the Child Welfare System*. Toronto: James Lorimer.

Joseph, Shirley. 1991. "Assimilation Tools: Then and Now." *BC Studies* 89.

Kamin, Leon J. 1974. *The Science and Politics of IQ*. Potomac, MD: Lawrence Erlbaum Associates.

Kane, Peter E. 1970. "The Group Libel Law Debate in the Canadian House of Commons." *Communication Quarterly* 18, 4.

Kastrup, Dieter. 2000. "From Nuremburg to Rome and Beyond: The Fight Against Genocide, War Crimes, and Crimes Against Humanity." *Fordham International Law Journal* 23, 404.

Katz, Steven. 1994. *The Holocaust in Historical Context: The Holocaust and Mass Death Before the Modern Age*. New York: Oxford University Press.

Kaufert, Patricia A., and John D. O'Neil. 1990 "Cooptation and Control: The Reconstruction of Inuit Birth," *Medical Anthropology Quarterly* 4, 4.

Kealey, Linda (ed.). 1979. *Not an Unreasonable Claim: Women and Reform in Canada, 1880s–1920s*. Toronto: Canadian Women's Educational Press.

____. 1984. "Canadian Socialism and the Woman Question 1900–14." *Labour/Le Travail* 13 (Spring).

Kelm, Mary Ellen. 2005. "Diagnosing the Discursive Indian: Medicine, Gender, and the Dying Race." *Ethnohistory* 52, 2.

____. 1998. *Colonizing Bodies: Aboriginal Health and Healing in British Columbia 1900–1950*. Vancouver: UBC Press.

Kevles, Daniel J. 1985. *In the Name of Eugenics*. New York: Alfred A. Knopf.

Kinsman, Gary, and Patrizia Gentile. 2010. *The Canadian War on Queers: National Security as Sexual Regulation*. Vancouver: UBC Press.

Klein, Allan. 1983. "The Political Economy of Gender: A 19th Century Plains Indian Case Study." In P. Albers and B. Medicine (eds.), *The Hidden Half: Studies in Plains Indian Women*. Washington, DC: University Press of America.

Kline, Marlee. 1993. "Complicating the Ideology of Motherhood: Child Welfare Law and

First Nation Women." *Queen's Law Journal* 18.

_____. 1992. "Child Welfare Law, 'Best Interest of the Child' Ideology, and First Nations." *Osgoode Hall Law Journal* 30.

Kline, Wendy. 2002. *Building a Better Race: Gender, Sexuality, and Eugenics from the Turn of the Century to the Baby Boom.* Los Angeles: University of California Press.

Kondro, Wayne. 1998. "Alberta Retreats over Sterilization Compensation." *Lancet,* March 21.

Kühl, Stefan. 1994. *The Nazi Connection: Eugenics, American Racism, and German National Socialism.* New York: Oxford University Press.

Kulba, Tracy. 2004. "New Woman, New Nation: Emily Murphy, the Famous 5 Foundation, and the Production of a Female Citizen." PhD diss., University of Alberta.

Kulchyski, Peter. 2005. *Like the Sound of a Drum: Aboriginal Cultural Politics in Denendeh and Nunavut.* Winnipeg: University of Manitoba Press.

_____. 1994. *Unjust Relations: Aboriginal Rights in Canadian Courts.* Toronto: Oxford University Press.

Kuper, Leo. 1981. *Genocide: Its Political Use in the Twentieth Century.* Harmondsworth: Penguin.

Lamberton, Ross. 2005. *Repression and Resistance: Canadian Human Rights Activists, 1930–1960.* Toronto: University of Toronto Press.

Lavoie, Judith. 2003. "B.C. Apologizes for Abuse at Mental-Health Facilities." *Times Colonist* (May 31).

Lawrence, Bonita. 2003. "Gender, Race, and the Regulation of Native Identity in Canada and the United States: An Overview." *Hypatia* 18, 2.

Lawrence, Jane. 2000. "Indian Health Service: Sterilization of Native American Women." *American Indian Quarterly* 24.

Leblanc, Lawrence J. 1991. *The United States and the Genocide Convention.* Durhman, N.C.: Duke University Press.

_____. 1984. "The Intent to Destroy Groups in the Genocide Convention: The Proposed US Understanding." *American Journal of International Law* 78.

Lechat, Robert. 1976. "Intensive Sterilization for the Inuit." *Eskimo* (Fall/Winter): 5–7.

Lemkin, Raphaël. 1947. "Genocide as a Crime Under International Law." *American Journal of International Law* 41.

_____. 1944. *Axis Rule in Occupied Europe: Laws of Occupation, Analysis of Government, Proposals for Redress.* Washington, DC: Carnegie Endowment for International Peace.

_____. 1933. "Acts Constituting a General (Transnational) Danger Considered as Offences Against the Laws of Nations" (originally written in French and presented in absentia at the International Conference for the Unification of Criminal Law, Madrid, October. <preventgenocide.org/lemkin/madrid1933-english.htm>

Lethbridge Herald. 1999. "Province Settles with Sterilization Victims." November 3.

Lewis, Deborah J. 1995. "Coercive Sterilization: Its Eugenical Underpinnings and Current Manifestation." MA diss., Carleton University.

Lewy, Guenter. 2005. *The Armenian Massacres in Ottoman Turkey: A Disputed Genocide.* Salt Lake City: University of Utah Press.

Lippman, Matthew. 1998. "The Convention on the Prevention and Punishment of the Crime of Genocide: Fifty Years Later." *Arizona Journal of International and Comparative Law* 15, 2.

_____. 1985. "The Drafting of the 1948 Convention on the Prevention and Punishment of the Crime of Genocide." *Boston University International Law Journal* 3, 1.

Loo, Tina. 1992. "Dan Cranmer's Potlatch: Law as Coercion, Symbol, and Rhetoric in British Columbia, 1884–1951." *Canadian Historical Review* 73, 2.

Lopez, Iris. 2008. *Matters of Choice: Puerto Rican Women's Struggle for Reproductive Freedom.* New Brunswick, NJ: Rutgers University Press.

Lougheed, Peter. 1998. "Why a Notwithstanding Clause?" *Point of View* 6.

Lowell, JoAnn. 1995. "NWT Abortion Review Puts Spotlight on the Politics of Medicine." *Herizons* 9, 1.

Lukacs, Martin. 2011. "Disappearing Aboriginal Women are Canada's Secret Shame." *The Huffington Post*, October 11. <huffingtonpost.ca/ martin-lukacs/aboriginal women_b_994185.html>.

Lux, Maureen K. 2001. *Medicine that Walks: Disease, Medicine, and Canadian Plains Native People, 1880–1940.* Toronto: University of Toronto Press.

____. 1998. "Perfect Subjects: Race, Tuberculosis, and the Qu'Appelle BCG Vaccine," *Canadian Bulletin of Medical History* 15.

MacLean's. 1998. "Sterilizing Klein's Legislation." March 23.

MacLennan, Christopher. 2003. *Toward the Charter: Canadians and the Demand for a National Bill of Rights, 1929–1960.* Montreal and Kingston: McGill-Queen's University Press.

MacLennan, Dave. 1987. "Beyond the Asylum: Professionalization and the Mental Hygiene Movement in Canada, 1914–1928." *Canadian Bulletin of Mental Health* 4.

MacMurchy, Helen. 1934. *Sterilization? Birth Control? A Book for Family Welfare and Safety.* Toronto: Macmillan Press.

____. 1912. *Infant Mortality.* Toronto: King's Printer.

Magnet, S. Rodgers. 1981. "Legislating for an Informed Consent to Medical Treatment by Competent Adults." *McGill Law Journal* 26.

Malloch, Lesley. 1989. "Indian Medicine, Indian Health." *Canadian Women Studies/Les Cahiers de la Femme* 10, 2 & 3.

Malthus, Thomas. 1878. *Essay on the Principle of Population.* London: Reeves and Turner.

Mann, Barbara A. 2000. *Iroquoian Women: The Gantowisas.* New York: Peter Lang.

Manuel, George, and Michael Posluns. 1974. *The Fourth World: An Indian Reality.* Don Mills, ON: Collier-Macmillan.

Marcus, Allan. 1995. *Relocating Eden: The Image and Politics of Inuit Exile in the Canadian Arctic.* Hanover, NH and London: University Press of New England.

Marx, Karl. 2009. *The Eighteenth Brumaire of Louis Bonaparte.* Maryland: Serenity Publishers.

____. 1990. *Capital: A Critique of Political Economy*, vol. I. London: Penguin Books.

Marx, Karl, and Frederick Engels. 1976. *Collected Works*, vol. V. Moscow: Progress Publishers.

McCallum, Dulcie. 2001. *The Need to Know: Woodlands School Report, an Administrative Review.* British Columbia: Ministry of Children and Family Development.

McCallum, Mary Jane. 2005. "The Last Frontier: Isolation and Aboriginal Health." *Canadian Bulletin of Medical History* 22, 1.

McClung, Nellie. 1945. *The Stream Runs Fast: My Own Story.* Toronto: Thomas Allen.

McConnachie, Kathleen. 1987. "Science and Ideology: The Mental Hygiene and Eugenics Movements in the Inter-war Years, 1919–1939." PhD diss., University of Toronto.

McCormack, Thelma. 1999. "Fetal Syndromes and the Charter: The Winnipeg Glue-Sniffing Case." *Canadian Journal of Law and Society* 14, 2.

McDonnell, Michael A., and Dirk A. Moses. 2005. "Raphael Lemkin as Historian of

Genocide in the Americas." *Journal of Genocide Research* 7, 4.

McGeer Edith, and Bluma Tischler. 1959. "Vitamin B 6 and Mental Deficiency: The Effects of Large Doses of B 6 (Pyridoxine) in Phenylketoburia." *Canadian Journal of Biochemistry and Physiology* 37, 3.

McLaren, Angus. 1991. "'Keep your Seats and Face Facts': Western Canadian Women's Discussion of Birth Control in the 1920s." *Canadian Bulletin of Medical History* 8.

____. 1990. *Our Own Master Race: Eugenics in Canada, 1885–1945.* Toronto: McClelland & Stewart.

McLaren, Angus, and Arlene Tigar McLaren. 1986. *The Bedroom and the State: The Changing Practices and Politics of Contraception and Abortion in Canada, 1880–1980.* Toronto: McClelland & Stewart.

McLaren, John. 2002. "The State, Child Snatching, and the Law: The Seizure and Indoctrination of Sons of Freedom Children in British Columbia, 1950–1960." In John McLaren, Robert Menzies and Dorothy E. Chunn (eds.), *Regulating Lives: Historical Essays on the State, Society, the Individual, and the Law.* Toronto: UBC Press.

McWhirter, K.G., and J. Weijer. 1969. "The Alberta Sterilization Act: A Genetic Critique." *University of Toronto Law Journal* 19.

Menzies, Robert, and Ted Palys. 2006. "Turbulent Spirits: Aboriginal Patients in the British Columbia Psychiatric System, 1879–1950." In James E. Moran and David Wright (eds.), *Mental Health and Canadian Society: Historical Perspectives.* Montreal & Kingston: McGill-Queen's University Press.

Mies, Maria. 1986. *Patriarchy and Accumulation on a World Scale: Women in the International Division of Labour.* London: Zed Books.

Miller, J.R. 1996. *Shingwauk's Vision: A History of Native Residential Schools.* Toronto: University of Toronto Press.

____. 1990. "Owen Glendower, Hotspur, and Canadian Indian Policy." *Ethnohistory* 37, 4.

Milloy, John. 1999. *A National Crime: The Canadian Government and the Residential School System, 1879 to 1986.* Winnipeg: University of Manitoba Press.

Mistral, Gabriela. 1956. "An Appeal to the World Conscience — The Genocide Convention." *United Nations Review* (June).

Mitchell, Andrew D. 2000. "Genocide, Human Rights Implementation and the Relationship Between International and Domestic Law: Nulyarimma v. Thompson." *Melbourne University Law Review* 24, 15.

Mitchinson, Wendy. 2002. *Giving Birth in Canada, 1900–1950.* Toronto: University of Toronto Press.

Moffitt, Pertice M. 2004. "Colonialization: A Health Determinant for Pregnant Dogrib Women." *Journal of Transcultural Nursing* 15.

Monture-Angus, Patricia. 1999. *Journeying Forward: Dreaming First Nations' Independence.* Halifax: Fernwood Publishing.

Monture, Patricia. 1991. *Thunder in My Soul: A Mohawk Woman Speaks.* Halifax: Fernwood Publishing.

____. 1989. "A Vicious Circle: Child Welfare and First Nations." *Canadian Journal of Women and the Law* 3, 1.

Moore, P.E. 1961. "No Longer Captain: A History of Tuberculosis and Its Control Among Canadian Indians." *Canadian Medical Association Journal* 84.

Morris, Alexander. 1991. *The Treaties of Canada with the Indians of Manitoba and the North-West Territories: Including the Negotiations on Which They were Based, and Other*

Information Relating Thereto. Saskatoon: Fifth House.

Morsink, Johannes. 1999. "Cultural Genocide, the Universal Declaration, and Minority Rights." *Human Rights Quarterly* 21.

Mosby, Ian. 2013. "Administering Colonial Science: Nutrition Research and Human Biomedical Experimentation in Aboriginal Communities and Residential Schools, 1942–1952." *Histoire Sociale/Social History* 46, 91.

Moses, A. Dirk (ed.). 2008. *Empire, Colony, Genocide: Conquest, Occupation, and Subaltern Resistance in World History.* New York: Berghahn Books.

____. 2004. *Genocide and Settler Society: Frontier Violence and Stolen Indigenous Children in Australian History.* New York: Berghahn Books.

____. 2000. "An Antipodean Genocide? The Origins of the Genocidal Moment in the Colonization of Australia." *Journal of Genocide Research* 2, 1.

NAHO (National Aboriginal Health Organization). 2008. *Celebrating Birth: Aboriginal Midwifery in Canada.* Ottawa, National Aboriginal Health Organization.

____. 2006. "First Nations, Métis, and Inuit Women's Health, No. 4." *Discussion Paper Series in Aboriginal Health: Legal Issues,* March. <naho.ca/documents/naho/english/publications/DP_womens_health.pdf>

____. 2004. "First Nations, Métis, and Inuit Health Care, No.2." *Discussion Paper Series in Aboriginal Health: Legal Issues,* June. <naho.ca/documents/naho/english/publications/DP_crowns_obligation.pdf>.

____. 2003. "Aboriginal Health: A Constitutional Rights Analysis, No. 1." *Discussion Paper Series in Aboriginal Health: Legal Issues,* June. <naho.ca/documents/naho/english/publications/DP_rights.pdf>.

National Institute on Mental Retardation. 1979. *Sterilization and Mental Handicap.* Proceedings of a Symposium Sponsored by the National Institute on Mental Retardation and the Ontario Association for the Mentally Retarded. York University, Toronto, Canada, May 24 and 25.

Neu, Dean. 2000. "Accounting and Accountability: Colonization, Genocide and Canada's First Nations." *Accounting, Auditing & Accountability Journal* 13, 3.

Neu, Dean, and Richard Therrien. 2003. *Accounting for Genocide: Canada's Bureaucratic Assault on Aboriginal Peoples.* Winnipeg: Fernwood Publishing.

Newman, Louise Michelle. 1999. *White Women's Rights: The Racial Origins of Feminism in the United States.* New York: Oxford University Press.

Nicholas, F.W. and J.M. 1989. *Charles Darwin in Australia.* London: Cambridge Press.

Niezen, Ronald. 2003. *Origins of Indigenism: Human Rights and the Politics of Identity.* London: University of California Press.

Nind, A. Naomi. 2003. "Solving an "Appalling" Problem: Social Reformers and the Campaign for the Alberta Sexual Sterilization Act, 1928." *Alberta Law Review* 38, 2.

Normandin, Sebastien. 1998. "Eugenics, McGill, and the Catholic Church in Montreal and Quebec: 1890-1942." *Canadian Bulletin of Medical History* 15.

O'Brien, Bev. 2013. *Birth on the Land — Memories of Inuit Elders and Traditional Midwives.* Nunavut Arctic College.

Pagden, Anthony. 1998. *Lords of All the World: Ideologies of Empire in Spain, Britain and France c. 1500–c. 1800.* Yale University Press.

Palmater, Pamela D. 2011a. *Beyond Blood: Rethinking Indigenous Identity.* Saskatoon: Purich Publishing Ltd.

____. 2011b. "Stretched Beyond Human Limits: Death by Poverty in First Nations."

Canadian Review of Social Policy 65/66.

Palmer, Brian D. 1992. *Working Class Experience: Rethinking the History of Canadian Labour, 1800–1991*. Toronto: McClelland and Stewart.

Parks, Deborah C., and John P. Radford. 1998. "From the Case Files: Reconstructing a History of Involuntary Sterilization." *Disability & Society* 13.

Paul, Daniel. 2000. *We Were Not the Savages: Collision Between European and Native American Civilizations*. Nova Scotia: Fernwood Publishing.

Paul, Diane. 1998. *Controlling Human Heredity: 1865 to the Present*. Amherst: Humanity Books.

Pearce, Maryanne. 2013. "An Awkward Silence: Missing and Murdered Vulnerable Women and the Canadian Justice System." PhD diss., University of Ottawa.

Pearson, Karl. 1888. *The Ethics of Freethought*. London: T.F. Unwin.

Peers, Laura. 1996. "Subsistence, Secondary Literature, and Gender Bias: The Saulteaux." In C. Miller and P. Chuchryk (eds.), *Women of the First Nations: Power, Wisdom & Strength*. Winnipeg: University of Manitoba Press.

Pemberton, Kim. 2003. "Woodlands Victims Get Apology, $2 Million: Advocates Say the Money Isn't Enough to 'Right the Wrong.'" *Vancouver Sun*, May 31.

Perelman, Michael. 2000. *The Invention of Capitalism: Classical Political Economy and the Secret History of Primitive Accumulation*. Durham, NC: Duke University Press.

____. 1985. "Marx, Malthus, and the Organic Composition of Capital." *History of Political Economy* 17, 3.

Perry, Thomas L., Shirley Hansen, Bluma Tischler and Rosamund Bunting. 1967. "Determination of Heterozygosity for Phenylketonuria on the Amino Acid Analyzer." *Clinica Chimica Acta* 18, 1.

Pringle, Heather. 1997. "Alberta Barren: The Mannings and Forced Sterilization in Canada." *Saturday Night Magazine*, June. <statismwatch.ca/1997/06/01/alberta-barren-the-mannings-and-forced-sterilization-in-canada/>.

Public Guardian and Trustee of British Columbia. 2004. *The Woodlands Project July 2002–June 2004: A Report of the Public Guardian and Trustee of British Columbia* (August).

Ralstin-Lewis, D. Marie. 2005. "The Continuing Struggle Against Genocide: Indigenous Women's Reproductive Rights." *Wicazo SA Review* 20, 1.

Ramírez de Arellano, Annette B., and Conrad Seipp. 1983. *Colonialism, Catholicism, and Contraception: A History of Birth Control in Puerto Rico*. Chapel Hill: University of North Carolina Press.

Ramos, Carlos, and Peta Henderson. 1975. "Political Ideology and Population Policy in Puerto Rico." In Stanley Ignman and Anthony Thomas (eds.), *Topias and Utopias in Health: Policy Studies*. The Hague: Mouton.

Regan, Paulette. 2006. "Unsettling the Settler Within: Canada's Peacemaker Myth, Reconciliation, and Transformative Pathways to Decolonization." PhD diss., University of Victoria.

____. 2005. "A Transformative Framework for Decolonizing Canada: A Non-Indigenous Approach." Speech given at the Indigenous Governance Doctoral Student Symposium, January 20. <web.uvic.ca/igov/research/pdfs/A%20Transformative%20Framework%20for%20Decolonizing%20Canada.pdf>.

Rehman, Javaid. 2003. *International Human Rights Law: A Practical Approach*. England: Pearson Education.

____. 2000. *The Weaknesses in the International Protection of Minority Rights*. Cambridge, MA:

Kluwer Law International.

Reiter, R.A. 1995. *The Law of Canadian Indian Treaties*. Edmonton: Juris Analytica.

Rensing, Susan M. 2006. "Feminist Eugenics in America: From Free Love to Birth Control, 1880–1930." PhD diss., University of Minnesota.

Revie, Linda. 2006. "More than Just Boots! The Eugenic and Commercial Concerns Behind A.R. Kaufman's Birth Controlling Activities." *Canadian Bulletin of Medical History* 23, 1.

Reynolds, Dave. 2005. "BC Sterilization Victims Win Settlement." *Inclusion Daily Press*, December 23. <www.inclusiondaily.com/archives/05/12/23/122305bceugenics. htm>.

Robinson, E. 1991. "Maternal Health and Obstetrical Services: Measuring Health Status and Quality of Care in Remote Areas." In B.D. Postl, P. Gilbert, J. Goodwill, M.E.K. Moffatt, J.D. O'Neil, P.A. Sarsfield, et al. (eds.), *Circumpolar Health 90*. Winnipeg: University of Manitoba Press for the Canadian Society for Circumpolar Health.

Robinson, Nehemiah. 1960. *The Genocide Convention: A Commentary*. New York: World Jewish Congress.

Rodney, Walter. 1973. *How Europe Underdeveloped Africa*. London: Bogle-L'Ouverture Publications.

Rosen, Philip. 2000. *Current Issue Review: Hate Propaganda*. Ottawa: Parliamentary Research Branch.

Ross, Brian L. 1981. "An Unusual Defeat: The Manitoba Controversy over Eugenical Sterilization in 1933." Paper presented at the annual conference of the Institute for the History and Philosophy of Science and Technology, University of Toronto.

Rousseau, Nicole. 2006. "A Historical Materialist Analysis of the Commodification of Black Women's Biological Reproduction in the United States." PhD diss., Howard University.

Rutherdale, Myra (ed.). 2010. *Caregiving on the Periphery: Historical Perspectives on Nursing and Midwifery in Canada*. Montreal: McGill-Queen's University Press.

Saleeby, Caleb. 1911. *Woman and Womanhood: A Search for Principles*. New York: Mitchell Kennerley.

Sanders, Byrne Hope. 1945. *Emily Murphy: Crusader*. Toronto: The Macmillan Company.

Sanders, Ronald. 1978. *Lost Tribes and Promised Lands: The Origins of American Racism*. Boston, Brown & Little.

Sandiford Grygier, Pat. 1994. *A Long Way from Home: The Tuberculosis Epidemic among the Inuit*. Montreal and Kingston: McGill-Queen's University Press.

Sangster, Joan. 2002. *Girl Trouble: Female 'Delinquency' in English Canada*. Toronto: Between the Lines Press.

____. 2001. *Regulating Girls and Women: Sexuality, Family and Law in Ontario, 1920–1960*. Toronto: University of Toronto Press.

____. 2000. "Girls in Conflict with the Law: Exploring the Construction of 'Delinquency' in Ontario, 1940–60." *Canadian Journal of Women & the Law* 12, 1.

____. 1999. "Criminalizing the Colonized: Ontario Native Women Confront the Criminal Justice System, 1920–1960." *The Canadian Historical Review* 80, 1.

Sarti, Robert. 1968. "Sterilization of Patients in Institutions Declines." *Vancouver Sun*, November 19.

Sartre, Jean-Paul. 1968. "On Genocide." In John Duffett (ed.), *Against the Crime of Silence: Proceedings of the International War Crimes Tribunal*. New York: Bertrand Russell Peace Foundation/Flanders, NJ: O'Hare Books.

Satzewich, Vic, and Terry Wotherspoon. 1993. *First Nations: Race, Class and Gender Relations*.

Toronto: Nelson.

Schabas, William A. 2008. "Origins of the Genocide Convention: from Nuremberg to Paris." *Case Western Reserve Journal of International Law* 40.

____. 2000. *Genocide in International Law: The Crime of Crimes.* Cambridge: Cambridge University Press.

____. 1998. "Canada and the Adoption of the Universal Declaration of Human Rights." *McGill Law Journal* 43.

Schoen, Johanna. 2006. "From Footnote to the Headlines: Sterilization Apologies and Their Lessons." *Sexuality Research & Social Policy* 3, 3.

Schwartz Cowan, Ruth. 1977. "Nature and Nurture: The Interplay of Biology and Politics in the Work of Francis Galton." *Studies in the History of Biology* 1.

Shah, Sonali B. 2002. "The Oversight of the Last Great International Institution of the Twentieth Century: The International Criminal Court's Definition of Genocide." *Emory International Law Review* 16, 1.

Shapiro, Thomas. 1985. *Population Control Politics: Women, Sterilization and Reproductive Rights.* Philadelphia: Temple University Press.

Shaw, Jessica. 2013. "The Medicalization of Birth and Midwifery as Resistance." *Health Care for Women International* 34.

Shea, Goldie. 1999. *Redress Programs Relating to Institutional Child Abuse in Canada.* Report Prepared for Law Commission of Canada (October).

Shewell, Hugh. 2004. *'Enough to Keep Them Alive': Indian Welfare in Canada, 1873–1965.* Toronto: University of Toronto Press.

Silliman, Jael, Marlene Gerber Fried, Loretta Ross and Elena Gutierez. 2004. *Undivided Rights: Women of Color Organize for Reproductive Justice.* Cambridge, MA: South End Press.

Silver, Michael G. 2004. "Eugenic and Compulsory Sterilization Laws Providing Redress for the Victims of a Shameful Era in United States History." *George Washington Law Review* 72, 4.

Simpson, Leanne. 2014. "Not Murdered and Not Missing," *Voices Rising,* March 4. <nationsrising.org/not-murdered-and-not-missing/>.

Slattery, Brian. 2007. "A Taxonomy of Aboriginal Rights." In Hamar Foster, Heather Raven and Jeremy Webber (eds.), *Let Right Be Done: Aboriginal Title, the Calder Case, and the Future of Indigenous Rights.* Vancouver: UBC Press.

Smith, Andrea. 2005a. *Conquest: Sexual Violence and American Indian Genocide.* Cambridge: South End Press.

____. 2005b. "Beyond Pro Choice versus Pro Life: Women of Color and Reproductive Justice." *NSWA Journal* 17, 1.

____. 2002. "Better Dead Than Pregnant: The Colonization of Native Women's Reproductive Health." In Jael M. Silliman (ed.), *Policing the National Body: Sex, Race, and Criminalization.* Cambridge: South End Press.

Smith, Keith D. 2009. *Liberalism, Surveillance, and Resistance: Indigenous Communities in Western Canada, 1877–1927.* Edmonton: Athabasca University Press.

Soltice, Alexis, A. 1996. "The United Farm Women of Alberta: Political and Educational Advocacy, 1915-1939." MA diss., University of Calgary.

Stannard, David E. 1992. *American Holocaust: The Conquest of the New World.* New York: Oxford University Press.

Stevens, Geoffrey. 1974a. "A Strange View of Law." *Globe and Mail,* October 24.

____. 1974b. "Warning on Abortion." *Globe and Mail,* October 23.

Stevenson, Winona. 1999. "Colonialism and First Nations Women in Canada." In E. Dua and A. Robertson (eds.), *Scratching the Surface: Canadian Anti-Racist Feminist Thought.* Toronto: Women's Press.

Sunga, Lyal S. 1997. *The Emerging System of International Law: Developments in Codification and Implementation.* Cambridge, MA: Kluwer Law International.

Tennant, C.C., and Mary Ellen Turpel. 1990. "A Case Study of Indigenous Peoples: Genocide, Ethnocide and Self-determination." *Nordic Journal of International Law* 59.

Tester, Frank James, and Peter Kulchyski. 1994. *Tammarniit (Mistakes): Inuit Relocation in the Eastern Arctic 1939–1963.* Vancouver: UBC Press.

Tester, Frank James, and Paule McNicoll. 2006. "'Why Don't They Get It?' Talk of Medicine as Science. St. Luke's Hospital, Panniqtuuq, Baffin Island." *Social History of Medicine* 19, 1.

Thomas, W.D.S. 1977. "The Badgley Report on the Abortion Law." *Canadian Medical Association Journal* 116.

Thornberry, Patrick. 1991. *International Law and the Rights of Minorities.* New York: Oxford University Press.

Titley, E. Brian. 1986. *A Narrow Vision: Duncan Campbell Scott and the Administration of Indian Affairs in Canada.* Vancouver: University of British Columbia Press.

Toovey, Karilyn. 2005. "Decolonizing or Recolonizing: Indigenous Peoples and the Law in Canada." MA diss., University of Victoria.

Torpey, John (ed.). 2003. *Politics and the Past: On Repairing Historical Injustices.* Oxford: Rowman & Littlefield Publishers.

Torpy, Sally. 2000. "Native American Women and Coerced Sterilizations: On the Trail of Tears in the 1970s." *American Indian Culture and Research Journal* 24, 2.

Tovias, Blanca. 2008. "Navigating the Cultural Encounter: Blackfoot Religious Resistance in Canada (c.1870–1930)." In A. Dirk Moses (ed.), *Empire, Colony, Genocide: Conquest, Occupation and Subaltern Resistance in World History.* New York: Berghahn Books.

Truth Commission into Genocide in Canada. 2001. *Hidden From History: The Canadian Holocaust.*

Tucker, William H. 1994. *The Science and Politics of Racial Research.* Chicago: Board of Trustees of the University of Illinois.

Turpel, Mary-Ellen. 1993. "Patriarchy and Paternalism: The Legacy of the State for First Nations Women." *Canadian Journal of Women and the Law* 6.

Upton, Leslie. 1977. "The Extermination of the Beothuks of Newfoundland." *Canadian Historical Review* LVIII.

Valverde, Marianna. 1992. "When the Mother of the Race is Free." In M. Valverde and F. Iacovetta (eds.), *Gender Conflict: New Essays in Women's History.* Toronto: University of Toronto Press.

____. 1991. *The Age of Light, Soap and Water: Moral Reform in English Canada, 1885–1925.* Toronto: McClelland & Stewart.

Van der Vyver, Johan D. 1999. "Prosecution and Punishment of the Crime of Genocide." *Fordham International Law Journal* 23, 287.

Van Heeswijk, Gail. 1994. "'An Act Respecting Sexual Sterilization:' Reasons for Enacting and Repealing the Act." MA diss., University of British Columbia.

Van Kirk, Sylvia. 1980. *Many Tender Ties: Women in Fur-Trade Society, 1670–1870.* Winnipeg: Watson & Dwyer.

Van Schaak, Beth. 1997. "The Crime of Political Genocide: Repairing the Genocide

Convention's Blind Spot." *The Yale Law Journal* 106, 7.

Vancouver Sun. 2010. "Court Approves Settlement for Woodlands Abuse Victims." July 9. <canada.com/vancouversun/news/westcoastnews/story.html?id=d28ef401-7243-4d28-aad8-4f3f4dc66ece>.

Volscho, Thomas W. 2010a. "The Continued Encroachment on Reproductive Rights." *Wicazo Sa Review* 25, 1.

___. 2010b. *Racism and Disparities in Women's Use of the Depo-Provera Injection in the Contemporary United States*. New York: City University of New York — College of Staten Island.

Wahlsten, Doug. 1997. "Leilani Muir versus the Philosopher Kings: Eugenics on Trial in Alberta." *Genetica* 99.

Waldram, J., D.A. Herring, T.K. Young. 1995. *Aboriginal Health in Canada: Historical, Cultural and Epidemiological Perspectives*. Toronto: University of Toronto Press.

Walker, Barrington. 2008. *The History of Immigration and Racism in Canada: Essential Readings*. Toronto: Canadian Scholars Press.

Walsh, Mary Williams. 1992. "Abortion Horror Stories Spur Inquiry — Canada: Questions Raised After Women Allege Hospital Denied them Anesthesia as Punishment." *LA Times*, April 3.

Westra, Laura. 2008. *Environmental Racism and the Rights of Indigenous Peoples: International and Domestic Perspectives*. London: Earthscan.

White, Pamela M. 1987. "Restructuring the Domestic Sphere — Prairie Indian Women on Reserves: Image, Ideology and State Policy, 1880–1930." PhD diss., McGill University.

Whyatt, Sabrina. 1998. "Sterilization Victims Urged to Come Forward." *Windspeaker* 16, 4.

Wicken, Bill. 1993. "26 August, 1726: A Case Study in Mi'kmaq-New England Relations in the Early 18th Century." *Acadiensis* 23, 1.

Wintonyk, Darcy. 2010. "Woodlands Victims Upset Over Settlement Exclusion." CTV *News*, January 27. <ctvbc.ctv.ca/servlet/an/local/CTVNews/20100127/bc_woodland_se ttlement_100127/20100127?hub=BritishColumbiaHome>.

Wittmeier, Carmen. 1999. "The Final Batch: Sterilization Claimants May Soon See Taxpayers Dollars, But Not Nearly What They've Demanded." *Alberta Report*, September 6.

Wolfe, Patrick. 2008. "Structure and Event: Settler Colonialism, Time, and the Question of Genocide." In A. Dirk Moses (ed.), *Empire, Colony, Genocide: Conquest, Occupation, and Subaltern Resistance in World History*. New York: Berghahn Books.

___. 2001. "Land, Labor, and Difference: Elementary Structures of Race." *American Historical Review* (June).

Woodsworth, James S. 1909. *Strangers Within Our Gates; or Coming Canadians*. Toronto: F.C. Stephenson.

Woodward, Joe. 1998. "When Sorry Isn't Enough." *Alberta Report* 25, 15.

Wosilius, Monica. 1995. "Eugenics, Insanity and Feeblemindedness: British Columbia's Sterilization Policy from 1933–1943." MA diss., University of Victoria.

Wright, Quincy. 1972. "The Law of the Nuremberg Trials." In Jay Baird (ed.), *From Nuremberg to My Lai*. Toronto: David Heath & Company.

Wylie, Lana. 2006. "We Care What They Think: Prestige and Canadian Foreign Policy." Paper presented at the Annual Meeting of the Canadian Political Science Association, York University, Toronto (June).

Ziegler, Mary. 2008. "Eugenic Feminism: Mental Hygiene, the Women's Movement, and the Campaign for Eugenic Legal Reform, 1900–1935." *Harvard Journal of Law & Gender* 31.

Index

Abbott, A.P., 74
Aboriginal children
  as gifts, 63
  Indian Act, 32
  nutrition/health, 90
  residential schools, 33–34, 37–38,
    145, 154
  state care, 6, 34, 42–43
  sterilization of, 53, 103
Aboriginal peoples
  Canadian citizenship, 149–150
  Canadian legal system, 120–121
  as culturally distinct, 137–139
  cultural repression of, 36–37
  economic opportunities, 160
  land rights, 30, 32
  living conditions, 90
  mental health care of, 49–50
  right to vote, 136
  role of Canadians, in survival of, 160,
    162–165
  society, 28–30, 63
  systemic *vs.* individual wrongs, 116,
    120, 123
  traditional medicine, 38, 40
Aboriginal women
  in Aboriginal society, 28–29, 31–33
  abortion, 75–77
  Canadian legal system, 118–119, 120
  consent, 62–63, 64–65
  marginalization of, 42, 43
  marriage, 34–35
  as "mentally defective," 48–49
  missing, 159–160
  nutrition/health, 39, 90
  sexual practices, 15, 40–42
  See also Birth control; Sterilization
Abortion, 75–77

Alberta
  Charles Camsell Hospital, 40, 71,
    74–75, 80, 81, 117
  D.L.W. v. Alberta, 107–108
  legal settlements, 108–111
  Muir v. Alberta, 106–107
  residents of the North, 117–118
  Sterilization Act, 46–50, 89, 101–103
Alfred, Taiaiake, 160–161
Anaya, James, 138
Anglo Saxon women
  feminism, 10–11, 22–26
  as "fit" mothers, 19
  sterilization of, 47
Apology
  Apology Act (B.C.), 114
  BC (Woodlands and 3 other institu-
    tions), 112
  "Expression of Regret" (Alberta),
    110
  and legal responsibility, 122–123
  Muir v. Alberta, 107, 108
Arishenkoff v. British Columbia, 113–114
Assimilation
  Aboriginal peoples, 23, 26, 29–31,
    36–40, 43–44
  defined, 29–30
  family structure, 34–35, 42, 62–63
  genocide, 133–134
  government policy, 32–33, 36–37,
    44, 70
  health care as, 38–39
  human rights, 138–139
  for land and resources, 160–162
  policy enforcement, 44
  reproductive control, 1–2, 5–9, 10,
    60–63, 92
  Western medicine, 38–40, 59, 75, 78
  See also Capitalism; Colonialism;